CONSERVATISM IN AMERICA

CONSERVATISM IN AMERICA

MAKING SENSE OF
THE AMERICAN RIGHT

Paul Edward Gottfried

CONSERVATISM IN AMERICA
Copyright © Paul Edward Gottfried, 2007, 2009.
All rights reserved.

First published in hardcover in 2007 by PALGRAVE
MACMILLAN® in the United States–a division of St. Martin's
Press LLC, 175 Fifth Avenue, New York, NY 10010.

Where this book is distributed in the UK, Europe and the rest of
the world, this is by Palgrave Macmillan, a division of Macmillan
Publishers Limited, registered in England, company number
785998, of Houndmills, Basingstoke, Hampshire RG21 6XS.

Palgrave Macmillan is the global academic imprint of the above
companies and has companies and representatives throughout the
world.

Palgrave® and Macmillan® are registered trademarks in the
United States, the United Kingdom, Europe and other countries.

ISBN-13: 978-0-230-61479-6

Library of Congress Cataloging-in-Publication Data is available
from the Library of Congress.

A catalogue record of the book is available from the British
Library.

Design by Scribe, Inc.

First PALGRAVE MACMILLAN paperback edition: May 2009
10 9 8 7 6 5 4 3 2 1
Printed in the United States of America.

Transferred to Digital Printing in 2009.

CONTENTS

ACKNOWLEDGMENTS

Duty and affection both require that I acknowledge friends and relatives without whose aid this book would still be unfinished. Professors Michael Long, David Gordon, David Brown, W. Wesley McDonald, Will Hay, and Matthew Woessner all examined various drafts of my chapters. Not all of their suggestions were taken, but I was gratified that my friends responded to my e-mail attachments with informative comments. Dr. Christopher Woltermann prepared the index and read a provisional draft from beginning to end; without his corrections, the following book would have been less comprehensible and certainly less felicitously worded. Chris convinced me to take my literary tics out of an earlier draft, and I take full responsibility if, contrary to his advice, some of these crept back in. Also worthy of mention is my daily German correspondent, Stefan Herrold. His detailed messages provide continuing insight into European politics. The librarians at Elizabethtown College graciously provided articles and references that were not easily accessible. Without their computer skills and those of Professors McDonald and Kathy Kelley and our house sitter Sara Robinson, I would still be struggling with the notes. I am also indebted to the Earhart Foundation, which has continued to fund my research after thirty years of support.

To my wife, Mary, I owe a special debt for putting up with my inattentiveness while I was researching this book. I shall henceforth try to spend less of my flextime at home on the word processor. To my older son Joseph, I remain grateful for the flak that he gave me for undertaking this project. Unlike his father, Joseph usually agrees with FOX News and the current conservative movement, and he believes that my book is disputing a truism. Indeed, those who call themselves "conservatives" are precisely what they say they are—as opposed to "liberals" or "extremists." Without our often-heated discussions, I would have felt less driven to formulate my response to interpretations that differ from mine. Note this book was written, among other reasons, to open a dialogue on the "conservative movement" with those who are willing and able to participate. It is unlikely, as my text makes clear, that those who would join this hypothetical discussion will emanate from either "conservative" organizations in the New York-Washington corridor or the neoconservative media.

A special acknowledgement is due to an intellectual tradition that cultural critic Allan Bloom calls the "German connection." Despite Bloom's admonitions, which are still in favor among American conservatives, I have happily drawn my insights from dead German thinkers. Their ideas have molded my approach to contemporary and chronologically more distant history; and instead of hiding my debts to Bloom's hated "historical relativists," I have chosen to acknowledge them openly. The rejection of such figures and their thought has been characteristic of the present generation of American conservatives, who seem invincibly ignorant of the sociohistorical dimension of their values. Spanish philosopher José Ortega y Gasset observed about his fellow Europeans in the 1930s that their present-mindedness betokened mass barbarism. Such a condition, far from being an indication of the quest for transcendent truth, is rather a mark of intellectual and cultural laziness. It is hard to think of any group that would benefit more thoroughly than self-described American conservatives from the historical-mindedness that they continue to oppose.

There are also sizeable debts that I owe to non-Germans for the concepts that enriched this book. Among these inspirations were Robert Nisbet, Eugene Genovese, M. E. Bradford, John Lukacs, Thomas Fleming, and Clyde N. Wilson, all of whom shared with me their valuable social perspectives. I also wish to acknowledge Samuel T. Francis, Paul Piccone, and Donald Livingston, whose social and ethical commentaries I read with profit, and Claes Ryn, George H. Nash, Murray N. Rothbard, and George Carey for their luminous insights about the American conservative movement. I should also respectfully mention my students, who discussed with me the major themes of this work while it was in progress. How I have chosen to use the ideas of others has more to do with my judgment than with theirs.

Paul Edward Gottfried
Elizabethtown, PA

INTRODUCTION

This book deals with the evolution of the American conservative movement from the 1950s to the present. The work highlights its successes and defects, examines what produced both, and explores how the two were related. Contrary to historian Clinton Rossiter's memorable 1962 description of American conservatism as the "thankless persuasion," today's conservative celebrities enjoy media access, personal wealth, and publishing fame.[1] Popular conservatives have at their disposal a widely available TV news channel and numerous heavily subsidized magazines. Their radio talk show hosts, typified by Rush Limbaugh, have made fortunes for themselves while dispensing their deeply felt views over the airwaves. Our Republican president loads his speeches with references to "values," which is a conservative movement buzzword; and the moral justification he gives for the American occupation of Iraq, when he talks about America's responsibility to implant its democratic institutions elsewhere, comes from "conservative" advisors and speech writers.

In contrast to these successes, which would have been inconceivable to earlier incarnations of the movement, it is necessary to take a closer look at the shadow side of the "conservative ascendancy." By doing so, we are dealing with an aspect of that ascendancy that the establishment press has generally ignored. This neglect has been the result of many factors, among them the liberal media's desire to push the conservative movement further in their direction. This is the source of the oft-heard complaint that the conservative movement has not moved far enough toward the liberal Left or that it remains insufficiently sensitive to designated minorities (blacks, Latinos, women, and gays).

This book approaches its subject from an entirely different angle by observing how frenetically the conservative movement has worked to accommodate its talking partners in the Left-Center. Although this has not always been apparent in the partisan tone of debates, it is certainly true for the conservative embrace of democratic egalitarian ideals and the current conservative appeal to great reforming presidents and to the lessons of the civil rights movement. Conservative leaders have marginalized their own right wing more than once as they have presented their movement as suitable for a dialogue with "moderates" on the other side. Therefore, we have reached a point where the widely respected conservative journalist and *Weekly Standard* senior editor David Brooks lavishes kind words on the "centrist" Hillary Clinton in the *New York Times* (May 11, 2006) while criticizing Republican conservatives for resisting moderate candidates John McCain and Rudolph Giuliani.[2]

For years the conservative movement has tried to appeal to its media talking partners by smoothing the movement's rough edges. It has tried to find common purpose with the liberal establishment by avoiding any appearance of extremism. Its affluent spokesmen have separated themselves from those who seem more "conservative" in their principles than the goal of bridge-building might render acceptable. Mainstream conservatives, especially those identified with foundations, have pursued this course not only to reassure liberal media colleagues but increasingly in recent decades to improve their place in the Republican Party. Since the 1980s, the conservative movement's association with the Republican Party has grown so tight that it is hard to imagine the movement surviving in the Washington Beltway without it.

The aforesaid changes in the movement have not always been clear to either outside observers or movement members. Although there is more than one reason for this blindness to change, one factor that this book accentuates is the use of values to create a sense of permanence. In this work I argue that the conservative movement's appeal to values has protected it from having to look more deeply at its own problems, most particularly its lack of connection to an older and more genuine conservatism and its general tendency to move leftward to accommodate those with whom it shares the public spotlight. By claiming to stand for "permanent values," the movement can treat its opportunistic politics as less significant than its allegedly enduring moral compass.

A survey of the American conservative movement in the twentieth century is neither needed nor provided here. I as well as others have prepared surveys for anyone seeking such a study. Moreover, the expanded (second) edition of George H. Nash's *The Conservative Intellectual Movement in America Since 1945* (Wilmington, DE: ISI, 1996) offers the most comprehensive and most balanced investigation of the subject. Readers cannot find a better general history of the conservative movement since 1945 than this work. Another useful source on the same theme is the anthology of readings introduced with informative commentaries by Gregory L. Schneider, *Conservatism in America Since 1930* (New York: New York University Press, 2003). Schneider picked his texts carefully to cover all historically significant conservative schools of thought, starting with those well before the rise of the *National Review* circle. Still one more reference work that readers ought to consult is the Intercollegiate Studies Institute's recently published *American Conservatism: An Encyclopedia*. Although it is possible to challenge the applicability of a "conservative" label for everything herein included, there is no disputing the volume's comprehensive and even-handed discussion of its chosen topics.

In addition to these studies, there are many impassioned examinations of sundry strains of the American conservative movement, particularly of those groups that battled each other for control in the 1980s. These books, most of which are highly polemical, suggest the presence of a highly contentious Right at a time when it was still open to exciting disputes. I do not retread the ground covered by these earlier studies. Rather, I seek to make sense of the movement as a whole by examining both how its adherents have defined their identity and what they have claimed about themselves as self-styled conservatives over the last fifty years.

The American conservative movement reveals far more ideological breaks than continuities. Much like the kingdom of ancient Egypt and the Byzantine Empire in the Middle Ages, it has developed a talent not only for presenting takeovers as the serene march of the past into the present but also for treating a general retreat from its original positions as a progression of victories. Like Egyptian or Byzantine chroniclers trying to make a series of invading rulers fit the story line of a steady dynastic succession, conservative movement historians emphasize the relentless progress of what we are told are timeless, ahistorical ideas. Despite the patent fact that the political landscape has been moving generally leftward since the fifties, conservatives celebrate a "Reagan revolution" while turning out books that hail their imagined transformation of American society. And while conservatives lunge toward many positions once held by the moderate Left, they make it appear as if they alone are standing up for "permanent values."

Nothing could be further from my intention than to denigrate the movement I discuss. I am simply trying to get to the bottom of a subject that has preoccupied me for decades. To some extent, this subject is autobiographical in that it encapsulates my own critical engagement with a persuasion to which I was once drawn in the past. My break from that movement was gradual but also so personally and professionally unsettling that it has left scars that continue to affect my social relations. Since the mid-eighties, I have written several books, starting with *The Search for Historical Meaning: Hegel and the Postwar Right*, in which I have focused on the perceived defects of the American Right. My original criticism, which social theorist Robert Nisbet examined in a detailed commentary for *National Review* (May 22, 1987), was that conservative theorists have abandoned the sense of a living historical past.[3] This legacy of Edmund Burke and of nineteenth-century conservatives had given way to the current preoccupation, which is particularly strong among neoconservatives, with "abstract universals," and this fateful turning has led to an association of American conservatism with certain eighteenth-century French revolutionary ideals. My concluding chapter, "A Conservative Farewell to History," earned the high praise of my book's illustrious reviewer and, later, former president Richard Nixon.[4] But contrary to Nisbet's impression that I had made definitive critical statement, I expanded my strictures in the second edition of my survey in 1993 to deal with the conservative movement's problematic beginnings and its decline into robot-like conformity. Although the earlier work seemed, in Nisbet's judgment, to be "the best and most provocative treatment of postwar conservatism yet written," the later work was still more "provocative."

By then in exile from the American Right, and increasingly banned from publishing in its magazines, I began to consider those peculiarities of my former comrades-in-arms that my earlier writings had missed. Why, for example, had there been so little internal resistance to the Right's occupation by neoconservatives, who had aroused no more than scant opposition against themselves as "interlopers"? Certainly the neoconservatives' views on a wide range of social and constitutional questions, and their hostility against those they could not drag over to their side, should have evoked more suspicion against their leadership than it did. If partisans on the Right had wished to be Truman Democrats, admirers of the Civil Rights Act of 1964, and relentless critics of southern conservatives and Taft Republicans, they could have become cold war liberals in the fifties or sixties. Why had they waited until the eighties to take over these positions held by the other side, and then under its highly imperious supervision, while claiming counterfactually that these had always been their views?

It was also obvious that there was a vigorous American Right before the 1950s, when William F. Buckley had reconfigured it around his newly founded fortnightly, *National Review*. My reading and my meetings with the aging representatives of the anti–New Deal Right convinced me that the shake-up of the eighties was not the first time self-described people of the Right had been "thrown off the bus." This practice, which I investigate in chapter 6, was formative for the movement that took shape in the fifties. What was less apparent was that those who had been hurled out of the movement suffered their fate as "extremists." They were, in most cases, the victims of a rewriting of history carried out by the movement in cooperation with its critics on the Left-Center. By branding ousted members of an older and more libertarian Right as "bigots" and "kooks," one could impose discipline on a movement that came to value this virtue above all others.

This book applies two distinct approaches to go beyond my earlier studies of what passes for the American establishment Right. One approach expands the frame of reference by contrasting the contemporary Right to its antecedents some fifty to seventy years ago. This analysis exposes fundamentally changed "conservative" tenets underlying a tendentious sense of continuity. My second approach examines the respectable Right in the United States in relation to other Rights and, even more revealingly, to the classical conservatism of the early nineteenth century. These comparisons are by no means arbitrary, for well into the sixties and seventies American conservative writers attempted to link genealogically their own movement to what European conservatives had espoused in the past. These extended comparisons make clear the utter futility of this enterprise. The evidence shows how little the American model shares with its alleged European antecedents.

In chapter 4 I aim to achieve terminological and historical clarification by dealing with the "Right" as something independent of both classical conservatism and its American namesake. The Right, as defined in this chapter, is a predominantly bourgeois reaction, explicitly against social and political radicalization, that has taken many forms. But these forms arose in societies in which the *ancien régime*, to which classical conservatism had rallied, was already tottering or had never existed. Whether one is discussing Italy on the eve of Mussolini's march on Rome in 1922 or the resistance to the New Deal, one is looking at postconservative bourgeois reactions to unwelcome changes or the threat of social disruption. Although this Right has survived as a weakened presence in the West, conservatism is no longer an option there, principally because of a multitude of social changes that have occurred since Burke inveighed against the French Revolution in 1790. The anti–New Deal Right defended bourgeois liberalism in its American form, against a centralized public administration that was bringing about a larger welfare state. Those who led this opposition described themselves as "Jeffersonians" and never pretended to be upholding European conservative traditions.

It was the decision of the postwar conservative movement, or its leaders, to construct some linkage between themselves and the Middle Ages or the European counterrevolution that led to their movement's convoluted history. Recognition of this fact does not require us to disparage what was borrowed. In fact, it may be hard to read my collected works without perceiving my sympathy for medieval and conservative ideas. My arguments here have nothing to do with their intrinsic merit. I address something vastly different, namely, the merging of anti-Communist and pro–free-market sentiments with a contrived "conservative" pedigree to produce a fictitious foundation for a political movement. That merger is fictitious in two senses: it has no firm social base and it rests on the claim of being "conservative" by virtue of standing above classes, tribes, and even nations. It is precisely the opposite of that which characterizes not only classical conservatism but also all genuine social and political movements, including European Communism and bourgeois liberalism.

This floating quality is nonetheless rendered tolerable by the fact that the "conservative movement" has a situational function, that of framing policies for the Republican Party and contributing to the administrative staff of Republican administrations. The movement also runs newspapers, Foxs News channel, and gargantuan think tanks—thanks to generous benefactors—and disseminates a recognizable kind of discourse, which this book examines. No matter how crudely partisan or rudely contemporary it may be, this rhetoric purports to be about eternal "values." It claims to reflect the moral high ground that movement conservatives supposedly occupy but that their opponents are viewed as ignoring or even scorning. These opponents suffer dismissal as "moral relativists" who favor permissive attitudes because, in contrast to conservatives, they cannot agree on the nature of the good.

The identification of conservatism with "values" and of the other side with "nonvalues" goes back to the structural weakness of the conservative cause, which is neither conservative nor an authentic historical movement. It is a collection of Republican Party partisans, think tank employees, and journalists who belong to one side of a changing political spectrum and political dialogue. Lacking either a stable social base or any tie to classical conservatism, self-styled conservatives champion "values" as a kind of moral glue for their network of associations. They also present their opponents as being without a moral position, which is a doubtful premise. As participants in the prevalent cultural strife in the United States and Western Europe, those on the Left have defined an identifiable post-Christian moral stance.

Value conservatism, which is the major theme of this book, arose to address one situation but has come to satisfy other needs. Its original function was to supply a base for a misnamed conservatism by decorating it with antirevolutionary and anti-Communist principles and rhetoric. This movement, quite broadly understood, did take on a certain gravitas as it tried to incorporate Catholic and Anglo-Catholic natural law thinking into its corpus of ideas. But that was generally a sideshow. Being part of the political conversation that took place in the media remained paramount for "conservatives" who could not identify themselves too closely with the Catholic Right without losing the possibility of broadening their political appeal. Moreover, there were Catholic philosophical and legal journals that treated ethical matters quite independently of the conservative movement.

Values were useful for giving conservative journalists and policy experts a leg up in the competition for political acceptance and popularity. By attaching "value permanence" to whatever one proposed, one could help make sympathetic political candidates and their electoral positions look venerable and high-minded. Even then one had to tailor one's "permanent values" to make them fit an increasingly less traditional and at least theoretically more egalitarian society. The style of debate nonetheless became so fixed that one's opponents routinely suffered depiction either as being less committed than oneself to values or as being prone to relativism. This style became all the more important as think tanks, many of them professing to be "conservative" or "value conservative," morphed into power centers in American and European political life. Berkeley's Manuel Castells, who has documented the shift of political decision making toward foundations and institutes generating "policies," has written widely on this trend.[4] One advantage over their opponents enjoyed by think tanks designating themselves as being on the Right is the effective use of value language. This exemplifies the practice of turning a onetime liability into an asset. A movement that has strayed opportunistically from its original ideological base has survived partly as a value construct. Its survival likewise reflects the accumulation of other strategic assets, including funding, access to the media and to politicians, and an unfailingly cooperative army of workers.

Lest anyone claim that I find nothing of merit in the subject of my study, I must note that some of the movement's byproducts have proved beneficial. Particularly in its early years it provided a forum for such outstanding political and social thinkers as Nisbet, James Burnham, M. E. Bradford, Forrest McDonald, and Frank Meyer. It also enabled Henry Regnery, an America First veteran of the anti–New Deal Right, to establish a publishing house that allowed Russell Kirk, Albert Jay Nock, Irving Babbitt, and other worthwhile men of letters to reach a larger public than otherwise might have been the case. The movement-affiliated Intercollegiate Studies Institute also engages in similar acts of cultural recovery, and its publications make available to students a variety of writings that politically conformist professors are not likely to put into their hands. It is also possible to find situations in which neoconservative-controlled think tanks have promoted freedom rather than spread democracy through war. From time to time, a member of the pre-Buckleyite Right may discover that he agrees with a position or string of positions held by the movement's power players in the New York–Washington axis. When he does not, he nonetheless learns from reading "conservative position papers" that the movement needs allies to "fight terror," or that Republicans have to be reelected, or else that we now live in the best of all worlds, a "democratic welfare state."

Nothing in the value critiques that punctuate this work should be read incorrectly as either a defense of "relativism" or a general attack on moral reasoning. The object of my criticism is partisan appeals to moral truth, which only rarely amount to ethical arguments with any substance. Indeed, most of time, the often cited "value game" never rises above the kind of name-calling heard from talk show hosts. Although those who choose to be honored as value-conservative intellectuals may wish to distinguish themselves from the vulgarizers, they typically bear a family resemblance to those whom they presume to disdain. This is because they both belong to the same movement, which provides financing and often mercenaries for electoral politics.

My conclusion asks whether some other opposition to the social democratic and later multicultural Left could have been possible. Certainly I would have preferred such an outcome. But any such hypothetical alternative might not have reached even the limited successes of the present version of the conservative movement. A strict constitutionalist Right, one that had stood where Senator Robert Taft did in 1950 and Congressman Ron Paul of Texas does today, might well have opposed the liberal Left even less effectively than the Heritage Foundation and the American Enterprise Institute do today. Although this idea will not please the remnants of a more genuine American Right, it is one that honesty requires us to consider.

Historical circumstances, namely, the establishment of a popular, expanding, and highly centralized public administration, may have foredoomed any attempt to keep alive an alternative American Right. By the same token, the recognition of this historical probability does not rule out the need to underscore the gulf between the achievements ascribed by the present conservative movement to itself and those misrepresentations from which it has benefited. Finally, one might note that the insertion of critical political variables into American life has altered the political discussion and the determination of policy. It is worth considering how political life in the United States might have differed had the neoconservatives not become the respectable Right in the eighties. Let us imagine, for example, a Right whose major concern was not a neo-Wilsonian foreign policy but rather restraint of the growth and reach of the central government. Such a Right, if it had taken off, might have contributed to a very different political debate from the one we now witness.

A qualifier is in order about the assertion, which I admit to having made in the past, that the postwar conservative movement has no real link to its beginnings. To be more accurate, the present media think tank movement does preserve or replicate the constructivist character of its postwar source. It is an artificial movement whose unity and support derive partly from manufacturing values. It also imposes solidarity by coming down hard on dissent, a practice it began in the fifties. In a sense then it continues, in altered circumstances and with new custodians, the attempt launched in that decade to fashion an anti-Communist Right, one that was intended to be more dynamic and timely than its anti–New Deal predecessor.

But that initial attempt did not entirely eradicate the older American Right, which penetrated the new structure. Not even bans of excommunication could keep this from occurring, and it took over a generation before the new in this case obliterated the traces of the old. If one searches through the views of Russell Kirk and Nisbet, both celebrities of the postwar conservative movement, one encounters the older tradition of anti–New Deal Republicanism ready to rise to the surface. That was the historically grounded American tradition from whence they and others whom Buckley drew into the New Covenant had come—and to which they periodically returned. Aside from misleading references to the "Far Right," Nisbet was speaking out of that older tradition, which was his own, when he penned this memorable passage in the eighties:

The Far Right is less interested in Burkean immunities from government power than it is in putting a maximum of government power in the hands of those who cannot be trusted. It is control of power, not diminution of power that ranks high. Thus when Reagan was elected conservatives hoped for the abolition of such government "monstrosities" as the Department of Energy, the Department of Education, and the two National Endowments of the Arts and Humanities, all creations of the political Left. The Far Right in the Reagan Phenomenon saw it differently, however; they saw it as an opportunity for retaining and enjoying the powers. And the Far Right prevailed. It seeks to prevail also in the establishment of a "national industrial strategy," a government corporation structure in which the conservative dream of free private enterprise would be extinguished.[5]

—◆—

CHAPTER 1

THE INVENTION OF
AMERICAN CONSERVATISM

AN AMERICAN CONSERVATIVE VALUE?

This chapter is built on a premise that gradually should seem self-evident: the American and European "conservative" experiences have been intrinsically different. It is therefore dubious and perhaps impossible to fit into a common political framework various European traditionalists, who defended aristocracy, social hierarchy, and ecclesiastical establishment, and the American advocates of such concerns as a market economy, an anti-Communist foreign policy, and a global democratic crusade. Nor are these differences reducible to varying historical backgrounds, even though the term "conservative" has proven sufficiently elastic to cover anything that people at any time may decide to call by this name.

Conservatism's putative antithesis reeks of comparable conceptual imprecision. In my book *After Liberalism*, I focused on the semantic confusion that has resulted from the overly free use of "liberalism," a movement that now refers to political programs and political ideals that would have appalled or perplexed liberals of a hundred years ago. Boston University sociologist Alan Wolfe, who reviewed my anatomy of a broken genealogy in the *New Republic*, expressed considerable shock at its "antiliberalism."[1] A very different response, however, came in a letter I received from Austrian classical liberal scholar Erik von Kuehnelt-Leddhin. This then almost ninety-year-old exponent of the European liberal tradition noted that my clarifications helped explain why "liberal" in the United States denotes something quite different from what it had for generations of Europeans. Unlike Wolfe, this correspondent had no desire to see the "dirty, stinking fungus that Americans in their semantic confusion mistake for liberalism" invade a truer liberal tradition in Europe.[2] Although my intention was not to be judgmental, I did attempt to draw distinctions that seemed necessary for understanding the politics of the present age. Today's proponents of liberalism ascribe to themselves a venerable tradition, that of limited government and bourgeois social norms, which is not really their own. The once established liberal position, formerly widely recognized as such, was not the "Gruppensituation" in which modern social "liberals" find or have placed themselves. The twenty-first century's social-moral world, inhabited by the urban advocates of expressive freedoms and the spokesmen for inner city blacks, is neither the same nor continuous with the group situation of the traditional bourgeoisie.[3]

In this book, I intend to investigate another equally blatant mislabeling, one that pertains to American "conservatives." In part, the use of this label took root in American discourse because the United States had once included various local societies or groups that were reminiscent of the European manorial system. The antebellum South and the Dutch patroons in the Hudson Valley in the eighteenth and early nineteenth centuries come most readily to mind here. Also reminiscent of the social base of European conservatism were a group of High Federalists at the end of the eighteenth century, men like Fisher Ames of Massachusetts, who feared the collapse of constitutional government into mob rule. Finally, there were old-stock British patricians, typified by the Adams family, who showed (or were thought to have shown) a family resemblance to European elites. And, like once dominant European classes that eventually underwent displacement, these Americans complained about their social eclipse and about what it boded for the country as a whole.

Drawing too uncritically on such examples, the postwar author Russell Kirk produced in 1953 the unexpected bestseller *The Conservative Mind, from Burke to T. S. Eliot*. This conservative mind or mentality had allegedly perpetuated itself in the Anglo-American world despite an apparent and much commented-on "conservative rout." Kirk purports to trace this tradition to the eighteenth-century Anglo-Irish statesman Edmund Burke, who had written vehemently against the French Revolution. With copious documentation, he then presents those variations on the

Burkean tradition that he discerns in later Anglophone authors and politicians. His examples, such as T. S. Eliot, Walter Bagehot, Edmund Randolph of Roanoke, and George Santayana, supposedly demonstrate that the United States has enjoyed a rich conservative legacy extending back to its British roots. And to indicate the lessons that this "conservative mind" can yield, Kirk, at the beginning of his volume (which he had submitted originally in a shorter form for a doctorate at St. Andrews University in Scotland), constructs for his reader's benefit six "canons of conservatism."[4] All of them stand in juxtaposition to the beliefs typical of a form of "radicalism [that] since 1790 has tended to attack the prescriptive arrangements of society." Leaving aside Kirk's qualifiers "in a hastily generalizing fashion" and "tended to," one can easily infer that he regarded those doctrines as the source of all of the radical movements that have bedeviled the West since the French Revolution. Among these beliefs are "the perfectability of man and the illimitable progress of society," "contempt for tradition" linked to faith in "reason, impulse, and materialistic determination," "political leveling" in the absence of "order and privilege," and "economic leveling" at the cost of private property. Burke's position on the state, however, was problematic for Kirk. Although he maintains that Burke saw in the state, properly understood, "a community of souls," he also suggests that Burke's sense of the state as a "moral bond between the dead, living and those yet to be born" had become unfashionable. It no longer corresponded to the "common radical view of the state's function," which Kirk, however, declined to examine.[5]

Kirk underlines that his canons are not entirely his own. He freely acknowledges that the "dozen principles of conservatism" listed in F. J. C. Hearnshaw's *Conservatism in England* were the source from which he had derived them. Even so, his repackaging of these principles as a "briefer catalogue" would become the most quoted part of his tract. To this catalogue belong principles that continue to appear in the seventh revised (1986) and most recent edition of Kirk's work. His tenets, we are assured, do not constitute an "ideology" but form "guidelines," which are "belief in transcendent order or body of natural law, which rules society as well as conscience"; "affection for the proliferating variety and mystery of the human experience"; "conviction that civilized society requires orders and classes as against the notion of a 'classless society'"; "persuasion that freedom and property are closely linked"; "faith in prescription and distrust of 'sophisters, calculators, and economists,' who would reconstruct society upon abstract design"; and "recognition that change must be salutary reform: hasty innovation may be a devouring conflagration, rather than a torch of progress."[6]

Burke and his *Reflections on the Revolution in France* (1790) were obviously on Kirk's mind when he put together his catalogue of conservative principles. The reference to "sophisters, calculators, and economists" comes directly from Burke's invectives against the Revolution, and the elaboration of every canon includes at least one paraphrase from passages in *Reflections*. The presumed dialectic is between defenders of English inherited liberties and legal procedures, what Burke and Kirk called "the politics of prescription," and the champions of radical transformation inspired by the French Revolution. Kirk ascribes such "hasty innovation" to the "rationalism of the philosophes and the romantic emancipation of Rousseau and his allies," but the list of villains grew to make room for "the utilitarianism of the Benthamites, the positivism of Comte's school, and the collectivistic materialism of Marx and other socialists."[7]

Although Kirk has a lot to say in his book about revolutionaries and the curses of modernity, the first edition of *The Conservative Mind* includes little about "liberalism" per se. The confrontation there is chiefly between Burkean prescriptive freedom and the ideas of the French Revolution. Moreover, the reader gets the impression that the fights against the "several radicalisms" offensive to Kirk are continuations of the war waged against that mother of revolutions that broke out in 1789. The American Revolution, we are told, was like the Glorious Revolution in 1688; Burke had seen in both of these events attempts to avert greater disturbances by dislodging or severing ties to troublesome monarchs. It is only in the last chapter, "Conservatives' Promise," that Kirk examines a then recently made observation by Columbia University English professor Lionel Trilling in *The Liberal Imagination* (1950): "In the United States at this time liberalism is not only the dominant but even the sole intellectual tradition. For it is the plain fact that nowadays there are no conservative or reactionary ideas in general circulation."[8]

Kirk retorts that it is the "liberal concepts that had gone dry and hollow," citing the Southern Agrarians and the other subjects of his work as counterexamples. He also refers to the fact that since 1950 "perhaps two-hundred serious books of a conservative cast have been published in America, and a goodly number in

Britain; several periodicals professedly conservative have appeared; and a bibliography of important conservative essays might require as many pages as this present volume contains."[9]

Kirk fails to address the observations of Trilling and his "liberal" critics because he neglects to ask about definitions; for example, what does one mean by liberal and liberalism, aside from vague humanistic generalities? In *The Liberal Imagination*, Trilling had designated liberalism as an "expansive" sensibility that had engendered a distinctive literary form. He certainly was not writing as an unqualified advocate of the object of his analysis; in fact, he devoted most of his anthology to exposing the weaknesses of the liberal sensibility. As Kirk's work went through five successive editions and gained notice in the national press, the political critics whom he provoked escaped rebuke for their shifting definitions of "liberalism." Whether it was Arthur Schlesinger, who mocked Kirk and other "new conservatives" as pawns of the "business community," or Louis Hartz, who in 1955 proclaimed "liberalism as the only American tradition," these exponents of the liberal persuasion rushed to give "liberal" a flexible meaning. And they were not the first to do so. A respected precursor of theirs was John Dewey, whose writings and lectures in the 1930s foreshadowed their own shell game. It was Dewey who had claimed that while he embraced liberalism going back to Jefferson, he wanted to clean off the scales in order to get at what was "vital" in the liberal tradition. In *Liberalism and Social Action*, which drew from his Page-Barbour Lectures of 1935, Dewey calls for "scientific liberalism," which would treat society as being "in continuous growth," and which would move beyond the free-market fixation in which liberals of the past had been 'frozen."[10] It is worth asking whether Jefferson would have recognized his own "vital" ideas in a "scientific" administrative state of the kind that Dewey outlines, a state featuring a governmentally instilled "democratic faith" as its religion.

While Dewey promoted the purely temporal image of a succession of liberal faiths taken from the Bible's two covenants, Schlesinger a generation later in *The Vital Center* (1949) offered a spatial image for relating his "liberalism" to the crisis of the cold war. Schlesinger's liberalism, which celebrates the "affirmative state" that has had to "fight conservatism at every step," sought "to control the business cycle and to reapportion income."[11] The holders of this position—who Schlesinger assures us were not ideologues, a term he reserved for Communists and conservatives—occupied a vital center between the Marxists and the defenders of laissez-faire and of the even more reactionary Right. Schlesinger showcased his preferred center and alternated "liberal democratic" with "liberal" to categorize it. Kirk, however, never confronted nor seemed to have noticed this game of wrapping a favored political cause in such high-sounding phrases as "liberal," "centrist" and "moderate." The suitable response, which Kirk could have given by referring to a slew of Anglophone articles on conservatism to prove that his cherished movement did exist, would have been to contest the unexamined or opportunistic use of terms. What right, he might have asked, has Mr. Schlesinger to exercise what the Germans call *Deutungshoheit*, the power to determine what words and symbols signify? By allowing his labels to stand, Schlesinger's critics permitted him in his second edition to announce what they could have semantically contested, namely that governmental "reconstruction had brought new phases of liberal thought to the forefront in the thirteen years since this book was published."[12]

Kirk did not contest this semantic appropriation because he was *not* offering a historically based understanding of liberalism or conservatism. He detested (and made no secret of it) German historical thinking, a category that he understood to include Teutonic philosophers like Hegel, German sociology, and anything containing the term "historicism."[13] He was, therefore, not prone to notice the changing definitions of "conservative" and "liberal." In a telling lack of curiosity, he never asked, at least not to my knowledge, how it was that Robert Taft, whom he considered an "American conservative" and about whom he wrote a biography, and Schlesinger, who attacked Taft and Kirk from the Left, both called themselves "liberals."[14]

Kirk might have also paid closer attention to Hartz's *The Liberal Tradition in America* when that interpretive study of the American political tradition came out in 1955. Although Hartz plays his own shell game (by subsuming the New Deal under a "happy pragmatism") and exaggerated the New Dealers' "faith in property, class unity, a suspicion of too much state power, [and a] hostility to the utopian mood," he also raises points that Kirk would have done well to address. According to Hartz, the United States from its inception was marked by two critical factors that would determine its later course as a political society, namely, "the absence of feudalism and the presence of the liberal idea." Furthermore, "the abstraction of the feudal force implies the natural development of liberalism, so that we are dealing with a single factor."[15] What the United States would become was different from both the hierarchical vision of "Southern feudalists" and the radically egalitarian society preached by the late nineteenth-century American socialist Daniel De Leon. Hartz's broad insight does not suffer a bit from either his defense of the progressive New Deal as being one with the American liberal past or his adulatory treatment of John Locke as the fountainhead of American political attitudes.[16]

It is possible, and indeed crucial for the present study, to frame an argument similar to Hartz's without replicating his polemics or overgeneralizations. For a start, one can acknowledge that a bourgeois liberal tradition, fed by American Protestantism, came to dominate American history quite early. Although not the exclusive tradition, it reigned for a long time, and even figures whom Kirk treats as personifying the "conservative mind," for example, James Fenimore Cooper and John Randolph, expressed essentially liberal views on the need to restrain or balance central government. In the voluminous study *Conservatism and Southern Intellectuals, 1789–1861*, young Southern scholar Adam L. Tate demonstrates the continued importance of liberal and rural democratic values even among the Southern planter class. Those whom Hartz dismisses as "Southern feudalists" did not entirely abandon a Jeffersonian yeoman self-image in the course of defending a slave economy.[17] Racialist views spread because they justified departures from principles of self-government, given the presence of a large servile class in parts of the South. But within the antebellum understanding of "liberty and the good society," certain liberal attitudes persisted, albeit with a generally Calvinist theology and a European romantic conservative flavoring. Arguing that the "conservative" position had not been routed, precisely because it had not been sufficiently prominent to require a route, does not refute or even significantly challenge the recognition of the dominance of liberal ideas in America from the eighteenth century onward.[18]

Equally relevant, the American Right that came forth to oppose the New Deal and, in some cases, to argue against American intervention in the Second World War hardly fits the Kirkian model, which draws on the images and personalities of the European counterrevolution. This specifically American Right attracted the opponents of the government's recently acquired power that the anti–New Dealers were then trying to shrink. Some of its representatives—Albert Jay Nock, Garet Garrett, and John T. Flynn—regarded themselves as latter-day Jeffersonians. At the same time, novelist Isabel Paterson; journalists H. L. Mencken, Henry Hazlitt, and John Chamberlain; and Haverford College president Felix Morley preferred to call themselves libertarians. But almost all such opponents of the New Deal, including Taft and former President Hoover, claimed to be addressing one particular, overriding task, namely, that of resisting the federal government's expansion, particularly its venture into regulatory and redistributionist programs.[19]

These anti–New Dealers did not share Burke's view of the state as the guardian of a mystical social bond. Even less did they incline toward the European restorationist view of political power as expressed, for example, by the French aristocrat Louis de Bonald (1754–1840). An author whose work whimsical postwar conservatives tried to revive, Bonald elevated the monarch to the status of "*le conservateur social.*" The French counterrevolutionary state, according to Bonald, was not an entity to be kept at bay but rather one worthy of being empowered to restore and protect traditional social orders. His "detheologized metaphysic of power," to use the term of one German critic, pointed to a political and social order that no longer exists—and indeed one that has never gained traction in the United States.[20] Equally foreign to American politics was the defense of feudal privilege against bureaucratizing monarchies, which had preoccupied early nineteenth-century conservatives in central and eastern Europe. Those conservatives who opposed centralized government were generally upholding aristocratic and manorial arrangements against the encroachments of royal administrators. Such a conservative mission could not be other than anachronistic in a country without a landed aristocracy invested with hereditary privilege. The weight of an American bourgeois liberal tradition, however, did not deter Kirk from interpreting a European conservative and antirevolutionary tradition as the dominant or crucial American one. This flew in the face of the fact that the social world of European conservatism was not the one favored or inhabited by the critics of FDR in the1930s and 1940s.

POSTWAR CONSERVATISM

Not until *after* World War II did those who claimed some kind of connection to the anti–New Deal or anti-FDR Right adopt for themselves the label "conservative." This fact cannot be overemphasized.

George Nash, in his study of the conservative movement, identifies three of its peculiarities: its grounding in the period after 1945, and particularly in the cold war; its heavy dependence on European émigré intellectuals; and its adoption of a "conservative" label.[21] A question that must be asked is why this growing alliance of anti–New Dealers, anti-Communists, and Catholic traditionalists decided to call themselves "conservative"—at the expense of other still usable and more American labels, including classical liberal, strict constitutionalist, and Jeffersonian. One plausible explanation, although there are others, lies in the movement's anti-Communist momentum. The effect of this momentum was to push other themes and purposes irreversibly into the background. Crystallizing around the organizational figure of William F. Buckley and his postwar conservative fortnightly *National Review* in 1955, the aborning movement redefined the American Right.[22] Postwar conservatives set about creating their own synthesis of free market capitalism, Christian morality and the global struggle against Communism. As a signature act, the wealthy and resourceful Buckley attracted a board of editors, including Frank Meyer, Willi Schlamm, James Burnham, and Will Herberg, who had gone from recovering Marxists into self-identified anti-Communists. Most of these figures supported Buckley's efforts to assist Senator Joseph McCarthy in his work of uncovering high-placed Communists in government and helped defend McCarthy's reputation against his adversaries in the press.

Distinguishing this postwar orientation from an older journalism on the American Right, for example, the weekly *Human Events*, which had appeared in Washington since 1944, and the libertarian magazine *The Freeman*, is first and foremost an affirmative view of the American state. Although the dismantling of the welfare state was their professed goal, the Buckleyites viewed that task as less urgent than fighting Communism. According to the Sharon Statement, drawn up in 1961 in Buckley's country home in northern Connecticut for the youth organization Young Americans for Freedom, "the United States should stress victory over, rather than coexistence with this [Communist] menace."[23] While the market economy was called "the single economic system compatible with the requirements of personal freedom and constitutional government," a less individualist defense of the market also appeared in the Sharon Statement: "When government interferes with the work of the market economy, it tends to reduce the physical and moral strength of the nation," and this might be a problem when "the national sovereignty of the United States" is what stands in the way of further Communist advances.[24] If there is any doubt about political priorities, one might look at Buckley's oft-quoted remark from *Commonweal* that American conservatives should "be willing to accept totalitarianism on these shores [presumably in the form of a highly intrusive government] for the duration [of the cold war]."[25]

The backing of an aggressive response to Communist threats led the postwar Right into a break with the remnants of the interwar isolationist Right. Those who held to a skeptical attitude about American overseas involvements, while harping on the need to dismantle the American welfare state, were soon driven into the wilderness. This often took the ritualistic form of being denounced in *National Review* as an apostate from the struggle against the enemies of freedom. Such an excommunication fell twice on the hapless libertarian isolationist Murray Rothbard, once in the fifties and again even more demonstratively after he died forty years later.[26]

Any fair inquiry must acknowledge that the postwar Right was forced to fight for recognition against cold war liberals, who were also competing for the intellectual and journalistic leadership of the anti-Communist side. Both Schlesinger's *The Vital Center* and the English Labour government of the late forties testified to the possibility at midcentury of being equally anti-Soviet and committed to left-of-center social programs. The postwar Right yoked its anti-Communism to a decidedly traditionalist and antisocialist worldview, and it pursued this fusion through certain characteristic positions. It emphasized the Christian origin of American liberties and cultivated a special relation to the Catholic Church as a respected bulwark against godless Marxism and as a source of "transcendent values." (This last term, which made a brief appearance in the Sharon Statement, has been a leitmotiv in conservative journalism ever since.) While some of the better known conservatives of the time were cradle Catholics, such as Burnham and Buckley, others, like Kirk, his libertarian adversary Meyer, and the sociologist Ernst van den Haag, would become Catholic converts; and still others, like Herberg and Schlamm (an Austrian Jew who leaned heavily in that direction), could be counted on to praise Catholic traditionalism. Historian Patrick Allitt has explored this Catholic-conservative connection in a book dealing with American conservatism and the Catholic Church in the fifties, when most American Catholics were New Deal

Democrats. The affinity of conservatives for Catholic thought was significant, though less pronounced than the nexus between anti-Communism and the Church.[27] The McCarthy movement, with its prominent Catholic backers, the impassioned remarks by Pope Pius XII about the Communist persecution of Christians, and the growing identification of Catholic ethics with the defense of moral absolutes, all fortified the postwar symbiosis between the church and the American Right.

Equally important, Catholic and pro-Catholic European intellectuals, such as Waldemar Gurian, Eric Voegelin, Eric von Kuehnelt-Leddhin, Thomas Molnar, and Stefan Possony, worked to strengthen the burgeoning conservative movement. They helped to build conceptual bridges between the struggle against Soviet and Chinese Communism and the threat of "totalitarianism," a concept that was then gaining currency among Christian Democrats in Europe as well as among the American readers of Hannah Arendt's *The Origins of Totalitarianism*. The Catholic and pro-Catholic intellectuals who joined the American conservatives depicted the war against a totalitarian enemy, a notion that embraced the Nazis and Communists alike, as something that affected the entire "Christian West." This once popular phrase was now made to stand for more than the geographical and demographical heartland of the anti-Communist side in the cold war. It also designated a repository of moral and spiritual wisdom, which the anti-Communists thought had come under attack from within and without.[28]

Causing this anti-Communist Right to be viewed as "conservative" were several tendencies that were simultaneously present within it: a pro-Catholic or at least pro-Christian cultural stance that was wedded to anti-Communism; a willingness to borrow heavily from European ideas in defining its character; and a reliance on the state, which was not gainsaid by its defense of the free market, to carry out foreign policy and domestic surveillance programs. At the same time, this anti-Communist front showed openness to other types of arguments that did not contradict or could be made to buttress its core concerns, for example, the cultural critiques of urbanism that Southern Agrarians had been propagating since the 1930s and the opposition to the federal attempt to enforce black voting in the American South. Almost all of the *National Review* editors in the fifties and sixties spoke critically about the modern obsession with equality, which had given new life, according to Meyer, to "the leviathan state of the French

Revolution." Egalitarian experiments were also viewed as a diversion from fighting Communism, a point that came up repeatedly in *National Review* in the sixties. While the Soviets and the Chinese Communists were poised to expand their servile empires, it seemed unwise to become embroiled in racial upheavals at home. It was widely thought in conservative circles that a large black electorate might adversely affect the balance of forces in the cold war. Such a development might keep the United States from maintaining a strong defensive perimeter against the Soviet empire or from staying on the alert against domestic Communist adventures as Negro voters threw their weight in the direction of social programs aimed at themselves. The presence of at least one Communist advisor on Martin Luther King Jr.'s staff was seen as a portent of a radicalized new electorate.[29]

It was in the framework of this attempt to define a postwar "conservative" movement, for which anti-Communism was the "big thing," that Kirk achieved his initial fame as a writer. The rise of Kirk from a solitary man of letters living in the Michigan pine barrens to instant celebrity came, as Nash noted, from the success of his *second* book, whereas his first, on the Virginia planter and self-proclaimed "Old Republican" John Randolph, in 1951 had received only sporadic notice. On July 5, 1953, *Time* magazine devoted its entire book section to Kirk's already briskly selling volume, and his publisher Henry Regnery, who spent his life putting out conservative works, including those of European counterrevolutionaries, rejoiced at how Kirk had given an unmistakable "identity" to the Left's "scattered, amorphous opposition." The Kirk success, which "came as rain after a long drought," also found its way into Regnery's memoirs, published twenty-six years later, and seems to have been a defining event in his life of political engagement.[30]

Nash speculated on the reason for this publishing coup, which would not be repeated in Kirk's lifetime, and offered the explanation that Kirk furnished the American Right with an "intellectually formidable and respectable ancestry." Significantly, "the dominant thrust of the new conservatism. . .was not toward America but toward Europe. The principle perspective in which to place Kirk's book was Europe and Burke; it was Kirk's argument, in fact, that the American tradition was fundamentally Burkean."[31] While Nash properly described Kirk's impact, the question remains why American "conservatives" would praise a work that told them that their "tradition" was to be found in Burke's defense of English prescriptive liberties and of English orders and degrees against the ranting of French revolutionaries. Why would Americans welcome such teachings, and why would the postwar conservative movement hold up Kirk as a teacher? Such questions are not intended to cast aspersions on the *Reflections* or to deny the applicability of much of what Burke wrote there and elsewhere to ethical and social matters. What is being questioned is the assumption that Burke in 1790 was defending a political society that still corresponded to the American one in the 1950s. There are ample grounds to challenge those who suggested that the United States during the cold war was struggling to uphold the kind of traditional society beloved of Burke a hundred and forty years earlier.

But these were not the comparative historical matters that concerned most self-identified conservatives in the fifties. Already by the middle of that decade, the celebrant of Burke the counterrevolutionary had become a regular contributor to *National Review* and a much sought-after guest at conservative gatherings. One critical reason for this prominence was that Kirk bestowed on the Buckleyites a genealogy deeply rooted in the European past. Such a pedigree is different from attributing humble New World antecedents to oneself and one's companions. It is by far more pleasurable than having to trace one's political traditionalism to the small-town dissenters, nonconformist isolationists and bohemian litterateurs who had made up the anti–New Deal Right. Although Kirk, who chose to live in a small Michigan town, would not have scorned them, the conservatism that he devised while claiming to have uncovered it with *The Conservative Mind* did not focus on such identifiably American types.

Receiving an Old World genealogy was, for the would-be conservative movement, like picking up a baron's title in the Austro-Hungarian Empire. It was a nice thing that hurt nobody but brought those looking for social status a needed lift. And the florid décor that Kirk conferred on his countrymen answered to individual as well as collective needs. Kirk's discovery of the conservative heritage came from, among other activities, visiting and meditating on European ruins, something that the French novelist Maurice Barrès had promoted in the 1870s. The frail esthete Barrès had brooded on French gravestones, about which he wrote lyrically, before he proceeded to found a French nationalist movement. This aesthetic stance was equally present in Kirk's version of the "new conservatism." Americans of a certain temperament could vibrate to Kirk's remembered experience when he had visited "Burke's house [in Dublin] or the sad scrap of it that remains" and lamented how "the past shrivels."[32] Kirk extolled "hierarchy," but avoided offending his countrymen, for example, when instead of injudiciously defending eighteenth-century British stratification or anything like it, he placed his anti-egalitarian value in opposition to "mediocrity" and "leveling." He explained that he and Burke were not champions of inequality in general but only admirers of one particularly commendable, and historically remote, example of orders and degrees, "the British upper classes of the eighteenth and nineteenth centuries," "as a body, honorable, intelligent, moral and vigorous."[33]

Becoming a Kirkian "conservative" was largely about embracing an experience and celebrating the six canons featured in *The Conservative Mind*. It was and is, ironically, a democratic option, in that respect similar to what Burke called the "unbought grace of life." It is available to all choosing to embrace it. Kirkean conservatism can be compared to American low-church Protestantism, which is equally democratic and equally open to those who subject themselves to certain transforming experiences. Kirk presented his sentiments with literary flair, and he helped his readers get past his flinty quotations from long-dead conservative exemplars by adding felicitous paraphrases. He also avoided saying anything that would hurt people's feelings, until Midge Decter in the late eighties noticed that Kirk had made fun of her obsessive Zionism (more her obsession than her Zionism) and went on to scold him, mostly to deaf ears, as an anti-Semite.[34] But his combination of Anglophilia, general indifference to party politics, and aesthetic sensibility made him popular with readers who had nothing to do with European aristocracy or aristocratic interests.

Kirk helped to bring into being an incipient value-conservatism. To become "conservative," one might infer from *The Conservative Mind*, was no longer a question of birth, or of social position, or of the worldview related to either. It was a matter of agreeing with sentiments and with passing a self-administered quiz on values. And this experiential and canon conservatism did not require the adherent to be against the modern state. In *Conservatism Revisited: The Revolt Against Revolt* (1949), Mt. Holyoke professor and occasional poet Peter Viereck foreshadowed some of the tendencies in Kirk's magnum opus by tracing a Euro-American conservative tradition that allows for an evolving government. Viereck went well beyond Kirk by opening conservatism's door to FDR, and in later editions of his book he showed the same magnanimity toward the "Tory Democrat" Adlai Stevenson.[35] Even before

Kirk, a "new conservatism" was emerging in the United States of which scholar Clinton Rossiter took note with mixed emotions and which supposedly broke from "Manchestrian liberalism" and "rugged individualism."[36] Although Kirk did not actually praise the welfare state, his wrangling with libertarians, whom he called "chirping sectaries," led to his being identified with progovernment conservatives.

A movement player, Kirk generally tried to adjust to the political situation. He made his living by writing and "speechifying," and after he married and fathered four daughters, his financial circumstances made him increasingly dependent on conservative foundations and philanthropies, in welcome addition to his customary readership. In his youth he had devoured the thoughts of the anarcho-libertarian Nock, whose memoirs he had taken along to read when he had served in the Second World War in Utah's Great Salt Desert. Yet none of Nock's isolationism entered Kirk's public statements during the cold war, despite the fact that, according to his biographer and onetime assistant W. Wesley McDonald, he never fully abandoned his youthful isolationist position.

Unbeknownst to those who did not read his autobiography *Sword of Imagination* (which came out posthumously in 1995), Kirk had cast his presidential votes for the Socialist Norman Thomas in 1940 and for his friend Eugene McCarthy in 1976 because both candidates shared his wariness of foreign military adventures.[37] But he sagely never publicized this isolationism as long as the cold war continued to rage. He also probably improved his conservative profile when he converted to Catholicism in the 1960s, partly under the influence of his devoutly Catholic fiancée. For the rest of his life and afterwards, Kirk and his descendants would enjoy the favor and adulation of Catholic devotees, who wished to place Catholic values and Catholic natural law conceptions at the heart of "cultural conservatism." (McDonald's biography may have created some cognitive dissonance in this circle by pointing to the non-Catholic core of ideas in Kirk's formative writing.[38])

Even more obligingly, Kirk amended key passages in successive editions of *The Conservative Mind* to keep up with a movement that was tending leftward. By the 1970s the neoconservatives had begun their trek from the New York liberal establishment and from the Democratic Party into the Nixon camp and, from there, into the conservative movement. By the eighties they would take over this movement, which by then was up for grabs to the highest anti-Communist bidder, and pressure the old guard into going along with their party line. Although, according to McDonald, Kirk had no fondness for the new masters of the house that Buckley had built, he did accommodate himself to some degree as a cultural and value conservative.

Kirk's first canon had been altered after his conversion from "belief that a divine interest rules society as well as conscience" to the more Catholic-sounding "belief in a transcendent order, or body of natural law."[39] In the seventh edition, the off-putting canon three underwent a transformation that would suit the neo-conservative preoccupation with democratic opportunity. To the defense of "orders and degrees" would be added this syntactical monstrosity: "Ultimate equality in the judgment of God and equality before courts of law are recognized by conservatives; but equality of condition, they think, means equality in servitude and boredom."[40] Whether or not Kirk, who was a brilliant English stylist, produced this phrasing is a question that cannot be answered. What is more certain, however, is that the revised wording plays up a by then regnant value of American value conservatism. From social hierarchy, the value of choice had become equality of opportunity, or at least that form of equality that had still not mutated into equality of result.

Despite his mild-mannered accommodations, Kirk did encounter some criticism on the American Right. One source was the antistatist, libertarian camp, exemplified by Rothbard and Meyer. A noted controversialist, Rothbard viewed Kirk, together with the German Jewish political thinker Leo Strauss, as part of "a recent trend in Locke, etc. historiography to sunder completely the 'bad,' individualistic natural-rights type of natural law in the 17th and 18th centuries from the 'good' classical-Christian type— good because it was presumably so vague and so 'prudential' that it offered very little chance of defending the individual against the state."[41] Rothbard recognized a signal weakness in the "new conservatism" that Kirk had pioneered; its attacks on John Locke and his notion of individual natural rights concealed an indifference to state power. What set him in opposition to these intellectuals, Rothbard made clear, is "valuational": "they are anti–natural rights and liberty and I am for them." Moreover, Kirk and his followers overlook the antiquity of the struggle over individual rights that they projected onto Locke and modernity. They failed to notice what Rothbard takes as obvious: "while Aristotle and

Plato were statists in their approach to natural law, the Stoics were fine individualists."[42]

Rothbard's discernment of the tendency of the "new conservatism" to acquiesce to the growth of state power in the twentieth century was well founded, but some of his criticism overshot the mark. He took liberties by projecting Lockean natural rights and the view that government is a dissolvable invention, made by contracting individuals, back into ancient times. Although it is possible to find a concern with the individual soul among the Stoics, Platonists, and in the early church, such an interest was never tantamount to favoring a social contract theory of government. Personalism and contractarianism, that is to say, are clearly different things. It is also certain that nothing like the modern "state," which arose in its modern form in the Middle Ages, existed institutionally in the ancient world. The terms $arx\bar{e}$ and *respublica* refer not to older versions of a modern administrative regime but to ancient forms of authority. In short, the past does not yield a "factual, historical" refutation of the attempt to locate natural right theory in early modern Europe. Even less does the past discredit those distinctions attributed to Kirk and Strauss, between medieval natural law, as a standard of moral valuation, and natural rights, as individual freedoms that are presumed to preexist political authority.[43] Notwithstanding these errors, Rothbard correctly appreciated how "conservatism" had evolved into a tool of state aggrandizement.

More compelling than Rothbard's editorializing against the anti-Lockean Right are Meyer's broadsides against Kirk in *In Defense of Freedom: A Conservative Credo* (1962). Meyer did not always argue with clarity, and he often left his readers with stretches of tortured prose. But he also effectively criticized Kirk's thought when he stressed the unlikeness between Burke's vindication in 1790, "a powerful, a solid constitution not seriously challenged at home" and the content of the New Conservatives' tradition. Kirk was fantasizing if he thought that his American countrymen were truly much concerned "with the salvation of their civilization and their country from the positivist and liberal-collectivist doctrines which are already far advanced in authority over the hearts and minds of men."[44] Kirk and his votaries faced a "rational decision" that they could not avoid by ascribing political institutions to a higher will. Either they would have to recognize that "the whole historical and social situation in which they find themselves, including the development of collectivism, statism, and intellectual anarchy, is Providential and all prescriptive attitudes, including the orthodox collectivist attitudes of the day, are right and true," or they would have to accept that "there are standards of truth and good by which men must make their ultimate judgment of ideas and institutions."[45]

Meyer faulted Kirk for constructing a mystique of the state, which applied equally well to modern welfare regimes and to eighteenth-century monarchies. While Kirk professed to despise Hegel as a false conservative, he had found a new application for the Hegelian dictum that "what is is rational."[46] He had invested the current American state with both the divine will and the cumulative wisdom of human experience. Instead of this fool's errand, Kirk should have been judging the present political life by how well it conformed to the Constitution. This was more important, Meyer thought, than falling back on a justification for the state devised for another regime in a different age.

Although Meyer showed a contradiction of his own, specifically between a willingness to empower the central state to do whatever was necessary to defeat Communism and a deep suspicion of the democratic welfare state, he did perceive the "powerlessness" of the Kirkian side. Its proponents could not be seriously critical of a regime that they had convinced themselves was "providential" and a veritable replica of the old British constitution. Meyer, a repentant former Communist, might have enjoyed the irony that his strictures about Kirk call to mind Marx's withering critique of Hegel's *Philosophy of the Right* in 1843. According to Marx, Hegel's treatment of the state under law, as the objectified ethical will, allowed politicians and bureaucrats to assume a second nature. They ceased to have mere transitory interests and became incarnated philosophical categories.[47]

A less penetrating but ultimately more significant attack on Kirk came from Strauss's student Harry V. Jaffa, who was then a renowned professor at Claremont College. Author of both *The Crisis of the House Divided* (1959), a book lauding Lincoln as the quintessentially American promoter of universal equality, and *Freedom and Equality* (1965), which derives an entire political philosophy from the Declaration of Independence's passage that "all men are created equal," Jaffa made his mark as an embattled moralist. In a famed 1965 debate with Meyer printed in *National Review* about Lincoln's statesmanship and the constitutional right to prevent Southern secession, Jaffa proclaimed two of his signature beliefs: that "anti-secessionism" was "the dominant trend in American statesmanship" and that Lincoln was "the great prophet of our tradition." Jaffa contended that Lincoln had seen "the inner connection between free, popular, constitutional government and the mighty proposition that 'all men are created equal.' Questions concerning the construction of the Constitution were absolutely subordinate to the principle which gave life and meaning to the whole regime."[48]

Jaffa's later comments on Kirk in *A New Birth of Freedom* came in the context of an exceedingly broad assault on other postwar conservative writers, including M. E. Bradford, Frank Meyer, George Carey, and Willmoore Kendall, all of whom had slighted the Declaration's passage about equality. But whereas these authors had accurately presented the Declaration as an historical document worth pondering, Kirk had dismissed it as an aberration. In *Intercollegiate Review* (Winter 1985/86), a journal for conservative students, he had accused Jefferson in his reference to natural equality of abandoning the solid legal ground of the colonists' "rights as Englishmen." Jefferson had left these Burkean grounds, which had furnished the basis of previously stated colonial grievances, for the "misty, debatable land of an abstract, liberty, equality, fraternity." Jaffa retorted that the Declaration and the Revolution justified by it were not about reclaiming English historical liberties. They were part of an upheaval intended to establish democratic government on universal principles, and the process that they began received additional impetus when Lincoln ended slavery by implementing the Declaration's affirmation of equality.[49]

In a collection of essays, *The American Conservation of the American Founding* (1984), Jaffa stated the view that "the uniqueness of the United States was uniquely dependent upon the implementing of the proposition of human equality. But the obstacle to its recognition lay above all in the separation of mankind arising from the sense of the discreteness of its patrimonies." Because of its emphasis on universal principles, chiefly on equality, "the regime of the American Founding was then the first in the history of the world fully consistent with the ground of the truth about man's nature."[50] Jaffa inveighed against Walter Berns, a fellow student of Strauss's, whose *Wall Street Journal* essay advocated an American mission to spread liberal democratic principles for the wrong reason, namely, for the sake of universal peace.[51] Berns had argued (with something less than historical rigor) that democracies had never gone to war against each other and that, therefore, any effort to increase their number would lead to a peaceful world society. Although in agreement with this conclusion, Jaffa condemned Berns's "false premises," which seemed to be that democracies should worry more about peace than principles. Jaffa recommended democratic bellicosity if such militance might help liberate mankind from life under non-democratic regimes.[52]

Some of his readers might have reacted with disbelief when Jaffa first presented his missionary ideas as preeminently conservative. Never one to hide his message, he devoted the first part of *How to Think About the American Revolution* (1978) to demonstrating that "equality is a conservative principle." He argued definitionally that "equality is a conservative principle because justice is conservative and equality is the principle of justice. Inequality, whether numerical or proportional, tends to disrupt and destroy political communities and equality tends toward their harmony and their preservation. Equality as the ground of justice is then both good in itself and good for its consequences."[53] The United States was now witnessing the rise of "New Conservatism," and Jaffa claimed, for those who bothered to look, that this conservatism was "identical with the Old Liberalism of the Founding Fathers of the American regime." The essence of both was the building and defense of a "new and more radically just political order" that privileged the principle of equality.[54]

For an historian of ideas, it does not matter whether Jaffa's explicit references to Aristotle on justice are accurate or whether the Old Liberalism of the Founding Fathers was mainly about equality. It is equally immaterial for my purposes whether the export of democratic equality is a "conservative" position or one that would in any way have satisfied the American Founders. Irrespective of these considerations, Jaffa's efforts to replace the "New Conservatism" of the fifties with his own version succeeded brilliantly. His chapter "Equality as a Conservative Principle" was scheduled for delivery at the annual meeting of the American Political Science Association in 1974 as part of the panel "Conservatism's Search for Meaning," then being put together by Buckley.[55] As the animating spirit of the postwar Right, Buckley was looking for new meaning for his drifting movement. He settled on Jaffa as someone who might help him. Buckley drew Jaffa and Jaffa's protégé Charles R. Kesler into his inner circle and prevailed on Kesler to compile in collaboration with him an anthology of "conservative" readings, *Keeping the Tablets* (1988).[56] Moreover, Buckley introduced *American Conservation and the American Founding* with an essay declaring that Jaffa's "observations have their roots in the Socratic understanding that virtue is necessary for citizenship." Any book offered by this patriotic, virtuous author, we are told, should be viewed as "a gift to the nation."[57]

In 1968, while I was sitting with Kirk in his library in Mecosta, Michigan, he showed me a copy of Buckley's anthology *Did You Ever See a Dream Walking?*, which included a contribution by Jaffa on equality and conservatism.[58] I asked Kirk if he liked the author, who was rumored to have ghosted Barry Goldwater's acceptance speech as the Republican presidential candidate in 1964. Kirk grimaced joylessly and responded, "not very much." Little did he know at the time that this figure in whom he found nothing pleasing would provide a successor value to his own in the progression of value conservatisms that has unfolded since the middle of the twentieth century. Hierarchy and prescriptive liberties would give way to democratic equality as well as to the corresponding obligation to wage wars to spread American ideals. Nor would Jaffa, and the neoconservatives, who took over his "conservative" arguments, abandon the cold war. Far from relaxing their vigilance after the collapse of the Soviet enemy, they would set this protracted struggle into a new moral framework, which included the American civil rights movement, Lincoln's victory over the slaveholding South, and the unfinished business of making over the world in an American egalitarian image.

The transition from Kirk's ideas about tradition and hierarchy to more up-to-date values placed him and his followers at the fringes of the conservative movement. Advocates of older conservative values were at a disadvantage amidst those who henceforth accentuated human rights and the advancement of "global democracy" and whose new values influenced the Reagan presidency. Unlike the neoconservatives and the Jaffaites, Kirk received no honors and only occasional promises of them from Ronald Reagan, whose ascendancy he had initially praised. And given Kirk's understanding of "conservatism" and of American electoral developments, his expectation prior to addressing the Heritage Foundation in June 1980 that "in both the great political parties, I suggest, conservative views will tend to dominate" seems truly startling.[59] The closing sections of McDonald's biography mince no words in plotting the relative decline of Kirk's reputation within the movement that he had once inspired.

The author of *The Conservative Mind* had contributed to a value approach to "conservatism" that proceeded to move beyond him. From its beginnings, this political orientation was doomed to ineffectiveness and to drifting leftward. This happened not only because of larger social forces, such as traditional bourgeois attitudes and institutions weakened, but also because of the character of value conservatism. This movement was a time-conditioned response to disruptive social change and to the international crisis posed by the expansion of Communism, but not a response grounded in either a dominant class or one effectively competing for dominance. When Burke invoked the "wardrobe of moral imagination" that bestowed honor and beauty on inherited social institutions, he was able to speak for a broad English national consensus. Monarchies, established churches, and social deference were the order of the day, and so there was nothing jarring about the images of continuity or the unbroken chain of generations united by veneration for its past that suffused Burke's *Reflections*. Meyer was right to point to the anachronism of such rhetoric in the United States in the second half of the twentieth century. What brought tears of pride to late eighteenth-century English eyes would not likely do the same for contemporary young urban professionals—or even for their parents who sold insurance, ran laundromats, or repaired TVs.

It should not be surprising, then, that the appeal to Burke eventually became connected to something other than historical imagination or nostalgia for social hierarchy. The lineaments of a quite different Burke revival became apparent in 1958 when a Catholic scholar and an eighteenth-century specialist, Peter Stanlis, unveiled *Edmund Burke and the Natural Law*.[60] The major focus thereafter in the elevation of Burke as a cultic figure, which went back to a circle of Catholic thinkers at Fordham University in the late forties, was the reinvigoration of a Catholic and Anglo-Catholic tradition of natural law. Burke emerged preeminently as a critic of moral relativism and individual natural rights, a critic who had opposed the French Revolution while expressing sympathy for the American colonists on the eve of the American Revolution.[61] His ties to the Irish Catholics, from whom he descended on both sides of his family, and his parliamentary crusades for a Catholic franchise in England and for Irish home rule, increased his ethnic and denominational appeals on the opposite side of the Atlantic. Burke's biography certainly suited the Irish Catholics who flocked to the postwar conservative cause—and who figure quite large in Allitt's monograph about Catholic intellectuals and the American Right.[62]

The new ethical emphasis had the obvious advantage of freeing "Burkean conservatism" from Burke's counterrevolutionary stance while relating it to a war over values. But this move would not avert or significantly slow down the slide toward the Left that overtook value conservatism in the seventies and eighties. The combination of Burkeanism, natural law talk, and grim warnings about the Communist temptation did not preclude the triumph of new "conservative" values, which centered upon equality and global democracy. Like other values that had once been in season, these victorious ideals were now destined to surge forth as newly discovered eternal truths.

A GERMAN DIGRESSION

A politics based on values, similar to what was then taking place in the United States, shaped the postwar "moderate" Right in Germany. It is therefore worthwhile to recount the fate of this German *Wertekonservatismus* to throw light on the American experience by elucidating the larger Western context in which it unfolded. German constitutional (in the European sense) liberals worked from the late forties well into the seventies to establish a moral and philosophical framework for postwar German constitutional democracy. Academics and other scholars, chiefly Joachim Ritter, Robert Spaemann, and Günter Rohrmoser, devised what they took to be a timely understanding of a distinctively German constitutionalism that incorporated Christian principles, bourgeois civic ethics, and jurisprudential understandings going back to early nineteenth-century German philosophy.[63] The thinkers involved in this enterprise were seeking a way to ground the West German state by furnishing their countrymen with both an image of a less than totally blemished national past and a meaningful sense of civilizational continuity. Another goal that engaged these German writers was to establish a political theoretical counterpoint to "totalitarianism" in its Stalinist as well as Hitlerian form, a goal that fit the strategic dimension of the ideological struggles of the time.

Since there was no significant remainder of an aristocratic order that might have shared in German leadership, the *Wertekonservative* placed their hopes for national renewal in what remained of an older bourgeois society. They appealed to the constitutional and cultural concerns of an educated *Bürgerstand* to help them rebuild their country on the foundations of lawfulness and family institutions. Their politics also spurred them to identify themselves with the Christian Democratic-Christian Social Union, which occupied the German Center-Right. Although the Union was an imperfect vehicle for promoting bourgeois culture and bourgeois interests, it was the best available. The *Wertekonservative*, who opposed the Center-Left Socialists as an antibourgeois force, warned that the socialization of industry and economic redistribution carried grave cultural implications. Unlike the American postwar Right, however, its German counterpart never assumed a counterrevolutionary pose. Rather, it sought to ward off attacks from the antifascist Left by affirming its loyalty to the " free, democratic foundations of the German Basic Law." It supported the German Constitution but tried to do so by advocating measures, or so it explained, that would strengthen a lawful, constitutional society.[64]

Like in the United States, the question arose about which "values" the defenders of the constitutional establishment should be teaching the public to uphold. And comparable to the way in which American conservative foundations became advisors and accessories to the Republican Party, the German *Wertekonservative* joined themselves so closely to the union and its think tanks that they progressively lost the ability to remain an independent force on the Right. The Union's party professionals meanwhile gradually watered down the "conservative values" that they dispensed, lest their expression of "extreme Right" views would cause offense to the media and/or voters. Angela Merkel, who heads the Christian Democrats, last year avoided taking much of any stand on whether the Germans should require immigrants to adopt a "dominant culture." Taking a sharp "conservative" position on this issue in the face of massive Muslim immigration, she and her strategists had calculated, would drive the German antinational Left into denouncing them as bigots.[65]

In December 2004, Wolfgang Bosbach, the head of the Union delegation in the German Bundestag, announced that Germany does indeed have a dominant culture, which needs to be passed on to those who choose to reside there. It consists of "liberal democracy" whose supporters "demand integration and oppose with determination all forms of extremism."[66] But this "conservative" stance, excepting only its label, *Leitkultur* (dominant culture), is indistinguishable from the Left opposition's own stance, namely, "living together on the basis of shared values" of diversity and loyalty to constitutional procedures. Beyond the Union's failed rhetorical attempt to position itself somewhere to the Right of the other side, there is nothing in its value statement that justifies conservative labeling.[67] This remains the case regardless of whether Germany, like much of Western Europe, has become a postbourgeois society, marked by a strongly antinationalist press and a declining birth and marriage rate, except among the 7 million Muslims who have settled there since the sixties.

DRIFTING "CONSERVATIVE" VALUES

Lest any belief to the contrary arise, it should be stressed that value replacements in postwar American conservatism generally have occurred by degrees. The changes have not required the precipitous ousting of one premier value, and the policies appertaining thereto, in favor of another. Instead, particular values have phased in and out, and the falling values have been allowed to coexist with the rising ones temporarily until the less favored "higher truth" is pushed out definitively. This pattern explains why it is still possible to find references to Catholic natural law alongside the affirmation of an American global democratic mission and Jaffa's tracts in *National Review*. Almost until the end of his life, Kirk received payment for his quarterly lectures at the neoconservative Heritage Foundation in Washington. His invocations of Burke and hallowed custom offered him the otherwise fruitless occasion to make the Heritage Foundation look inclusive without diverting its staff from their crusade for democratic progress and economic growth. Similarly today, proabortionists and advocates of gay marriage can rise in the conservative movement, but socially traditional critics of an American democratic mission to the Middle East are less welcome. This reality reflects equally the relative weight now assigned to a neo-Wilsonian foreign policy and the dwindling importance of domestic social agendas tied to biblical and natural law points of reference.[68]

Beyond these policy preferences, a different conception of conservatism now prevails as measured against the one that existed forty years ago. In 2000 and again in 2002, *National Review Online* editor Jonah Goldberg prepared commentaries on the kinship between leftwing supporters of group rights and the European

self-admitted counterrevolutionary Joseph de Maistre. Goldberg
asserted that Maistre, an early nineteenth-century figure who had
noted the essential distinctiveness of nations and classes, foreshadowed the present Left: "It goes without saying that the Left sub-
scribes precisely to this point. Along with nationality, they
emphasize ethnicity, race, and various other identity politics, but
the principle is the same." Furthermore, " Maistre would have
no trouble saying 'people of color' because that is how he largely
saw the world."[69] Goldberg strongly implied that Maistre could
not have been a conservative given the extent of his disagreement
with the current *National Review* editorial board. What unites
conservatives, Goldberg explained, is the belief in "universal values" and "human rights," sacred ideals that French reactionaries no
less than the postmodern Left have scorned. At least philosophically,
Goldberg concluded, Maistre should have embraced the now fashionable plan to award special rights to women and blacks.

This, mind you, is not any man's opinion about Maistre's
Leftist persona but rather that of a leading conservative journalist,
indeed one who by his late twenties had become a conservative
media celebrity. It not incidentally coincides with Jaffa's negative
judgment about Maistre in *New Birth of Freedom*.[70] Jaffa and his
disciples also produce the *Claremont Review of Books*, a well-
funded publication that subsumes the Marxist Left and essentially
all the critics of human rights doctrines and the ideal of universal
equality into a single villainous company. Readers find in the
Claremont Review a tendency to link together fascism, Marxism,
and the Confederate cause as morally related evils. These wicked
forces appear in stark opposition to democratic equality.[71] The
Review's contributors' practice of what seems random linkage
proves the power of the present "conservative" fixation on
selected abstract values detached from historical circumstances.
Those who stand outside the chosen value framework of the value
selector are uniformly condemned if not dehumanized.

This practice is hardly restricted to obscure groupies. Jaffa's
fellow Straussian Allan Bloom undertook another sweeping linkage in a "conservative" book of social criticism long on the *New
York Times* best-seller list, *The Closing of the American Mind*
(1987). In Bloom's version of converging bad values, it is the
"German connection" that has led to our present civilizational
woes. Rightwing Teutonic critics of democratic equality, Friedrich
Nietzsche and Martin Heidegger, inflicted on later generations
their combination of moral relativity and hatred for democracy.

This German background engendered both Nazism and the student Left, Bloom argued, and he urged his fellow Americans to stand up for equality and human rights against the antidemocratic miasma from abroad: "And when we Americans speak seriously about politics, we mean that our principles of freedom and equality and the rights based on them are rational and everywhere applicable. World War II was really an educational experiment undertaken to force those who do not accept these principles to do so."[72]

Bloom also explained, to the resounding cheers of hundreds of thousands of American conservatives who bought his book, what it means to be an American but what is alien to German-influenced relativists and historicists. According to Bloom's understanding of American identity, "by recognizing and accepting man's natural rights, men found a fundamental basis of unity and sameness. Class, race, religion, national origin or culture all disappear or become dim when bathed in the light of natural rights, which give men common interests and make them truly brothers. . . . There was a tendency, if not a necessity, to homogenize nature itself."[73] This statement unfolds like a creed going back to the Jacobins of the French Revolution. According to political theorist Claes Ryn in *America the Virtuous*, the reader cannot avoid wondering about the accuracy of defining it as "conservative."[74] Equally perplexing in 1989 was the proposal of *National Review*'s longtime contributing editor Ernst van den Haag for a putative middle ground between the neoconservatives and the conservatives on the Right whom they were then displacing.[75] The proposed middle ground, namely, a commitment to make democracy universally accepted, was in fact a capitulation to the neoconservatives who were then on the rise. Van den Haag had advanced his proposal despite his longtime friendship with Kirk and their shared interest in reversing the eroding unity of conservatives after the fall of the Soviet Empire.

The qualified endorsement of the Trotskyite tradition in *National Review Online* (June 3, 2003) is indicative of where mutating value conservatism may be leading. This praise of the ideas and career of onetime Communist leader Leon Trotsky came from *National Review* contributor and movement conservative critic of "Islamofascism" Stephen Schwartz. Summoning the democracies to fight Islamic fundamentalism, which he categorizes as "fascist," Schwartz holds up Trotsky for special commendation. He judges Trotsky's scorners on the Right, particularly those who do not share Schwartz's revulsion for "Islamofascism," to be themselves "neofascists" and he heaps ridicule on those who refuse to call these people by their proper name.

Schwartz's timid allies stood accused of not being willing to recognize Trotsky's accomplishments. Like the "neofascist" Right, they focus on Trotsky's considerable contribution toward a Communist dictatorship in Russia, while they ignore how staunchly he opposed the antidemocratic Right. Were he still alive today, Schwartz contends, he would be lending his energies to fighting fanatical Muslims:

> To my last breath, I will defend Trotsky who alone and pur- sued from country to country, and finally laid low in his own blood in a hideously hot little house in Mexico City, said no to Soviet coddling to Hitlerism, to the Moscow purges, and to the betrayal of the Spanish Republic, and who had the capacity to admit that he had been wrong about the imposition of single-party state as well as about the fate of the Jewish people. To my last breath, and without apology. Let the neofascists, and Stalinists in their second childhood, make of it what they will.[76]

Although whitewashed images of Trotsky and his revolution- ary Left have not yet joined other "new conservative" icons, *National Review* has welcomed Schwartz's journalism in a way that it has not done with that of an older Right. Significantly enough, there is nothing that the rising generation of conservative journalists should find offensive in the remodeled Trotsky, a Jewish radical who gains posthumous entry into the democratic Left for having fought fascism and Stalinism. As early as 1987 in the *New Republic*, Michael Massing noticed how "Trotsky's orphans" had moved into the Reagan camp as the sworn enemies of Soviet "Stalinism."[77] The American Right was falling under the sway of partly disenchanted Leftists who hated the Soviets for hav- ing betrayed their vision of a reformed humanity. These apparent converts from the Left aroused little opposition on the Right, although their rhetoric sometimes retained an inflammatory Trotskyist tone. Schwartz, who has pushed the succession of val- ues and their corresponding icons exactly in the direction outlined by Massing, has contributed to a process affecting the conservative movement that had begun decades earlier.

This critical look at the parade of "conservative" values that have been changing since the 1950s is not intended to demonize the late Russell Kirk. Whatever the defects of his quest for a conservative pedigree, Kirk stood out as someone who often sounded like an authentic English conservative. He also had affinities to Taft Republicanism, which was evident in his desire to avoid foreign military engagements and in his small-town American tastes. For all of his laments about a lost aristocratic age, Kirk belonged to the isolationist and relatively classless Midwest. His contribution to the value game that overtook the "Right" was in large measure unwitting—or undertaken without foreknowledge of the end result. Despite the conservatives' "rout," Kirk believed, these American counterparts to the British Tories and Old Whigs had genuine, centuries-old roots in their society. The conservative mind supposedly continued to influence American politics into the 1980s, and those who personified it perceived the conceptual and historical overlaps between the British and American constitutions. Kirk strove mightily to keep alive this shared conservative tradition, which he felt was now under siege.

The problem, as the next chapter will try to clarify, is that those who looked for this "conservative" link among English-speaking societies had to search beyond the questionable evidence of social continuity. American conservatism could not be anchored in anything as concrete as the social world in which European conservatives had lived and defended their orders and degrees. Kirk and his disciples thus had to focus on alternative continuities. Initially they focused on moral and aesthetic sentiments but ultimately settled on shared values, an amalgamation of ideas and preferences that came to be known as "cultural conservatism." But this amorphous combination of ideas never fully detached itself from what it claimed it was not. While Kirkians have always been eager to declare that their concerns, like those of T. S. Eliot, are "the permanent things," usually they also have consorted with relatively worldly types as they self-consciously cultivated their ties to the Republican Party. With unflagging zeal, they have thrown themselves behind party candidates whom they have tried to associate with their own programs.

Ryn once observed with puzzled amusement the behavior of his graduate students at Catholic University of America who identify themselves as Kirkian conservatives. Such students typically "make a fuss over the GOP" while " also preparing to be received into the Catholic Church."[78] There arises the question of the extent to which this partisan affiliation and this religious involvement can be separated from a "conservative" identity. Can one be a "cultural conservative" while being likewise a Protestant and a Democrat, or a nonpartisan Deist? If so, are such types mere anomalies in the group? Despite their loyalties, the Republican "value-conservative" activists have not gained the political and philanthropic rewards that they have obviously sought, and those they have garnered have depended on the whims of neoconservative mediators. The Kirkian and cultural conservatives have not been able to compete effectively for influence against the bearers of more up-to-date "conservative" values and position papers.

But this falling behind has not been the result of choosing an *entirely* different course from the one taken by groups deemed more progressive. Cultural conservatives have remained in the same general political movement with the others while engaging in their own value talk. They have not become a strictly bookish alternative to those who are freezing them out or controlling their lifeline. No school of conservatism that has gained attention in the last fifty years has left the political arena for monkish or contemplative lives. Save for the remnants of the anti–New Deal Right, all contemporary forms of conservatism have their lineage in what Buckley and his comrades worked inventively to put together. Most of these forms also reflect the periodic revisions undergone by the positions once embedded in the postwar conservative movement.

———◆———

CHAPTER 2

CONSERVATIVE THEORY IN CONTEXT

DIFFERENT ERAS

One does not require a fixed definition of conservatism to recognize the postwar American movement's misapplication of that term. So loose was its usage that the meaning of "conservative" continued to change over several decades. As the foregoing review of these changes demonstrates, any attempt to create conservative rallying points by appealing to values independently of social authorities is doomed to one of two outcomes: either being bypassed in a phantasmagoria of competing values or succumbing to pressures or artifices to affirm identifiably Leftist notions as eternal "conservative" truths. This is not because those who engage in these actions necessarily wish to deceive. The neoconservatives who took over the American establishment Right resisted the "conservative" label before eventually having it thrust on them. Throughout the seventies and into the eighties, they made distinctions between themselves as Harry Truman and Scoop Jackson Democrats and Zionists and the older American Right. Although by the present century they had come to consider themselves the only proper conservatives and to treat anyone to their right as an "extremist," this was not always their attitude. The older generation of neoconservatives had winced at the term "conservative" for its alleged association with the nativist or anti–New Deal Right; only when they were able to impose their dominant values and policies did this initial distaste turn into an eager acceptance of their conferred identity.

This development owed little or nothing to the intellectual maturation of the newly minted conservatives. In truth, personnel no less than value orientation changed as urban, Jewish, erstwhile Democratic proponents of the welfare state took over a conservative movement that had been largely in the hands of Catholic, pro-McCarthy and (more or less) anti–New Deal Republicans. That the older movement collapsed into the newer one is a demonstrable fact. Less obvious are the claims that the second movement is more intellectual than the first (both having been run predominantly by journalists) and that the transformed movement is ethically more advanced. All that can be observed in a nonpartisan manner is a process by which one value package has been replaced by another in a movement that defines itself as "conservative."

The media attach "conservative" colors to groups of their own choosing, and this practice may be compared to giving names such as Guelfs and Ghibellines to our political factions, assuming that there were a hypothetical surge in the popularity of the designations of these once-feuding medieval parties. Would these designations continue to be applicable simply because influential people have taken a liking to them, although the names themselves pertain to rival factions that had existed in thirteenth-century Florence? And if those terms were used, would they indicate what they originally referred to or would they be merely labels affixed to groupings that have nothing in common with those factions from whom they have drawn their names? There has arisen a situation such as Thomas Hobbes noted centuries ago, when he denounced calling wisdom what "another man calleth fear and cruelty what another justice." Where semantic confusion reigns, Hobbes observes, there are no steady "grounds of ratiocination," for arbitrary names lead to inconstancy in meaning.[1]

An examination of conservatism requires a return to the era and society that gave birth to that concept. Indispensable for this study is a vast and growing body of interpretive literature about the conservative reaction to the French Revolution and the spread of revolutionary ideas across Europe. Like the rationalists, who had prepared the way for the revolution and its bureaucratically imposed reforms, the Revolution's critics formed a conceptually distinctive school of thought. And though this school ranged from moderate reformers such as Edmund Burke in England, to self-proclaimed counterrevolutionaries Joseph de Maistre and Louis de Bonald in France, to defenders of organic aristocratic societies, represented by Adam Müller (1779–1829), Karl Albrecht von Haller, and Friedrich Stahl, in Germanophone Europe, there were certain commonalities among its exponents. All such critics of revolutionary change took up a manner of thinking that Burke had predicated in his *Reflections.* These thinkers placed their own ideal of a traditional society in stark contrast to a nontraditional one. They also advanced a different epistemology from the one developed by rationalist reformers. The resulting conservative discourse, as Karl Mannheim explained in what may be the most penetrating study of the conservative mind yet produced, *Das konservative Denken,* focused on concreteness, particularity, vitalism, hierarchy, historicity, and collective consciousness. Although not all of these perspectives surfaced simultaneously in every writer, Mannheim demonstrated that they appeared widely, starting with Burke's critique and then advancing especially in German-speaking regions, until they formed a distinctive conservative worldview.[2]

Mannheim's analysis yields three characteristics about the "conservative mode of thought," all of which clarify its essence. One, the conservative *Denkweise* (way of thinking), emerged as a reaction to bourgeois rationalism as European aristocrats and their theoretical apologists reacted against liberal and revolutionary democratic reformers and their political designs. In opposition to these reformers, conservative critics on the continent upheld the inalienability of aristocratic estates, guild restrictions on trade practices, and seigniorial rights to dispense justice on noble land. More generally, they took aim at the materialist scientific approach to government and to economics embodied by the rising bourgeoisie, and they worked on alternative explanations for the evolution of human relations. Against an analytical epistemology and a moral perspective predicated on abstract universals, they conceptualized situational and genetic approaches to topical issues. The truth of a proposition, they asserted, had to be uncovered by looking at the historical particularities and conditions that had shaped its content.[3] Conservatives resisted any appeal to universal definitions of human rights, as demonstrated by the skepticism expressed by Maistre about "mankind in general" as the bearer of rights in general. This rejection of such universals went far beyond justifications for particularistic manorial and guild privileges the defense of manorial and guild privileges. With Burke, it entered the picture in the context of defending the "historical liberties" of

Englishmen, including the right of English subjects to practice commerce, which Burke set over the universal rights proclaimed by the French Revolution.

Another characteristic attributed by Mannheim to the conservative mode of thought referred to its practitioners, intellectuals who offered their services to a threatened social class. Crucial to Mannheim's insight is his controversial concept of "free-floating intellectuals [*freischwebende Intelligenz*]," which does not signify exclusively that which it is often misunderstood to mean. Mannheim did not suggest that intellectuals are more selfless than other specimens of humanity; rather, his point was that intellectuals, ever since the Middle Ages when they were tied firmly to the Catholic Church as theologians and priests, have been moving around looking for classes and institutions to which they could attach themselves. Although most of them in the West during the twentieth century gravitated toward the Left and particularly toward Marxism, this has not always been true of other intellectuals at other times. In the early nineteenth century, some intellectuals moved into the conservative camp as spokesmen for aristocratic and manorial interests.[4] Mannheim saw at work here the overlap of layered interests. Such German publicists as Müller, Friedrich Gentz, and the converted Jewish Prussian jurist Stahl, gained access to the upper class and were even ennobled after they had turned their talents toward a defense of the ancien régime. At the same time, they identified themselves with their overt beneficiaries, partly because of the ideological framework they had constructed and embraced and partly because they took their bearings from the class whose defenders they had chosen to become. An incipient social attachment, which was also a professional one, thus evolved over time into an existential commitment (*Seinsverbundenheit*). Their intellectual, imaginative and social involvements all came to have the same reference point.[5]

The final characteristic of the conservative mode of thought, according to Mannheim, is that it did not disappear with the vanishing of the order that it was meant to justify. It not only survived, it thrived, and the methods and thought processes that Mannheim found in his subjects had profound impact on a wide range of movements and intellectual currents, from Hegelian philosophy and the Historical School in nineteenth-century Germany to Marxism and modern sociology. Like American social theorist Robert Nisbet, Mannheim viewed the classical conservatives as forerunners of later attempts to explain individual behavior

through social and historical particularities. He credited these conservatives with the recognition that there is a group consciousness
that transcends and shapes the individual. And he noticed how
throughout the nineteenth and twentieth centuries, the European
bourgeoisie moved away from the atomistic rationalism and the
abstract way of framing moral questions, an approach that had
once been their tradition, toward a more organic and historically
based understanding of morals and behavior. The conservative
intellectual crusade, whether it marched under the banner of
"Mind," "History," or "Life," was effectively a struggle waged
against "mere rationalism." For as long as battles for supremacy
among competing ideas lasted, both rationalism and its rival
would show up, as Mannheim states, in "philosophical systems
that were nurtured and brought together by standpoints extending back to the political polarities between liberal and conservative
world aspirations."[6]

THE MISSING FIT

American "conservative thinking" has kept and, over time, increased its distance from the European conservative tradition. For
Allan Bloom, it reeks of the "German connection," and he and
other heroes of postwar American conservatism have railed at
"historicism" as being antithetical to values.[7] Not only is Mannheim's notion of conservatism offensive to the American establishment Right it also provides, when discerned in those whom
American conservatives oppose, the hobgoblins of "value relativism." Significantly the self-proclaimed Burkean Russell Kirk
sneered at those continental conservatives (save for Gentz) who
had embraced Burke's ideas about revolution and tradition. Kirk's
readers are not allowed to forget that Burke was not a continental
conservative but rather a stalwart of Anglo-American culture.
Modern American conservatism has so rigidly entrenched this perspective that an unequivocal rejection of European historical conservatism is the admission price one pays to join a movement
centered on "Anglo-American" values.

Ironically, Kirk and a number of Southern conservatives
favored themes and perspectives that Mannheim had accentuated
in his study of classical conservatism. Whether Kirk talked about
sentiment and intuition as the wellspring of moral behavior,
inveighed against abstract rights that purport to be universal, or

wrote "gothic" ghost stories, he fit without having to be stretched into Mannheim's conservative romantic typology.[8] Kirk's avoidance of this problematic association does not prove the opposite, given the resemblance between his conservative traits and Mannheim's. The Southern conservative historical tradition is likewise full of the type of thinking that Mannheim associated with classical conservatism. Exemplified in recent years by M. E. Bradford, Clyde Wilson, and Donald Livingston, modern Southern conservatives have focused on their region's landowners, who were the presumed leaders of likeminded communities and were supposedly oblivious to the "principles of the Declaration."[9] Although these Southerners probably never read Justus Möser (1720–1794), the eighteenth-century German progenitor of conservative ideas and a legal counselor to the estates assembly in the principality of Osnabrück, they and he spoke with seemingly the same voice. The modern Southerners and the eighteenth-century German stress identical themes, namely, localism, inherited authority, and a profound disdain for universal, rationalist thinking applied to politics.[10] There is one major difference: while Möser defended the remnants of serfdom in his principality, the Southern conservatives gingerly evaded the question of Negro slavery. But, as the historian of the South Eugene Genovese emphasized, such diplomatic subterfuge cannot work for those who are looking at the fabric of antebellum Southern life. For better or for worse, a servile class and a manorial economy shaped Southern culture and manners, and no overview of the Southern past or Southern tradition can exclude these facts from a comprehensive, historically valid understanding.[11]

In *Ideas Have Consequences* (1947), Richard Weaver (1910–1963), a yet more reactionary thinker from the South, traced "the dissolution of the West" back to an "evil decision" that had occurred centuries before. This decision had been reached in the fourteenth century, when the belief in universals gave way to nominalist philosophy. Such thinkers as William of Ockham were allowed to assail what scholars had considered the ideal nature of reality, thereby doing violence to a Western structure of thinking going back to Plato and Aristotle. A method of inquiry that aimed at grasping individual objects had taken the place of an older one, which had examined the particular in relation to its unchanging essence. According to Weaver, this intellectual change had led to the fall into modernity. Both material acquisition and the calculation of interest thereafter had driven an identifiably modern society. But Weaver viewed the rural South, out of which he himself had come, as the "last non-materialist civilization" and one that had lost in a struggle against a Northern capitalist empire.[12]

Although his attack on Ockham still resonates among Catholic cultural conservatives, and although as late as 1970 Frank Meyer characterized *Ideas Have Consequences* as "the fons et origo of the contemporary American conservative movement," Weaver's antimodernism has little or nothing to do with today's conservative politics.[13] Significantly, it also rejects classical conservative thinking in its appeal to Platonic and scholastic paradigms, the rejection of which, according to Weaver, brought about the descent into the modern period. In his moral-historical stance, Weaver, a once revered traditionalist, showed the same distaste for historical conservatism that later movement conservatives would exhibit for other, more progressive reasons.

Thinkers and ideas bearing classical conservative trademarks have, in any case, little appeal at the present time. This is due, in part, to the necessary failure of any attempt to cordon off a zone of nonpolitical conservative thought. Conservatism in either its real or fictitious form has been inescapably about politics. Being conservative is not the same as being "traditional," which can refer to a wide variety of cultures, not all of them Western, but involves sharing the common identity of being nonmodern and socially prescriptive. There is, of course, vast literature on the subject of tradition, and there are a multiplicity of anthropological studies dealing with the oddities of traditional societies.

But the particularities of all such traditional societies do not add up to the Western movement that arose in reaction to the Enlightenment and the French Revolution—or so we learn from reading Nisbet, Mannheim, Carlo Galli, Panajotis Kondylis, and Kirk.[14] Such authors, who eschew examining anything as remote as gender relations among central Asian tribes, described a reaction in the Western world to Western events. The French upheaval and the reactions that followed assumed definite historical forms, and what came to be known as conservatism was the political movement that emerged to challenge a specific kind of revolutionary thinking and revolutionary politics. To say that conservatism has ceased to be political and thereby has become essentially apolitical is itself a political tactic, one to which those who are losing the value war have sometimes resorted. It is a case of appearing to turn one's back on the world after one's enemy has shifted the meaning of conservatism and moved the relevant discussion toward the Left. But this response is essentially a political one, and this remains the case particularly when those who wish to give the impression of leaving the political game are still visibly continuing to play it.

Another term that needs to be distinguished from self-styled cultural conservative is cultural traditionalist. The latter are those who seek to preserve a literate Western civilization but are not even conscious of political battles. *The Conservative Mind* is full of cultural traditionalists, such as philosopher and man of letters George Santayana and long-active Princeton Christian Platonist Paul Elmer More, who lived in a world of ideas and great books. Such figures did not ghost speeches or ring doorbells for political candidates, and if they had done so, they would not have considered such behavior seemly nor would they think it had anything to do with cultural traditionalism. Santayana's occasional political stands seem to have been too idiosyncratic to fit any firm ideological pattern. The Harvard professor, in the course of his very long life, expressed mild sympathy for the Soviet Union as an attempted postnational empire but also admired the perceived counterrevolutionary stance of the Italian fascists. Santayana generally supported the Nationalists during the period of the Spanish Civil War but, as a Spaniard on his maternal side, admired equally the Latin courage of the "rojos" and particularly the anarchists. His statements about politics were never those of an activist but of someone whose interests and passions lay elsewhere, namely, in his efforts to reconcile his philosophical naturalism with the aesthetic and ascetic implications of his thought.

The New Critic interpreter of early modern English poetry, as well as student of the Southern Agrarians, Cleanth Brooks, whom I met during my graduate studies at Yale, had no political inclinations known to his students beyond occasionally casting a vote for the Democratic Party. His strongest commitments were neither to an ideology nor to a party but to the Anglican Book of Common Prayer, whose original wording he worked for decades to keep in use at Episcopal services. It was impossible while listening to his lectures on Keats or Donne to fathom which of the two American national parties Brooks supported. Someone equally unlikely to be taken for a failed political activist is another cultural traditionalist of my acquaintance, George Panichas, a Christian Neo-Platonist and an exponent of More and Irving Babbitt. Although a longtime chairman of the English Department at the University of Maryland and the perennial editor of *Modern Age*, Panichas has remained blissfully ignorant of both academic infighting and the presumed differences between our two national parties. He has justified his deliberate neglect of such matters by dismissing them as "passing doxai," in contrast to the deeper truths that he finds in mystics and in such religious authors as Dostoyevski, Simon Weil, and Alexander Solzhenitsyn.

Nineteenth-century conservatism, in sharp contrast to contemporary value conservatism, exerted much greater influence on its surrounding culture. Its ideas spread rapidly into universities, churches, and civil institutions before making headway among the socially triumphant bourgeoisie. This diffusion of ideas, however, did not result from political conservatives having presented themselves as "value conservatives." It succeeded because of a fit between what they taught, which was not strictly partisan, and the views of reality that had come to find favor among the nonaristocratic classes.

By the second half of the nineteenth century, both the working class and the bourgeoisie discovered various aspects of conservative romantic thinking that suited their needs and confirmed their perceptions. The middle class embraced the conservatives' passion for national antiquities as well as their vitalist, evolutionary understanding of society that came out of the conservative reaction to the Enlightenment. Conservative romantic thinking also proved adaptable to the spokesmen for the proletariat, starting with Marx and Engels, who drew from it their conceptions of historical concreteness and historically conditioned ideologies, while substituting for the conservative idea of national consciousness the collective consciousness of the working class.[15] There is no comparable impact on the surrounding world of ideas that is coming from today's cultural conservatism, in spite of its attempted escape from political labels.

There is another reason, beyond the aforementioned implausible attempt to appear apolitical, that all bearers of classical conservatism have little impact on our society. Simply put, those who do not sound sufficiently progressive in their "conservative values" call attention to their incompatibility with their social milieu. Especially in America, people evidencing attitudes or behavior reminiscent of Europe's old landed aristocracy mark themselves for ridicule. The Greek Germanophone intellectual historian Kondylis, for example, recognized the labored efforts of some American men of letters to resurrect the culture of the British landed class or the etiquette of antebellum Southern planters, who

were vanquished by an alliance of Northern free-soilers and industrialists. Kondylis criticized Kirk's *The Conservative Mind* for its
presentation of a "living conservative tradition" without a landed
aristocracy behind it.[16] While Kirk's tract may be of literary interest, Kondylis saw it as reflecting a contradiction between an idealized tradition and social realities that were utterly different.

The German legal thinker Carl Schmitt leveled a similar criticism
against classical European conservatives in *Political Romanticism*
(1919). Seemingly to counter Schmitt, especially his disparaging
opinions about Adam Müller, Mannheim dwelled at special length
on Müller's theoretical contributions in *Das konservative Denken*.
Schmitt had ridiculed any description of the romantic conservatives of the early nineteenth century as sober theoretical minds.[17]
Like Müller, Schmitt claimed, those writers had suffered from idle
imaginations. Thus they evoked, on the basis of flimsy evidence, a
world of spiraling, interpenetrating polarities, which they applied
to political life. The politics of the time furnished them with the
"occasion" to vent their arbitrary images and rhetorical flights. As
long as the French Revolution fired their imaginations, they were
captivated by it but later abandoned it for another object of
delight, in this case, the reactionary mystique. Always aesthetic
adventurers, the romantic conservatives served more than one set
of masters.

Mannheim argued that the imaginative style so distasteful to
Schmitt belonged to a *Denkweise* deserving of respect. One
thinker influenced by the romantics was Friedrich Carl von
Savigny (1779–1861), a famed jurist and the author of widely read
studies on Roman law. In both his criticism of legal codifications
and his appeal to custom and popular faith as the basis of legality,
Savigny depicted law in the romantic manner, as the product "of
quietly working forces" within the unfolding of national histories.
A Prussian state minister and a Catholic nobleman from the
Rhineland, he understood the role of the jurist to be dependent
on intuition.[18] This imaginative resource arose from sensitivity to
historical continuities, a quality that Savigny found equally in
Burke, the German historical philosopher Johann Gottfried Herder,
and the romantics of the early nineteenth century. For both
Savigny and Mannheim, a passage from Müller's work pertaining
to the Prussian king and dating from 1810 insightfully expressed
"the continuing motif of all conservative thought that came out
of the romantic era." Müller had written: "State constitutions
cannot be invented. The cleverest calculation must fail here as

utter ignorance. For there is no substitute for the spirit of a people and for the power and order that spring from it."[19]

Müller undoubtedly had his faults. Calculating his interests, he changed his homeland by going from Berlin to Dresden and then back again to Berlin. He was a footloose man of ambition. He later went to work for the Austrian government in Catholic Vienna after he had become a Catholic in Dresden, a conversion he sometimes hid when its disclosure would have been inopportune. Müller also frequented the company of aristocrats in the hope of cutting a figure in high society, and he laced his depictions of an aristocratically controlled regime with flattering artistic effects. But whatever his social failings, explained Mannheim, Müller wrote of historical consciousness in a way that shaped intellectual discourse in the early nineteenth century. He brought his forceful language and images to the aid of a once dominant class in its battle against a looming bureaucratic state. His work had a direct, vital relation to a social struggle in which he participated.[20]

Kirk and the Southern conservatives had no such societal relevance. Even if they were no less profound than Müller and even if they did not leave behind duller acolytes, their work has not played a key role in any social confrontation. Political theorist Mark Henrie, the Intercollegiate Studies Institute Director of Publications, has tried to turn this around by alleging the utility of a persuasive "traditionalist conservatism" for contemporary America. Henrie constructs an ambitious synthesis of conservative principles, drawing on Kirk, Burke, Nisbet, Adam Müller, Maistre, and Bonald, which he believes can be applied to American social problems. He expounds these principles in his brief survey of American conservative thought, "Understanding Traditionalist Conservatism," beginning with the postwar New Conservatives.[21] In his judgment, this founding generation can still contribute to the rebirth of a traditionalist political life. He contrasts the New Conservative teachings that he presents to liberalism, understood in the rationalist and atomistic sense in which Mannheim had applied that term, and he identifies liberals with libertarians, who are seeking "aggressively to expand the principle of consent through all spheres of human interest." Against these forces, Henrie unfurls a traditionalist banner on the Right. He places neoconservatives somewhere in between, as "prudent or responsible liberals who understand that the tendency of liberal regimes to totalize their central principle constitutes a danger." This neoconservative perspective, Henrie opines, might lead to tempering acquisitive individualism through administrative control and public teachings about virtue.

Henrie proposes several ways in which traditionalist conservatism could be put into practice, for example, by "encourag[ing] experiments in alternatives of all kinds that might allow schools to reflect comprehensive conceptions of the good" and even by tolerating "the worst-case scenarios of Islamist or Wiccan schools." But it is never made clear that he and classical conservatives said the same things or could do so given their differing historical situations. One consideration is that they had very different opponents. Nineteenth-century liberals, whom classical conservatives resisted, stood well to the Right of today's respectable or even conceivable ideological polarities. While Henrie's willingness to tolerate Wiccan schools may come from living in an age that defies his wishes, he definitely has not revived the arguments of the nineteenth-century classical conservatives whom he invokes. The conservatives of the past were defending established churches and social hierarchies— not trying to cut a deal with a multicultural regime. Certainly they were not laying out individual choices for their reader's perusal but were hoping to patch up an intricately ordered society that had come under attack.

To his credit, as an historically minded theorist, Henrie understands this difference and, to address it, stresses the need to reverse current habits of thinking. Americans are apparently too infatuated with their "exceptionalism," he acknowledges, and only when "the sun will set" on their illusions will "those who have placed their fondest hopes in the promises of ideological politics" feel "dispossessed and demoralized." At that point, according to Henrie, "those who have hearkened to the teachings of the traditionalists may find themselves, at last, at home." This is a comforting thought, but Henrie also voices the more realistic opinion that "with America incontestably the greatest power on earth and American popular culture driving all before it, such a project of self-limitation may seem a fantasy."[22]

Stated still more bluntly, it is hard to imagine that even if those whom Henrie warns against were to disappear, the result would be a Burkean society—or what Maistre poetically described as "pas une contre-révolution mais le contraire de la révolution." Our historical situation differs so fundamentally from that of the classical conservatives that neither public support for religious institutions nor the promotion of educational diversity seems likely to bring about the desired moral change. It may be relevant

that Henrie and other unreconstructed New Conservatives nowa-
days fail to resonate with self-designated American conservatives.
In February 2005, one third of those who expressed support for
Hillary Clinton for president in a *New York Times* survey called
themselves "conservative." And they apparently approved of
Clinton because of her supposedly conservative values.[23]

THE NEOCONSERVATIVE VALUE TURN

Until the neoconservatives came to command the American
Right, their predecessors struggled continuously for support.
Among other tasks was a search for constituencies capable of
assisting them to rise politically and journalistically. The core
groups they targeted ranged from Irish Catholic McCarthyites to
the "emerging Republican majority," which journalist Kevin
Phillips in 1965 had claimed was naturally conservative, to
Nixon's Moral Majority.[24] These and other groupings for whom
the postwar conservatives tried to speak have either dwindled as
conservative constituencies, as in the case of blue-collar Catholics,
or turned out to be Republicans by other names.

Distinguishing the neoconservatives with respect to their
backing has been their success in forging a sizable media and foundation empire. They have also given themselves credit, as their
spokesman Murray Friedman did on their behalf in *The Neoconservative Revolution*, for "creating an intellectual underpinning for
more traditional values." Only a few and isolated voices on the
Right had addressed cultural and moral issues, Friedman alleged,
until Gertrude Himmelfarb, Allan Bloom, James Q. Wilson, and
others in the neoconservative camp aimed their shafts at the New
Class and at the New Left's moral revolution. Friedman then
offers this surprising observation, that most of the neoconservatives "have said little about the hot-button issue of abortion" and
"steered clear of writing about homosexuality." Although perpet-
ually embroiled with other East Coast publicists, Friedman's neoconservatives are not really "a moralistic lot."[25] This occasions the
question: how exactly have they engaged the cultural Left while
avoiding hot-button issues?

Friedman throws up partisan charges: the older Right, which
resisted the neoconservatives, dripped with both anti-Semitism
and Holocaust denial. Moreover, "in the cultural arena neocons
barely disguised their contempt for older-style conservatives,

whom they viewed as philistines."[26] Friedman cites as proof of this assertion an undocumented statement attributed to William F. Buckley that " the neocons' social scientific expertise helped buttress his conservative ideology."[27] But the recent past differed from Friedman's forced reconstruction. *National Review* and other conservative publications, particularly *Modern Age*, abounded in cultural, literary, and artistic reflections before the neocons absorbed the establishment Right. The latecomers disseminated the literary and aesthetic concerns of New York intellectuals, but the older postwar Right had been equally diligent in publicizing the Southern Agrarians. The late Bradford, who fell victim to neoconservative slander in 1981 while apparently on his way to becoming Ronald Reagan's Director of the National Endowment for the Humanities, made this point repeatedly.[28] As John B. Judis recognized in *The New Republic* in 1987, "the conservative wars" have produced ugliness on both sides, such that, as sociologist I. L. Horowitz observed, these exercises in hostility during the late eighties became "the rhetorical equivalent of the Spanish Civil War."[29] Writing as the descendant of Jewish refugees from the Nazis, I must report that I have never detected the virulent anti-Semitism that Friedman and other neoconservatives have ascribed to their adversaries. That accusation may be wearing thin. It has become an all-purpose charge that Jewish neoconservatives and their Christian allies routinely throw at Leftist critics as well as at those on their right.

Friedman stood on firmer ground when he stressed that neoconservatives have made even stronger inroads in the George W. Bush administration than they had achieved under President Reagan. They now have a greater number and more influential point people in high places than they used to, going from Jeane Kirkpatrick, Elliot Abrams, William Bennett, and the managers of the National Endowment for Democracy in the Reagan administration to their current stars, Bush's Paul Wolfowitz, Douglas Feith, the vice president's wife, Lynne Cheney, and Condoleezza Rice. The president's recent and ongoing rhetoric about spreading democracy globally and exporting American democratic capitalism reveals how deeply neoconservative personalities and neoconservative concepts have become embedded in Republican administrations. Neoconservatives have won their positions and influence while avoiding much of the criticism that the media have directed at Republican politicians who have adopted neoconservative ideas. Despite the spleen vented on the Bush presidency by the national press and network TV, neoconservatives continue to write for the editorial pages of the *Washington Post* and the *New York Times*, and they have usually fared well in the feature sections of the *New York Times Sunday Magazine*. Moreover, as Friedman tellingly remarked, such authors associated with the Left as Frank Rich and Michael Walzer have spoken well of the neoconservatives' braininess and style.[30] Nor has the older Right criticism of the Iraq War, in more indignant language than that dared by the Left, caused the slightest change in this alignment. Not even the feverish denunciation of President George W. Bush as a warmonger by *American Conservative*'s Old Right critics of the war, former Undersecretary of the Treasury Paul Craig Roberts, and Pat Buchanan has spurred the "liberal establishment" to reconsider its debating partners.[31] Although Mick Jagger's new song "A Bigger Bang," with its line, "my sweet neocon, where's the money gone in the Pentagon?" may raise some eyebrows, it has not changed the media-preferred political mix. Jagger's "sweet neocons" have not been told to vacate their spot in the authorized political conversation on TV in favor of what is sometimes called a "harder Right."

The exclusion of this "harder Right" from respectable political dialogue is not the only reason why the neoconservatives have become the official media opposition. There is the additional consideration that neoconservatives stand closer ideologically and sociologically to the Center-Left than any other group identified with the "conservative" side. As Gary Dorrien explained in his book *The Neoconservative Mind: Politics, Culture and the War of Ideology* (1993), "[neoconservatives] did not convert existing conservatism but rather created an alternative to it."[32] Because of their idealization of the "democratic welfare state," their pursuit of a neo-Wilsonian foreign policy, and their adulation of Martin Luther King Jr. as a cultic figure in their version of American greatness, neoconservatives have nothing in common with the Anti–New Deal Right; nor do they bear much resemblance to those whose views were reflected in *National Review* at the time of its founding. Then, too, neoconservatives cultivate a distinctly imprecatory style derived from the predominantly Jewish Left, out of which their older generation had come. From the standpoint of these publicists, the antiwar Right that had flourished in the thirties and forties was riddled with anti-Semites and fascist fellow travelers. Clearly, the Left's acceptance of neoconservatives as debating and often social companions is due to factors other than shared interests in the arts and cuisine or the mutual desire for a lively exchange of ideas.[33] Comparable to the corporate donors who applaud neoconservative trade policies and support for reduced marginal tax rates, the Left does not have to reach far to get along with those who have beaten down a less compatible Right.

In his autobiography, *Nation* editor Victor Navasky speaks tenderly about Richard Lowry, the young editor-in-chief of *National Review*. Lowry's respectfulness toward a lifelong anti–anti-Communist and his admission of similarities between the goals of Navasky's periodical and his own caused the *Nation*'s editor to reflect on how much more agreeable Lowry is than those "spewing rightwing propaganda he had spent his life fighting."[34] Neoconservatives had opposed the Soviet Empire, but they had usually done so for nonrightist reasons; for example, it kept Jews from leaving Russia, it suppressed labor unions, and it opposed "basic human rights." Never did neoconservative journalists annoy Navasky by railing against "godless Communism" or evoking images of a global struggle between Christian civilization and its enemies.

What exactly are the lines of continuity between this camp and the older movement that they swallowed up institutionally and ideologically? Although much of the older Right folded in the face of financial rewards and a new party line, many of its members also found something familiar about neoconservative teachings. Here were anti-Communists who supported the Republican Party (in return for influence) and who spoke about "values" nonstop. Contrary to Friedman's contention, it was not the neocons but the older Right who began to moralize about values. Figures like Leo Strauss, who became a neocon guru, had once been heroes to the postwar Right for confronting the danger of "value relativism." For twenty years, one of America's leading aesthetic and moral philosophers Eliseo Vivas had written for *National Review* and had discussed precisely those subjects that the editors of the neoconservative *New Criterion* credit their side with having brought to American conservatism. A graduate professor at Northwestern, Vivas produced books, including *The Moral Life and the Ethical Life*, addressing "the ontological status of values." Moreover, the postwar Right, with the aid of publisher Henry Regnery, had turned its critical attention to "relativists" in the context of identifying and fighting totalitarian enemies. The German-Italian cleric Romano Guardini, thanks to Regnery's publishing services, achieved posthumous fame on American shores as a Catholic critic of value breakdown.[35] This postwar emphasis on values appeared elsewhere as well. Austrian libertarian economist Ludwig von Mises, whose work Rothbard recapitulated and expanded, found disciples who took up the value implications of his work. Among his disciples Mises would receive a facelift, transforming him from a utilitarian proponent of economic freedom to a defender of human rationality and of the moral order derived therefrom. Postwar conservatives, and even the extreme libertarians whom they drove from their midst, undeniably dealt with value questions.[36] It is arrant nonsense, therefore, to pretend that the neoconservatives were the first on the Right to address moral and aesthetic subjects.

More to the point, the neoconservatives gave value questions their own spin. Although not especially inclined toward social hot-button issues, they took moral stands of a different kind, above all, on the need to defend a democratic way of life by adopting a strong internationalist posture and by opposing antiwar groups on college campuses. Friedman and Dorrien both underlined the neoconservatives' value mission to campuses and to the world of journalism as defenders of democracy during the Vietnam and Iraq Wars. There was generally much less interest in personal moral principles unless they could be tied to a larger political mission. Neoconservative founding father Norman Podhoretz had denounced homosexuality, primarily in the seventies, because he thought that it was linked to the "culture of appeasement."[37] Podhoretz might also have shared his ancestral Hebraic distaste for this practice, but his major concern, as seen by his reference to George Orwell on homosexual pacifists in England on the eve of the Second World War, was the imagined effect of homosexuality on the American will to prosecute the cold war.

The neoconservatives' battles for academic freedom also cast a revealing light on their approach to values. To be fair, there are some neoconservative-funded activists, like Steve Balch, Allan Kors, and Herbert London, who have stood up for a freer academic environment. And the ardent neoconservative David Horowitz has used his organization Students for Academic Freedom, among other purposes, to publicize academic discrimination against religious Christians. However, much of the neoconservative funding to uphold academic freedom has been aimed at the like-minded, that is, the pro-Israeli professors who are dealing in their jobs with Arab sympathizers or defending President

Bush's policy of exporting democracy against his Democratic detractors.[38] Only one case known to me breaks dramatically with this pattern. It occurred at the University of Pennsylvania, where the spirited Professor Kors came to the aid of an undergraduate standing to the Right of the neoconservatives. But this may be a solitary exception. To the extent that universities follow the prescriptions of Bloom's *Closing of the American Mind*, moreover, they may degenerate into centers for neo-Wilsonian missionizing. It is hard to see how Bloom's defense of indoctrinating Americans in Straussian civics lessons can promote an honest battle of ideas.

A partial explanation for both the open-endedness of neoconservative value discussions and their relation to current events appears in Peter Steinfels's study from the late seventies, *The Neoconservatives*. Although the first-generation neoconservatives, according to Steinfels, stressed "a cultural crisis, a matter of values manners, and morals" more than any problem "at the level of socio-economic structures," their framework of judgment was both local and time-bound.[39] Neoconservative authors were then grouped around *Commentary* magazine, under whose aegis they battled "the adversary culture," which they associated with such particular evils as being soft on the PLO, vandalizing university buildings, and breaking up classroom lectures with exhibitionist vulgarity. Lionel Trilling, A neoconservative mentor at Columbia, had written on this antibourgeois revolt against taste and moderation but, unlike his student Podhoretz, had not raised it to a public cause. Nor had anyone else done so until the neoconservatives elevated the struggle against hippies and antiwar protestors to a major cultural event.

But this cultural war was about less than it seemed. It involved a quarrel among groups that often had more in common with each other socially and culturally than they had with those who were observing their spat. The major fallout of his "breaking ranks," according to Podhoretz, was quarreling at cocktail parties and having to turn down dinner invitations that would have brought him into contact with those who had ridiculed him in print.[40] The stage on which these mock-heroics unfolded was remarkably narrow, and it featured storms in teapots that now look quite dated. In fact, while the splits at the cocktail parties were in some sense value-related, the neoconservatives were less concerned about hedonism or the decline of religion than they were about displays of "unanimity" in the face of the adversary culture. This was the enemy that they thought they encountered in the form of erstwhile friends who either had been moving leftward or had not turned sufficiently in the direction that they themselves were going.

Despite the space that they gave to bioethicists and sociologists of morals in their numerous magazines, the neoconservatives have never pursued moral debate with the degree of philosophical earnestness found among some Thomists or on the older Right. Hard moral absolutes, distinct from such political programs as exposing the New Class of antipatriots or demanding a politics of moderation, have never been their driving interest. More to their taste have been civics lessons centered on their policies and personal goals and enabling them to avoid the third rail of indelicate social issues. And much of their morality, and hence their value-related discussions, have been in the context of being for or against certain politicians or getting along with "our crowd," as neoconservatives once affectionately referred to themselves.[41] Critical journalist Samuel T. Francis observed that neoconservative loyalties come straight out of Lewis Namier's depiction of eighteenth-century British politics. Like Namier's family histories, the neoconservative world exemplifies a "prosopography" based on whom one knows and whom one follows. Discourse in such a circle tends to stand at several removes from any abstract theory about morals.[42]

Neoconservatives chanced upon value language almost in the same way that they took the label "conservative," that is, by accident. Their precursors in the fifties and sixties, S. M. Lipset, Irving Kristol, and Daniel Bell, had argued that the United States was moving beyond the "age of ideology."[43] They defined ideology narrowly as fighting intensely over economic redistribution and over whether the American government should move from a welfare state democracy toward a more systematic state control of productive forces. As representatives of a moderate New Deal liberalism, the incipient neoconservatives had warned against the kind of ideas-driven politics that their East Coast acquaintances still relished. They called for the reduction of debates dealing with broad political principles to policy issues and lessons about civic virtue, and even after the onset of their feud with the adversary culture and its "New Class spokesmen," they looked for an appropriate moral concept in which to clothe their "end-of-ideology" position. Thus they settled on values, and their values became "conservative" ones after the neoconservatives were able to dominate the establishment Right.

AT WAR WITH VALUE RELATIVISTS

Neoconservatives as moralists have excelled at riveting their movement's attention on value relativism. But here their achievement has been to set up and combat what is often a straw man. Typical of these attacks are Professor Jaffa's much-publicized orations at Lincoln Day conferences in Washington. These lectures feature seemingly obligatory attacks on "value relativists," namely, those who refuse to identify American history with his (and presumably Lincoln's) moral mission. For the affront of viewing the American past in a less progressive manner, Jaffa has repeatedly tarred Southern Agrarians and states-rightists with the relativist brush. While Jaffa's opinions now enjoy more popularity in the court of public opinion, those thinkers he is criticizing are neither amoral nor practicing a relativist moral standard.

Jaffa and his devotees energize their value-based commentaries with a didacticism meant to shame their opponents. Thus Jaffa's contribution to *Did You Ever See a Dream Walking?* treats value relativists as likely defenders of cannibals and mass murderers. Jaffa contrasts such types to America's founders: "The men who found our system of government were not moral or political relativists as those terms are understood today."[44] Jaffa then proceeds to his "apodictic" assumption that the founders had based their state-building on the axiom that "all men are created equal." According to linguistic analyst David Gordon, this may or may not be true, but it does not follow in any case from the unknowable premise that the founders had rejected the current notion of relativism.[45] Perceptive readers may discern in Jaffa's prose a train of moral sentiments from which one finds it hard to dissent publicly while keeping one's reputation as an academic or journalist.

Rhetoric to the contrary notwithstanding, there is no significant, ongoing debate between relativists and antirelativists wherein the neoconservatives are intervening on the antirelativist side. When Pat Buchanan, at the 1992 Republican presidential convention, spoke of the "cultural war" in the course of taking on the gay lobby, no major neoconservative journalist seconded him about the need to pursue this struggle. This fact is noteworthy, given that such sympathetic historians as Mark Gerson and Murray

Friedman have credited the neoconservatives with taking the conservative movement beyond the cold war into a new cultural war. The movement's direction, if it still has one, becomes still more problematic in light of the declaration by the neoconservative gray eminence Kristol in the *Wall Street Journal* that Buchanan was oblivious to the fact that the cultural wars had been lost. "The Left had won," Kristol maintained, among this present "hands-on" generation. Kristol urged the Religious Right to emulate the Orthodox Jews in Israel—who apparently would never stoop to coercion in their opposition to abortion but instead try to convert others to Orthodox Judaism.[46]

Kristol's featuring of the Orthodox Rabbinate in Israel as a model of tolerance for American Christians is so grotesque that it leaves the reader gaping with wonder. Aside from the fact that abortion is not as morally grave or divisive an issue among Orthodox Jews as it is among traditional Christians, there is another inconvenient truth. Orthodox authorities in Israel have exercised the kind of power over the legal, marital, and even ethnic status of Israelis that no single Christian denomination has been able to do in the United States. Among the tactics that the Orthodox in Israel have blatantly applied is the imposition of their will through the power they have demanded and have been given in parliamentary coalitions.[47]

In an equally puzzling manner, Kristol followed his announcement that the Left has won the cultural war because "the culture is too liberal" with the joyous announcement, three months later in the *Wall Street Journal,* that Americans were now rushing into "the Coming Conservative Century."[48] Kristol then added to the confusion of any critical reader by publishing "America's Exceptional Conservatism," in his 1995 book, *Neoconservatism: The Autobiography of an Idea*, celebrating an American conservatism seen as both populist and religious. So advanced is this unique Right that "conservative political thinking has not yet caught up with it."[49] Beyond providing mixed signals, Kristol's zigzagging implicitly made the old *argumentum ad auctoritatem*. Because we are in charge, the moral values that matter are ours. What bothers the Religious Right does not have to concern the neoconservatives. They may occasionally pay lip service to it, but they are also free to retire or bring back as a public issue any value or moral issue that serves their changing needs.

As for the apparent value struggle to which the neoconservatives wish to turn our attention, who exactly are the moral relativists whom we are supposed to resist? Certainly it is not the multicul-turalists whom the neoconservatives denounce in their magazines. Those who advocate supplanting the neoconservatives' own gov-ernmentally protected pluralism with a more extensive form of the same are not against value preferences; they are simply asserting their own choices in a posttraditional and by now increasingly postbourgeois society. One can dispute which set of values is nicer or more tasteful, but it is ludicrous to infer that someone who dis-agrees about a particular value choice has thereby revealed himself to be a relativist.

The neoconservative line of reasoning, to the contrary, did not start the day before yesterday. Willmoore Kendall, Buckley's professor at Yale and an outspoken McCarthyite, anticipated this move in his essay "Do We Want an Open Society?" written for *National Review* (January 31, 1959). In this polemic criticizing John Stuart Mill and his latter-day adherents, Kendall portrays Mill as a relativist who launched liberal society on a steep path toward total skepticism. Mill popularized the ideal of an "all ques-tions-are-open-questions society" and opened the door not only to tolerance for American Communists but to the even more omi-nous development of a society that "would descend ineluctably into ever-deepening differences of opinion, into progressive breakdown of those common premises upon which alone a society can conduct its affairs by discussion, and so into the abandonment of the discussion process and the arbitrament of public questions by violence and civil war."[50]

This glum assessment of the impact of Mill's advocacy of pub-lic discussion is wrong for three reasons, all of which are relevant to the opportunistic imputation of value relativism. One, as Joseph Hamburger, Maurice Cowling, and Linda Raeder have noted in detailed works on him, Mill prescribed open discussion as an instrumental good in order to build a postmetaphysical society committed to scientific reasoning.[51] He was not the addled free spirit that Kendall assumes he was. In fact, he was pushing thought-control and did so through a highly original ruse, by giv-ing the appearance that he was advancing free inquiry. Two, those who advocated total freedom for Communists to organize in the 1950s were rarely unadulterated civil libertarians. Many of them, as William Donahue documented in his study of the American Civil Liberties Union, had long histories of involvement with Leftist causes and exhibited concern about the expressive freedom of the Communists, a concern that they had generally withheld from those suspected of having had fascist sympathies.[52] Finally, even if one located the only a relatively small number of consistent First Amendment absolutists at the time that Kendall was writing, it would be inaccurate to designate them as "relativistic." They were choosing to privilege a value that Kendall rejected because he thought it was detrimental to social harmony and national security. Whether or not his judgment was correct, there is no reason to assume that his opponents were value-relativists.

Certainly some multiculturalists have presented themselves as relativists, but they have done so with clumsy and transparent inconsistency. They have hidden their "foundations" while they have happily moralized about oppressed genders and races and, moreover, at least implicitly expressed moral predilections for non-Western religions over Christianity. Such multiculturalists typically equivocate about their moral intentions and often illustrate the problem discussed by Mannheim, that a self-consciously value-free person keeps stumbling on his own "intellectual horizons."[53] These horizons remain a given, no matter how detached the observer hopes or pretends to be. But Mannheim is examining a methodological *Problematik* as opposed to dissembling about his ideology. By the time that the generally disingenuous politically correct advocates of openness entered the debate, the neoconservatives might have stopped flogging the dying horse of relativism. That was not and is not the true object of their hostility.

Their choice to act differently reflects a politically driven line of moral reasoning. Their "shtik" (to use a pointed Yiddish colloquialism!) is to be for "values" and against "relativism" while keeping their options open as to which values need defending. Bloom's *Closing of the American Mind* generated a mass readership by pouring scorn on "nihilism, American style" and on values reduced to mere choices. But his book left Bloom's personal traditionalism murky at best, despite his praise of the United States as a propositional nation and his complaints about druggies listening to rock music, presumably while getting high on German fascist ideas. Bloom's homoeroticism, which Saul Bellow, his longtime literary friend, exposed in a novel after his death, is apparently not a taboo, or at least not one that renders him ineligible to lead the war against relativism.

The Closing of the American Mind's statements about nihilism manufactured in Germany, and traced back to "the cultural relativist" Nietzsche, reveals more about Bloom's sociological anxieties than it does about what ailed the United States in 1987. Bloom's fear and dislike for the country that perpetrated the Holocaust and its tainted legacy suffuse his picture of modern America and its cultural ills. Those who follow Nietzsche, readers are told, are inviting "war, great cruelty rather than great compassion," because "cultures [as interpreted by relativists] fight wars with each other." Furthermore, "liberal democracies do not fight wars with one another because they see human nature and the same rights applicable everywhere and to everyone."[54] Bloom obviously begged the question of whether liberal democracies, by the current understanding, existed in the West in 1700 or even as recently as a hundred years ago. But as critic Barry Shain quipped, Straussians—and not only their most successful author, Bloom—avoid history out of principle.[55] To illustrate this flaw, let us take one of Bloom's implied accusation and subject it to critical examination: did the hippies, whom Bloom considers to be Nietzschean relativists, incite international strife among national cultures because they were ingesting *Genealogy of Morals* and *Beyond Good and Evil*—in addition to cannabis? It would seem to all appearances that Bloom and his neoconservative fans have been more eager to invade other countries than the customary targets of their attacks, whom they condemn for meditating on dead German authors.

Bloom also denounced the "value relativism" of those who had criticized President Reagan for stressing the "value differences" between the United States and the Soviet Union. Referring to such a misperception as a form of relativism, Bloom wrote that it "must be taken to be a great release from the perpetual tyranny of good and evil, with their cargo of shame and guilt, and the endless effort that the pursuit of the one and the avoidance of the other enjoin. . . .And this longing to shuck off constraints and have one peaceful world is the first of the affinities between our real American world and that of German philosophy in its most advanced form, given expression by the President's speech."[56] Actually, one may agree with the former president's foreign policy, as I did no less than Bloom, and concurrently find nothing relativistic about those taking a more conciliatory stand in relation to the Soviets. Such people may have taken their position for tactical reasons or may have had a more sympathetic view of the enemy than we did, but there is no reason to assume, absent proof to the contrary, that they espoused their position because of "value relativism" or because of the hated "German connection." Although I personally disagreed with the late George Kennan on which policy the United States should have pursued in the seventies and eighties toward the Soviets, it is impossible for me to think of anyone whose ethical beliefs I respected more deeply. I similarly balked at the extreme isolationism of the late Robert Taft but also saw it as the expression of high principles.

An appreciation of the possibility that prudential judgments may differ seems to have eluded Bloom's imagination. It is altogether possible for two persons to hold widely divergent views on a policy issue but be generally in moral agreement. And it is certainly possible to take an ill-advised position on some issue because of a faulty assessment without being a cultural relativist. Finally, it is possible for two value-ascribing and value-interpreting individuals to arrive at the same practical position for different motives or on different moral grounds. Bloom and his fellow neoconservatives strongly supported the cold war, but they did so for presumably different reasons from those of General Francisco Franco, the authoritarian traditionalist victor of the Spanish Civil War.

Kristol launched antirelativist diatribes in "The Machiavellian Profanation of Politics," his 1961 essay reflecting the work that Bloom's teacher Strauss had just completed on Machiavelli and political modernity. Apparently in the writings of both Kristol and Bloom is the same formulaic approach to political morality, divorced from any concrete understanding of historical change. Machiavelli is declared guilty, without any demonstration of a causal chain, of the current positivist belief that "it is right for political knowledge to be divorced from moral knowledge." Furthermore, "there have been three major figures during the last five centuries who have rejected Christianity, not for its failure to live up to its values, but because they repudiated those values themselves. The three are Machiavelli, de Sade and Nietzsche. A great part of the intellectual history of the modern era can be told in terms of the effort of a civilization, still Christian, to come to terms with Machiavelli in politics, de Sade in sex, Nietzsche in philosophy." Kristol fears that Nietzsche's disciple Heidegger is right, "that the 'slave morality' of Christianity is constantly in retreat before the revolt of the 'masters.'"[57]

One may ask how Kristol's and Bloom's undocumented generalizations fare in comparison to serious studies that are replete with historical illustrations and coherent arguments. To raise a question still more damaging to their assertions, is there any compelling reason to think that Nietzschean despisers of equality now rule Western societies and are imposing their elitist rule? In the anthology wherein Kristol expressed his fear about the revolt against slave morality, he also complained against the growing obsession with "equality."[58] He offered no attempt, however, to explain this apparent contradiction about where he discerned his chief enemy—among worshippers of the will to power or among radical egalitarians.

But such moralizing is less striking than the travesties on value discussions that emanate from Republican operatives and Republican foundations. Here analytic standards get thrown recklessly to the wind. In *The Third Generation*, a short volume published in 1987 and celebrating the accomplishments of "the Third Generation," Heritage Foundation official Benjamin Hart heaps praise on the conservative campaign for values. Having already carried conservative "issues and values" to new public recognition over two generations, the movement is now passing leadership to a third generation, one that cares passionately about "issues and values." These youthful conservatives were working with President Reagan, who, in his greeting to the group, had expressed his own interest in "values and programs."[59]

Hart wrote his overview to stress that all three generations of conservatives have marched behind the same moral preferences. Nonetheless, neither his exposition nor his (for such a slim volume) disproportionately long bibliography—which lists in a mystifying jumble Catholic corporatists, anarcho-capitalists, Southern Agrarians, and Zionist neoconservatives—suggests the presence of any shared worldview.[60] When Hart comes to discuss the war for values, which must be waged against the "value-free quality of American life" advocated by pornographers, he pummels the reader with electoral issues, such as being for voluntary prayer in public schools and resisting government subsidies for abortion. He then urges blacks to embrace such conservatism, for among other reasons because conservatives oppose raising the minimum wage. Apparently, high minimum wages impact negatively on black employment.

Hart then provides a defense of what he presents as "conservative" value outcomes resembling positions that crop up in electoral debate. These positions belong in party leaflets aimed at blocs of voters, but they have nothing to do with ethical argument; nor do they demonstrate that American value conservatives have stood for the same moral interests for the preceding fifty years. One is reminded here of George Will's retort to a complaint that the Senate majority leader was not listening to "'social conservatives' who represent 'value voters.'" Will responded by posing the rhetorical question, "What voters do not intend their political choices to advance their values?"[61]

The attempt to wrap ethical questions in movement-tailored slogans and to isolate them there has cheapened discussions that might otherwise be worth pursuing. Neoconservative warhorse Bennett's *Broken Hearth* engaged issues that go well beyond electoral sound bites about the permanence of family patterns. Bennett, who might have consulted social anthropologists David Popenoe and Grace Goodall, presented the bare bones of a response to the claim that the nuclear family is of recent origin. According to Bennett, the structure of familial relations now under attack builds on behavioral patterns and human needs that have prevailed for thousands of years. Because of this, cautious scholars see problems with seeking to change long-established family arrangements at the behest of feminists.[62] But rather than fleshing out this traditionalist proposition, Bennett rushes on to other topics, having apparently discussed "family values" as far as his advisors or editors deemed prudent.

Value conservatism has entered a downward spiral regarding the characteristic arguments to which it has become attached. From the privileging of certain social preferences rashly assumed to function independently of a dominant class, value conservatives proceeded to adopt a combative stance against "value relativists." At this point, the value content began to shift as the representatives of "conservative values" moved ideologically leftward or toward overt identification with the neoconservatives.[63] The battle would henceforth be against those who were "value-free." It would be, in part, against certain demonized German thinkers, chiefly Nietzsche and Heiddegger, who supposedly paved the way for the adversary culture. Conservatives continue to fight against these sinister figures, although a convincing demonstration of their responsibility for the ills mechanically attributed to them has not yet graced any of the multitudinous conservative journals. From these windy attacks, the exercise in value assertion has fallen to lower depths yet. The upholding of values has become a series of noises, like the puffs of air to which Ockham likened the resort to universals among fourteenth-century schoolmen. "Values" now go together with "family" as an electoral slogan aimed at wheedling whatever rewards the electoral market will yield.

———◆———

CHAPTER 3

ON TOP OF THE HEAP

CONSERVATIVE PHILANTHROPY

In a comment on New York philanthropist Bruce Kovner, one of America's richest people and, after Rupert Murdoch, perhaps the most generous supporter of neoconservative causes, *American Conservative* editor Scott McConnell stated this about the neoconservative infrastructure: "One thing the neocons have that both other factions of conservatives and liberals don't have is they can employ a lot of people. AEI [American Enterprise Institute] provides a seat for the kind of midlevel intellectuals who can produce op-ed pieces. It's 50 to 100 people with decent prose styles or Ph.D.'s and they form a critical mass. They help create the reality of being the dominant strain of conservatism."[1]

McConnell's observation is noteworthy for both its content and its inclusion in an essay in *New York* by Phil Weiss detailing Kovner's connection to AEI, one of the largest neocon foundations and a source of many policy positions and policymakers for the Bush administration. Although the title of Weiss's essay, "The George Soros of the Right," may be overblown (Weiss never clarifies how Kovner and his beneficiaries are rightwing except in their Zionist opinions), he does document the targeting of enormous wealth for certain propagandistic ends. Kovner, who gives heavily to the neoconservative newspaper *New York Sun* and has his hand in the neocon-directed Manhattan Institute as well as in AEI, supports journalism expected to promote his "ideological projects." Moreover, contrary to the Soros analogy, "Kovner has always been comfortable with radical ideas." The reference here is not to radically *conservative* ideas. "Understanding the Kovner communists of the forties and fifties and their scene [Bruce's family] is a key to understanding the neocons and their scene. As there is today, there was talk then of cabals and fellow travelers. Both causes were heavily Jewish. The ideas of both the neocons and the communists were Utopian and revolutionary. Neocons would carry the torch of revolution out into the world, with scant attention paid to the disparate natures of the affected societies. Communists had similarly inflexible ideological goals."[2]

As McConnell points out, those who have undertaken this project "can employ lots of people" for their purposes, which continues to make it possible. The possibility for such employment, as my book *The American Conservative Movement* (1994) demonstrated, was dependent upon annual funding from philanthropic foundations well in excess of 50 million dollars, plus patronage from the World Unification Church, Australian press baron Murdoch, and foreign governments opposed to American protectionism. Also enhancing employment opportunities was the availability of government positions, particularly in Republican administrations, courtesy of the National Endowment for the Humanities (NEH), National Endowment for Democracy (NED), United States Information Agency, and Department of Education. In all of these government sectors, especially in NEH and NED, key patronage posts have gone to reliable neoconservative types who can do favors for their benefactors, as was their wont in the Reagan years and afterward.[3]

The sources of neoconservative funding have changed over the last decade, and reliance on grants and subsidies from organizations with obliging staffs, for example, those at the Scaife, Bradley, and Olin Foundations, has shifted to dependence on individual benefactors who now finance the neoconservative media empire. This transition occurred as neoconservative persuasive efforts increasingly came to entail the use of TV broadcasts and mass-circulation newspapers typified by the *New York Post* and *New York Sun*. There is now less resort to the glossy periodicals favored twenty years ago, although the paradigmatically neoconservative *Weekly Standard*, funded by Murdoch and headed by Bill Kristol, is an exception. At that earlier point there was an interest in demonstrating that the converts to neoconservatism were ripe for national leadership because they were extraordinarily thoughtful, as attested by their capacity to run periodicals and to gain influence as book publishers. They were taking over the Right supposedly because of the depth and impact of their thinking, and by walking around Dupont Square in Washington in the eighties, one was exposed to the magazines that young neoconservatives were then creating and staffing. Typical of most of their publication was the prominence of the word "democracy" in their titles (e.g., *Journal of Democracy*) and table of contents. Generally speaking, these periodicals were all but invisible outside of the New York–Washington corridor.[4] To give their views a wider audience and greater impact, neoconservatives built a national news network. This had the effect, among other advantages, of rendering the Republican Party dependent on neoconservative publicity. It was and remains an expensive accomplishment. Weiss has repeatedly emphasized that the neoconservatives have had to find benefactors with deep pockets in order to make their ventures fly. In conversation with me, he suggested that my figures on annual neoconservative funding might have to be revised dramatically upward.[5]

More significant than the extent of the neoconservatives' funding is the reason why their ideas have caught on as well as they have. Surely not everyone who buys them is a recovering Communist of Russian Jewish ancestry who has made a fortune in bond trading. Murdoch is an Australian Presbyterian, and Bush, who is the most neoconservative-sounding president to date, is a born-again Christian from Texas. While no sensible person would deny the ethnic, regional, and culturally specific nature of neoconservative thinking, equally obvious is its expansion beyond its original base. Simply put, others outside the circle inhabited by Irving Kristol, Norman Podhoretz, and Midge Decter find neoconservative ideas compelling. In fact, the conservative movement, with the exception of the now marginalized dissenters, has come to accept the neoconservatives' leadership since the early eighties, and it never publicly broke with it. In the late eighties and early nineties, there appeared numerous books and articles dealing with "conservative wars" and the "conservative breakdown" that followed the fall of the Soviet empire and the demise of anti-Communism as an issue on the Right. Such a conflict did take place, and both neoconservatives and their opponents on the older postwar Right defended their prerogative to speak for the American conservative movement. For the older Right, the neoconservatives were "interlopers" who represented an aberrant Leftist position that the rest of the Left had moved beyond. Their residual

Marxist phraseology (some of which seemed borrowed from Leon Trotsky speaking on the prospect of socialist world revolution) no less than their blend of cold war liberalism with Zionist enthusiasms betokened the alien character of their contribution to the older movement.[6] No matter how far apart on some issues the old-fashioned libertarians like Murray Rothbard were from Southern Agrarians M. E. Bradford and Clyde Wilson and the Kirkian value conservatives, all of them stood together as a *cordon sanitaire* against the neoconservative invasion.

Ranged on the other side, the neoconservatives set about presenting the history of the American Right, before their ascendancy in it, as heavily anti-Semitic, nativist, and racist. Well into the late eighties, *Commentary* featured attacks on the conservative organizational leader who later rallied to them, William F. Buckley, for his comments in the decades before he had come over to their side.[7] The neoconservatives stood in the same relation to the Right that they replaced as the Bolsheviks did to Tsarist Russia. Never did they show anything but disdain for Taft Republicans, anti–New Deal Buckleyites of the 1950s, Southern Agrarians, or American isolationists during the First or Second World War. They continue to offer their own history of the American past in the magazines under their control. Whether they are portraying the Civil War as a struggle for world democratic ideals against Southern racists or they retrospectively are justifying the dropping of the atomic bombs as necessary for carrying American ideals to benighted Japanese, the neoconservatives have imposed their own perspectives, often in glaring opposition to older conservative beliefs. They have also espoused the Leftist habit of branding those whom they oppose internationally as "fascists." The *Weekly Standard* has favored the term "fascist" to characterize both anti-American resistance in Iraq and Islamic opponents of Israel.[8]

Lest anyone forget the disjunction between the neoconservatives and their predecessors on the Right, Irving Kristol dwelt on this matter in a feature essay, "The Neoconservative Persuasion," published August 25, 2003, in his son Bill's fortnightly, *The Weekly Standard*. According to Kristol, "the historical task and political purpose of neoconservatism would seem to be this: to convert the Republican Party and American conservatism, generally against their respective wills, into a new kind of conservative politics suitable to governing a modern democracy."[9] This conservatism differs in kind from any European or American conservatism that has hitherto existed. It can prevail only by displacing that which conservatives had admired in the past. "[Neoconservatism] is hopeful, not lugubrious; forward-looking, not nostalgic; and its general tone is cheerful, not grim or dyspeptic. Its twentieth-century heroes tend to be TR, FDR, and Ronald Reagan. Such Republican and conservative worthies as Calvin Coolidge, Herbert Hoover, Dwight Eisenhower, and Barry Goldwater are politely overlooked."[10]

A TAKEOVER

The neoconservatives' rejection of the older conservative hagiography and their general indifference to a limited, balanced constitutional government need to be stressed in order to underscore their achievement in rebuilding the conservative movement. Much of this success goes back to resources. By the mid-eighties, the neoconservatives had been able to achieve a near stranglehold on funds targeted for conservative activism; and unlike other groups on the Right, they did not have to worry about direct mailings for money. Already in control of old conservative philanthropies like the Smith Richardson Foundation, once identified with anti–New Deal isolationism, neoconservative operatives moved into commanding positions at AEI and Heritage, which had started off in association with the older postwar Right. Those who rushed to do their bidding in Washington were often government employees, some of whom came with the "Reagan Revolution" and who decided that they liked the oxymoron soon to be called "big-government conservatism."[11] Why push for limitations on the central government when the result might cost them their jobs? Far better to collect a salary while working, or claiming to work, to make the federal administration receptive to "conservative values." The roles assumed by self-identified "movement conservatives" during the Reagan presidency would affect their attitude toward public administration and their places within it.

The lack of leadership alternatives within the conservative movement, which was undergoing a generational transition during the eighties, also facilitated the takeover. By the late seventies, there was a noticeable dearth of figures who could effectively represent conservative causes and conservative values on the national level. Most of the founding generation of the postwar conservative ideology, for example, Frank Meyer, James Burnham, Russell Kirk, and Will Herberg, were dead, incapacitated, or simply uninterested in the leadership role that the neoconservatives assumed. There did exist a New Right and, later, a Religious Right, but neither had the social presence for leadership. The New Right functioned in the seventies and eighties as a direct-mail organization, led in Washington by Richard Viguerie and Paul Weyrich, who mobilized grassroots opposition to abortion and to the now largely forgotten Equal Rights Amendment. The Religious Right, identified in the eighties with Jerry Falwell and the Christian Coalition's Ralph Reed and Pat Robertson, also failed to offer leaders capable of winning respect in the world of conservative advocacy journalism. Like the New Right but even more so, the Religious Right has usually rallied behind Republican presidential candidates and tried to stay in line with their neoconservative associates.[12]

Also favoring the neoconservatives was the fact that they preached values closer to the journalistic mainstream than those taught by cultural conservatives or by the enemies of the welfare state. For persons wishing for whatever reason to call themselves "conservative" while cultivating respectability, sounding like the *Wall Street Journal*'s editorial page on the universal need for democracy or professing admiration for Martin Luther King Jr. and his unproved opposition to racial quotas was better than being on the same side with those who had equivocated on segregation or had failed to condemn Joe McCarthy sufficiently. Neoconservatism seemed to provide a *juste milieu* between a Left-Center moving fashionably leftward and an older Right that was becoming socially unacceptable. It also permitted recognition of such victims of Western Christian civilization as blacks, Jews, and, to a lesser extent, women, but it did not push the victim card quite as aggressively as did the Left. Although the West had persecuted certain groups, whose suffering was to be duly acknowledged, conservatives of the respectable sort could admire Western teachings, particularly insofar as they had led toward the present-day belief in human rights and the acceptance of America as a "universal nation based on the proposition that all men are created equal." A member of the older postwar Right, Samuel Francis inadvertently recognized the neoconservatives' strength when he contemptuously referred to them as the "harmless persuasion" because of their incorporation of Truman-Humphrey Democratic thinking and their devotion to a democratic welfare state. Francis's well-positioned opponents made converts to a moderate, centrist kind of American patriotism by not leaning excessively to the Right.[13]

Still another strength of the neoconservatives was that they could effectively push issues that the older Right was less advantageously situated to bring before the public, for example, accelerating the arms race with the Soviets and reconsidering affirmative action programs. Throughout the seventies and into the eighties, neoconservative-run *Commentary* and *Public Interest* published numerous outstanding articles on foreign policy and race-related issues. Among the authors featured were Edward Banfield, James Q. Wilson, Charles Murray, Elie Kedourie, Patrick Moynihan, and Jeane Kirkpatrick. The work of these authors lent credibility to the assertion that the neoconservatives were, as Murray Friedman claimed, intellectually gifted successors to the older Right.[14]

But this assessment is only partly justified. There is no reason to assume that the articles produced by these authors would not have drawn attention if they had been printed elsewhere. Indeed, most of these authors wrote for other publications as well. Nor is there reason to ascribe high intellectuality to the organizers of neoconservative foundations and publications just because they used the funds to secure noteworthy articles and then successfully advertised them. Although nothing was reprehensible about any of this, only a sycophant or simpleton would equate such self-promotion with erudition—or with bringing class to the American Right. It might be nice to bring to one's hometown a concert given by Isaac Stern, but being an impresario is not the same as being a great violinist.

The daily responsibility of producing neoconservative publications has been the duty of assistants boasting less-than-stellar intellectual attainments. As McConnell observed, the grunge work usually falls on middle-level types, who solicit and restate polemics that the reader, in all probability, has encountered before. Much of what one finds in neoconservative publications is very old hat, for example, accusing those who disagree with the neoconservatives on Middle Eastern politics of being anti-Semitic or verging on it. In one particularly striking example of name-calling, journalist Charles Krauthammer used his pulpit in *National Interest* (Fall 2004) to scold the once favored neoconservative author Francis Fukuyama for suggesting that the United States should not always identify its foreign interests with those of the Israeli government. Krauthammer accused Fukuyama of being obsessed with the Jewishness of some of his colleagues. Nonetheless, Krauthammer commended Fukuyama for not quite sinking to the "crudeness" of Pat Buchanan, a despised embodiment of a truly "poisonous strain of conservatism."[15] A distinctly neoconservative intramural debate erupted in 2004 about whether those who referred to "neoconservatives," especially in its shortened form as "neocon," were guilty of an anti-Semitic faux pas. *National Review* abandoned this line of attack after prominent neoconservatives made clear that they had decided to hold on to their name.[16]

References to neoconservative intellectuality sometimes seem to be retrospective justifications for the stampede of conservative activists into the neoconservatives' camp. Their alleged cerebral accomplishments receive considerable attention in *The Conservative Revolution* (1999) by Lee Edwards, whose research and writing were sponsored by Heritage Foundation. Like other chroniclers of recent events in the conservative movement, Edwards is accounting for a fact that may still baffle his readers, namely, the willingness of lifelong conservative activists to fall meekly into line behind journalists who had come from the Left.[17] By the end of 1992, neoconservatives had mopped up most of the resistance to their control. It was then that their chief nemesis Buchanan went down to defeat in the Republican presidential primaries. Thereafter Buchanan's intellectual advisors, whom he had recruited from a then recently established Old Right organization, the John Randolph Club, disappeared from public notice—except as targets of neoconservative tirades.[18]

Conservative organizations and magazines also purged from their staffs and stable of writers those who were offensive to or displeased "Norman and Midge." By the late nineties, *National Review* had extended this policy to those who criticized high levels of immigration, such as the author of *Alien Nation* Peter Brimelow, and demoted its usually obliging editor, John O'Sullivan, for commissioning essays on immigration that jarred with the neoconservative pro-immigration position.[19] Much earlier exclusionary measures had preceded these. In 1981, Mark Gerson recounted in his study of neoconservatism, Heritage Foundation chief Edwin Feulner Jr. and Buckley intervened with President Reagan for purposes of dissuasion. They persuaded the new president *not* to nominate the Southern conservative literary scholar Bradford as NEH director but to give that slot to William Bennett, a friend of Irving Kristol and Kristol's wife, Gertrude Himmelfarb. Looking at this mission twenty-five years later, it is still hard to understand the degree of accommodation to neoconservative wishes that then took place. Bradford was far better qualified as a published scholar. Unlike Bennett, he had not been a liberal Democrat before

switching over to the Republican side. Bradford had also frequently contributed to *National Review* and, as he later told me,
considered "Bill a really close friend."[20] While the Democratic
press went after the Texan Bradford for his criticism of Lincoln's
imputed role in fomenting the Civil War, the campaign against
Bradford had begun with tirades from George Will and other
journalists in or near the neoconservative camp. Buckley and
Feulner could have honorably stayed neutral, but their intervention
against a friend and political ally of many years still remains a mystery.

One explanation for this defection is that Buckley and
Feulner, and others who stood with the neoconservatives against
Bradford, thought (properly, as it turned out) that they had allied
themselves to the future. In the 1980s the neoconservatives were
establishing themselves in the Reagan administration, even in
high-visibility posts up to and including those occupied by such
figures as Bennett and Eliot Abrams, and were flooding the "movement" with funding that had not been previously available. This
victory brought about a sharp redirection in the way that the history of postwar conservatism had been understood. Among neoconservatives it ceased to be important to justify their takeover of
the conservative movement from the older Right. Although such
pronouncements pervaded neoconservative narratives until the
late nineties, they had disappeared by the new millennium. In
place of "conservative wars," in, for example, Friedman's account,
there appeared a sense of entitlement and a tendency to treat the
neoconservatives' opposition on the Right as being beneath contempt. This triumphalist perspective sharply departed from the
measured tone of George H. Nash's *The American Conservative
Intellectual Movement* (1996), which stands out as the most fair-
minded and balanced study of its subject available. Having covered the twists and turns of the "conservative wars," Nash
suggests that these verbal encounters remain significant because
they underscore a dramatic battle of ideas that would continue to
shape or reshape American conservatism.[21] In reality, one of
Nash's two sides has all but collapsed or, in the case of some paleoconservatives, moved toward a Catholic antimodernist posture.
This tendency, which has manifested itself in multiple conversions
to Latin Mass Catholicism (often combined with attacks on the
Protestant foundations of American society) on the marginalized
Right, was not yet apparent when Nash wrote his second edition
in the midnineties. Much of the opposition then to the neoconservatives came from sociobiologists and analysts of the modern

managerial state.[22] The latest turn by the once embattled Right may indicate an understandable fatalism among former activists who can no longer enter into dialogue with movement conservatives. Other remnants of the older Right have survived in varying degrees of privation. Some unreconciled Libertarians lean rightward on cultural matters, and they and other isolationists reminiscent of the interwar Right have nurtured the Ludwig von Mises Institute based in Auburn, Alabama. Antiwar publicists grouped around *The American Conservative*, as well as their own anti-Bush Web site, persist in their heterodoxies. Nonetheless, as long as the neoconservatives and those further on the Left can limit the impact of their voices, all of these dissenters are unlikely to influence or even penetrate the national media.[23]

It is therefore explainable and not simply politically expedient that the recent histories of the American conservative movement, for example, Jonathan M. Schoenwald's *A Time for Choosing: The Rise of Neoconservatism* (2001), try to present neoconservatism as a natural stage, the latest in the formation of the postwar conservative movement. This choice is at least partly dictated by the accomplished fact of neoconservative control.[24] Prominent "conservatives," those whom historians are likely to interview, would treat the neoconservative ascendancy as a refinement of the movement's nascent tendencies. Typically omitted from this interpretation is the scorn that neoconservatives have expressed for the early history of the movement now under their thumb. Though in the end a friendly takeover did occur, for the neoconservatives what they were doing resembled a kind of "white man's burden." Their job was to reeducate the members of a backward culture who, contrary to Kristol's account, actually welcomed their instruction.

NEOCONSERVATIVE VALUES TRIUMPHANT

One critical factor behind this accommodation was that neoconservatives were following a movement precedent, without media disapproval in their case. They were teaching a constructivist form of conservatism, similar as such to its postwar predecessor in its appeal to values. At stake was not the future of a real social class but competition among foundations and newspapers to influence public policy. Drawing in interest groups that would support their polemical activities became the daily concern of the Washington policy community. Separating Brookings from Heritage or AEI was mostly a fight over funds—and over enjoying access to politicians. The differences revolved around nothing as concrete as the grand political battles of the past, when, for example, one side fought for the proletariat and the other for the bourgeoisie or one side spoke for the Church of Rome and the other for the Calvinists. In sharp contrast, the Prussian conservative Friedrich von Stahl in the 1860s could easily divide Germany's political class into those who wished to follow the French Revolution and those who were fighting its ideas.[25] There was nothing as decisive as Stahl's distinction that stood between "conservative' and "liberal" foundations by the time that neoconservatives came on the scene. Their major contribution as leaders of a cause was to blow up differences in values and policies with the Left in order to give credibility to an already costly conservative establishment. By the mideighties, Heritage each year needed about 13 million dollars in order to meet its operational expenses.

At the same time, the neoconservatives were effective at narrowing the range of difference with their putative opponents. Despite their tracts about "family values," Himmelfarb, Bennett, Lynne Cheney, and, more recently, former Senator Rick Santorum of Pennsylvania have not moved out on a rightwing limb with respect to the value question. Neoconservatives have merely competed with the Left-Center as interpreters of values widely avowed by the Left. This is the source of the frequently heard distinction between "moderate" and "radical" feminisms.[26] Again, in competition with the Left, the establishment Right depicts itself as being better able to implement the ideal of equality. Conflicts with the Left, as critics on the older Right have observed, are nowadays immanentist duels fought out among the would-be implementers of already agreed-on values. Clear evidence on behalf of this assessment comes from the characteristically neoconservative Secretary of State Condoleezza Rice, that the United States was set up by "flawed men, but they were men who gave us institutions that were capable of correcting those flaws." Furthermore, "through two-plus centuries of American history, it has been a history of people struggling to correct those flaws," two of which, Rice specified, are racism and the longtime refusal to give women the vote. Even as the United States works to carry its political accomplishments to other countries, the secretary of state emphasized, "we're still struggling. We're struggling every day for equality for our races and equality of men and women."[27] The struggle for equality seems to benefit from the diligent efforts since the

1980s of neoconservative journalists and public figures to misrepresent Martin Luther King Jr. as an exemplar of neoconservative values. In particular, Lynne Cheney, Bennett, and David Horowitz are known for associating King with "equal opportunity" but not "equality of result." Such adulation persists, despite the fact that virtually all positions ascribed by the neoconservatives to the civil rights leader as one of their own finds little support in King's own words.[28]

Like the Bush administration that they typically defend, neoconservative journalists have presented themselves as the perfecters of the American past. External wars have been an opportunity to transform other societies in a way that Americans are doing at home. *New York Post* columnist Ralph Peters, in his recently published book *New Glory: Expanding America's Global Supremacy*, speaks proudly of the "many revolutions," including feminist and civil rights upheavals, which the United States has imposed upon its own society. Henceforth, according to Peters, who is a retired military officer, the American government has an obligation to bring our revolutionary experiences to other continents.[29] In a similar vein, Rich Lowry has praised the secretary of state for viewing the Iraqi War as an opportunity to actualize in the Middle East the civil rights cause that she had supported as a girl in Birmingham, Alabama.[30] Such examples, which can be multiplied, prove that neoconservatives do not allow their grumbling about Leftist relativism to distract them from affirming the Left's values, ostensibly in order to pursue those values worldwide in the most consistent manner.

Neoconservatives of the older generation in particular linked their argument with the Left to a persistent social difference. They were standing their ground against what Norman Podhoretz and Lionel Trilling had called the "adversary culture" and what Irving Kristol identified as "the new class." This form of self-description, which Peter Steinfels considers fundamental to how the neoconservatives saw their break with a radicalized Left, suffused the original neoconservative identity.[31] But this demonology did not, according to prominent European Leftist Jürgen Habermas, give evidence of a real social conflict.[32] Such tension as there was did not rise above the trivial. Much of it transpired within an insular circle of New York acquaintances. Even when it moved beyond this arena, the war against the "new class" was directed against the pursuers of a certain lifestyle that had come to elicit neoconservative scorn. It is worth asking why David Brooks, who is a syndicated columnist for the *New York Times* and who approves of gay marriage and much of the Left's social agenda, is not part of this "new class."[33] The only obstacles that would keep him from being thus classified are his support for the Iraqi War and his cordial relations with the editorial staffs of *National Review* and *Commentary*. It is only shifting taxonomy that allows him to be called a "conservative" and by indirection a presumed enemy of the "new class." Given his opinions on a wide range of topics, it would seem that Brooks is no successor of any kind to Kirk, let alone to Carl von Savigny or Stahl.

The dissonance between older conservative traditions and the changing contemporary appeals to "conservative" principles casts some light on Irving Kristol's latest formulation in 2003 of his "idea" or "persuasion." Endeavoring to explain the "idea" that is supposedly electrifying the American Right, Kristol reveals some glaring misconceptions: "There is nothing like neoconservatism in Europe, and most Europeans are highly skeptical of its legitimacy. The fact that conservatism in the United States is so much healthier than in Europe, so much more politically effective, surely has something to do with the existence of neoconservatism. But Europeans, who think it absurd to look for the United States for lessons in political innovation, resolutely confuse to consider this possibility."[34]

Why, one may ask, should Europeans be anything but puzzled by an ideology that is alien to their experience of conservative thought and indeed has nothing in common with it? There are, of course, European exceptions, such as Alexandre Adler, an editor for *Le Figaro* in Paris and a devotee at the altar of "American democracy, globalization, and Zionism," and the critic of French anti-Americanism Jean-Francois Revel, who was a personal friend of the American neoconservatives.[35] But these are the exceptions on a continent that once exhibited, even if it later rejected, a genuine conservative tradition. Here neoconservatives likely would not be identified with such a venerable tradition not only because of their "neoliberalism" and Zionist views but also because of their enthusiasm for American democratic crusades.

Kristol never demonstrated that he was praising anything other than that which he had helped concoct. For some reason (perhaps mere self-importance), he expected his readers to understand his own "political innovation" as a conservative accomplishment. This was despite the fact that he expressed disdain for those "lugubrious" things that the American Right admired in the past but that the neoconservatives hope have been permanently displaced by

the march of history. Readers learn that Kristol's fellow neoconservatives, by "reaching out beyond the traditional political base,
have helped make the very idea of political conservatism more
acceptable to a majority of American voters." To dispel any doubts
about his drift, Kristol finally declared: "it is the neoconservative
public policies, not the traditional Republican ones, that result in
popular Republican presidencies."[36]

At the very least, Kristol's claims rest on inconclusive evidence
that he alternates with self-praise. Two of the Reagan administration's policies for which Kristol and other neoconservatives take
credit, namely, tax relief by way of supply-side economics and a
tough containment approach toward the Soviets, were entirely
imaginable without them. Such major advocates of tax relief as
Undersecretary of the Treasury Paul Craig Roberts and the economist Jude Wanniski were so far from being neoconservatives that
both of these players in the Reagan administration had persistently
stormy relations with them.[37] Reagan's approach toward bargain-
ing with the Soviets, which may have contributed to the collapse
of the Soviet Empire, had been standard Republican operating
procedure before Richard Nixon and Henry Kissinger replaced it
with détente. It is doubtful that the former president, who had
made a name for himself as an anti-Communist, needed neoconservative advisors to act on his long-held principles.

Other questions arise as one reads Kristol's glorification of his
"persuasion." Why, for example, should anyone believe that a
higher percentage of Americans consider themselves "conservative" now than before because of neoconservative outreach?
Approximately one-third of Americans have considered themselves
to be moderately "conservative" for several decades. Neoconservatives have not caused this figure to soar upward, but they
have succeeded in dictating the content of acceptable conservative
thinking. They have pushed that content, for better or for worse,
steadily toward the Center-Left.

Neoconservatives belong to larger historical trends that they
themselves affect only minimally. Over the last thirty years in the
United States and in Western Europe, conventional industrial
welfare states have seen the rise of service economies. At the same
time, they have expanded their social and educational activities in
such a sweeping manner that some European scholars now speak
of a "security state." The security at issue goes well beyond material entitlements; it extends to a proliferating variety of governmental programs aimed at the family, health-care choices, and behavioral

or attitudinal control intended to render citizens "sensitive" as well as physically sound. Having devoted my last three books to this development, I am astonished by how thoroughly the neoconservatives ignore it, while they rush to praise Western managerial democracies. One would like to know whether fundamental changes in the structures and reach of government mean anything in terms of either Kristol's "idea" or the justification of a neoconservative crusade for the current Western version of "liberal democracy."[38]

But neoconservatives have no interest in addressing these matters. They are too busy adapting their internal politics to lifestyle changes—now that we've lost the culture wars—and to the administrative state, which has sponsored much of the cultural change that has rattled the Right. The fact they generally treat "culture" as something separate from public administration gives their game away. Like Bill Kristol, they deal with "democratic government" in a way that recalls Mussolini's florid invocations of the *stato totalitario*. Kristol remarks, "In sum, national greatness conservatism does not despise government. How could it? How can Americans love their nation if they hate its government?"[39] Falling back on such rhetoric makes it unnecessary for neoconservatives to notice that the modern state accelerates social and cultural changes.[40] Because they wish to use the state as a source of employment and as a vehicle for an adventurous foreign policy, they respond to criticism about its enlargement with levity or contempt. Over the last few decades, the neoconservatives' desire to protect the American government in every sense has displaced their once admired but even then exaggerated capacity for critical thinking.

Neoconservatism's shifting attitudes and positions reveal the problem of attaching to it an immutable content or even a coherent ideology. It has become philosophically minimal in proportion to its increased political clout, its enhanced philanthropic resources, and its tendency to celebrate ever more lavishly "the neoconservative persuasion," "the neoconservative imagination," and neoconservative readings in ostentatious volumes distributed among its dependents. Toward grasping the present situation, two brief concluding observations may be in order. Neoconservatism's generally leftward drift has not entailed a generational rift between its founders and their successors. Although the founding generation went from a youthful embrace of Marxism (particularly in its Trotskyist form) toward the anti-Communist Left or Left-Center, they nonetheless steadily espoused bourgeois social values, which they had probably received from their parents. The support of these values, to put it mildly, was far less evident in the cultural stands of the younger neoconservatives, and it may be family loyalty that has kept the older generation from calling attention to this glaring cultural-political difference.

A MISREPRESENTED DISENGAGEMENT

Moreover, an even larger discrepancy emerges between the neo-conservatives who were disengaging from the intellectual Left and the ones who assumed leadership of a transformed American Right. The neoconservatives in their preconservative phase expressed views that were often more rightwing than those they later permitted to their followers. Examples abound. In the fifties, Podhoretz lamented black political influence and black violence. Then, in the sixties, he and his wife attacked homosexuals and their culture of military appeasement. The first neoconservatives showed no reverence for Martin Luther King Jr. or the civil rights movement; nor did the senior Podhoretzes show support for their son when he declared himself for gay marriage. Nor is it simply the case that neoconservatives in the early seventies were objecting to the excesses of the civil rights movement but hoped to elevate that movement, shorn of its excesses, to respectability. This is the neo-conservative version of their role in the "good" civil rights move-ment, which, despite King's example and their own warnings against immoderateness, strayed into both anti-Israeli politics and quotas for blacks. But early neoconservatives had no great interest in the civil rights movement; they involved themselves with it mostly as critical observers. Their angry attacks on blacks in *Commentary* are difficult to reconcile with their critical position against the older Right for being insufficiently receptive to the civil rights movement.

Podhoretz's outburst expressing his own insensitivity comes to the fore in "My Negro Problem—and Ours" (1963) in *Commentary*, when he tried to deal with his "hatred" for blacks. He recounted, without apparent embarrassment, "the disgusting prurience that stirs in me at the sight of a mixed couple" and "the violence that can stir in me whenever I encounter the special brand of paranoid touchiness to which many Negroes are prone."[41] The retort here is almost too obvious: It is strange to hear someone who has devoted his life to calling opponents anti-Semites and to comparing them to Nazis, but living in a country that has done no special harm to Jews, denying the descendants of American slaves a right to complain. What gives Podhoretz and his acolytes the moral high ground to assault the character of Southern conservatives in the early eighties for not being sufficiently sympathetic to American blacks? Why is his special pleading on behalf of his fellow Jews any more legitimate than that of the "touchy" blacks who annoy him?

The intergenerational aspect of the neoconservatives' hypocrisy again appears in their efforts to expose those on the Right who formerly supported Senator McCarthy and chided President Truman for shielding Communists and Communist sympathizers in government. There should be no confusion about the editorializing against the pro-McCarthy Right that the neoconservatives even now continue to pursue.[42] As they do so, they ignore fact that some neoconservatives and others now claimed for their movement, for example, Jewish theologian Herberg, were not exactly in the forefront of the opposition to McCarthy or McCarthyism. As late as 1969, Irving Kristol in "The New York Intellectuals," published in *Commentary*, let the obvious be known: "McCarthy himself [for me] was never really an issue."[43]

Note that my citation of this material is intended as neither an endorsement nor a condemnation of McCarthyism. How publicists related to this issue fifty years ago is a matter of historical fact, not something to be addressed as a moral question. By the same token, ongoing political agendas should not be read backward by exaggerating the distance between the neoconservatives and the older Right on certain apparently divisive questions. Ironically, one of the strongest reproaches against anti-McCarthyites came from the then moderate Leftist Irving Kristol and was placed in *Commentary* (March, 1952): "For there is one thing that the American people know about Senator McCarthy; he, like them, is unequivocally anti-Communist. About the spokesmen for American liberalism, they feel they know no such thing, and with some justification."[44]

Dated rhetoric about McCarthy would no longer be relevant were it not for the zeal with which Ronald Radosh and other neoconservative historians have gone after those who were McCarthyites or failed to defend President Truman and his administration against McCarthy's charges. Against the backdrop of this fervent, belated rallying to the anti-McCarthy side, critical observers of neoconservatism should recognize that its older representatives rarely displayed that contempt for McCarthy that the movement they created would later do. Confronting neoconservatives with their documented opinions in this matter may draw attention to another embarrassing feature of their past, namely, a series of anti-Christian essays published in *Commentary* in the eighties tracing the roots of the Holocaust back to the Gospels and Pauline Epistles. Such troubled journeys into the Christian past came before the neoconservatives chose to champion the Religious Right, a position that the Zionist fervor of the Fundamentalists may help to explain. To the neoconservatives' credit, they would be the first to recognize this reason for their changed hearts.[45]

It is unimaginable that another group will take over the American conservative movement in the near future. Those who swarm around the neoconservatives personify Aristotle's notion of the "natural slave." And they will not probably alter their behavior by overthrowing their masters. What is more, many "conservative" professionals are now serving the national Republican Party while simultaneously working for neoconservative foundations or magazines. These professionals experience enormous pressures to accommodate themselves to electoral strategies and to heed the instructions of their employers. It is doubtful that the neoconservatives' opponents on the Right will successfully challenge their dominance. This opposition is now battered and without friends in high place. Most importantly, it cannot do favors—least of all persuasive favors. The neoconservative ascendancy has brought in its wake a "conservative" media presence, resting upon a proliferation of well-paid careers. Indeed, if "our crowd" had not reached the top of the heap, a visible "conservative" media, with its own TV network, likely would not have come into existence. Nor would the public have listened to a second inaugural given by a president, whether a Republican or a Democrat, that featured neoconservative value language in celebration of America's world democratic mission. For these monetary and other contributions to value conservatism, neoconservatism's beneficiaries should feel appropriate gratitude.

CHAPTER 4

---•---

WHITHER THE RIGHT?

THE FASCIST RIGHT

Essential to understanding conservatism is the distinction between it and the Right. While conservatism arose as a militant response to the French Revolution and its doctrine of universal rights and found an eloquent precursor in the 1790s in Edmund Burke, the Right emerged in the twentieth century in reaction to the progress of the Left. Unlike conservatism, the Right drew its strength primarily from the bourgeoisie but also from remnants of the aristocracy and those members of the working class who rejected socialist internationalism. The alliance that became the Right developed by joining together the concerns of the bourgeoisie and parts of the working class with various nationalist ideas and goals. Particularly as this process unfolded in the twenties and thirties, it helped nurture the Marxist critique that fascism and other real or alleged rightwing movements characterized an advanced form of capitalism trying to stave off a worker's revolution.

Even though this argument, which often takes the form of an accusation, overlooks the deep human attachments and widely held sentiments to which the Right has appealed, sentiments that, as the historian John Lukacs noted, are more real to more people than socialist internationalism or the dubious achievements of the now vanished Soviet economy—the Marxist interpretation of fascism includes some measure of truth.[1] In interwar Europe and in South America, what there was of a professional and commercial class was attracted to authoritarian regimes that promised social stability. The bourgeois typically had to share power in ruling coalitions with other forces (e.g., landowners, the military, the Church, and cooperative labor unions) and accepted this arrangement in return for economic security and at least the appearance of a defense against the radical Left. The Left then was either Communist or anarchist but, in the demonology of the time, incorporated such other disturbers of the peace as Masons, Protestants, Jews, or clericalists. The demons varied according to both the type of authoritarianism established and the inherited political culture.

Fascism was only one variant of this phenomenon, albeit the most strident and perhaps most interesting example. Particularly in its Mussolinian *Urform*, fascism took the form of mobilizing opposition to Leftist revolution. Contrary views suggesting the fascists' revolutionary origins and goals must be understood in this context. The Italian fascist model claimed to be revolutionary, and indeed more genuinely so than the Left because of its national and popular character: Mussolini's Carta del Lavoro, enacted in April 1927, was supposed to have integrated workers and much of management into a syndicalist structure under state supervision. Moreover, the hard-line Italian fascists like Giovanni Bottai, Massimo Rocco, and Augusto Turati, often referred to as *arditi*, never hid their anticapitalism as they endeavored to construct a system of state socialism. Were it not for Mussolini's attempt to reassure his capitalist base, the Carta del Lavoro, as historian Renzo De Felice explained, might have turned out to be a far more radical document.[2]

But more relevant for the future was the anti-Leftist side of the fascist project, what Ernst Nolte, when discussing the interwar period, has fittingly called its "counterrevolutionary imitation of the Left." Whatever Italian, Spanish, and other predominantly Latin fascists may have initially hoped to do, and no matter how well they attracted nationalists from the working class, they came to be seen as the protectors of the bourgeoisie against revolutionary dangers.[3] This was the role that the fascist squadristi had already necessarily assumed in Italy by the time Mussolini took power in 1922. His paramilitary bands had battled the anarchist Left in street fights after the First World War, when the Italian economy was crippled by massive strikes. Somewhat later, after the national party had come into being, Mussolini had to balance its antibourgeois and working-class elements against a large middle-class base that swelled the ranks of his triumphant movement. This base of what Felice called, perhaps unfairly, "fiancheggiatori [hangers-on]," typified by the large industrialist lobby Confindustria, was an economic foundation stone for the new Italian regime. Mussolini accordingly had to assure Emilio Olivetti, who directed Confindustria, that "fascism believes in the sanctity of property." National syndicalism would do nothing to interfere with the right of employers to "terminate the tasks" of their employees. In addition, prior to the Carta, the fascist government had imposed stringent deflationary measures, to the detriment of the working class. These measures dealt no real blow to the owners of Italian industries, who anticipated increased prosperity once the Italian currency had been stabilized.[4]

Fascism strengthened, in an exaggerated manner, developments that the Italian and other European bourgeoisies had supported in the nineteenth century: the nation and the state. The first was to become a revolutionary principle, whereas the second would be totalized, at least in theory, in the framework of a national revolution. While this fusion was often messy and hastily improvised, and while some bourgeois preferences, like liberal parliamentary institutions, were denounced by the fascists for being decadent or politically counterproductive, some continuity between bourgeois and fascist societies is not hard to find. A relatively liberal economy in some fascist countries, the functioning of representative bodies even in fascist Italy into the thirties, however attenuated, and the preservation of a nation-state structure that the bourgeoisie had helped build made fascist rule something that its bourgeois critics Benedetto Croce and Vilfredo Pareto could at least tolerate.[5] In its mild, clerical fascist form in Austria, this interwar fascist authoritarianism gained the favor of the classical liberal Austrian school of economics for saving the country from the revolutionary Left. The clerical fascist emphasis in Austria in the thirties on neo-Thomist and corporatist socioeconomic policy mattered less to the liberal bourgeoisie than did the efforts of Christian Social Chancellor Engelbert Dollfuss (1892–1934) to protect the Austrian state. Dollfuss, who ruled by emergency decrees, sought to control Nazi infiltration of the Austrian government while keeping the Social Democratic paramilitary organization from seizing political control in a civil war. Dollfuss became a firm ally of fascist Italy before it changed sides to join the Axis and before Dollfuss fell victim to Nazi assassination. He and his followers belonged emphatically to the anti-Marxist and Catholic Right, a loyalty that led them into struggling to prevent Hitler's takeover of their country.[6]

Disagreement about whether fascism was essentially "counter-revolutionary" in the 1990s moved two prominent European historians, Nolte and François Furet, to take up the contested subject in an exchange of correspondence. In the magazine *Commentaire*, they published the fruits of their exchange, which dealt with the following themes: whether fascism should be viewed for the most part as an interwar development that gained currency in reaction to Soviet Communism and its supporters; whether it contained a revolutionary potential similar to that of Bolshevism; and whether Nazism represented a general fascist phenomenon that emerged in response to the Soviet revolution.[7] At least two points made by the corresponding historians in *Commentaire* and elsewhere are pertinent to the present discussion. Furet argued on the basis of Nolte's first major work, *Three Faces of Fascism*, that (1) the intellectual foundations for interwar fascism were laid before the First World War, that is, prior to the Bolshevik Revolution, and (2) the Nazi variant of this movement was far more virulent than Mussolini's version or the Spanish Falange. Nazism exemplified a violent, genocidal radicalization of an older fascism, Furet argued, and it differed qualitatively from the movements to which Nolte, a German, linked it. Despite Nolte's courageous originality as a thinker who has been badly abused by the German "antifascist" Left, Furet insisted (with justification, in my opinion) that his colleague could not escape the feeling of obligation as a "patriotic German" to render less abhorrent German Nazi crimes, which were immeasurably worse than those committed by Italian fascists before the Germans took over their country. It was his desire to normalize the aberrant authoritarianism that took over Germany in the thirties that impelled Nolte to treat Nazism in a general context, as just another form of extreme anti-Communism or, in his earlier work, as a German absorption of a counterrevolutionary body of ideas that affected other European peoples as well.[8] Furet made this observation sympathetically, while deploring the antifascist intolerance that has gripped German academic life—and perhaps, to a lesser extent, scholarship in his own country.

But the difference between Nazism and some kind of generic fascism cannot be ignored. The Nazi variation on fascism was not only vicious and aggressive, but it also brought to power similar movements wherever Hitler extended his empire. In interwar Germany, those who most closely resembled Mussolinian fascists, like the Black Front of the Strasser brothers or the would-be putschists grouped around General Kurt von Schleicher, fell in a Nazi purge in 1934. And throughout Nazi-occupied Europe—including Hungary, which the Germans only directly occupied as late as 1944 after overthrowing the Rightist but non-Nazi regime of Admiral Miklos Horthy—violent anti-Semitic groups had to be mobilized to carry out Hitler's final solution against the Jews. The re-creation of a German-controlled Italian fascist government, the Salo Republic in 1943, resulted in similar mass murder. One may be excused for speculating about Italian fascism and how it might have evolved under different circumstances, that is, if Mussolini had not been seduced in 1936 into a self-destructive alliance with Hitler. That alliance, however, came about only after Mussolini had reversed his earlier course as the European leader of the anti-Nazi front. He had assumed this role in the wake of Dollfuss's murder in 1934. And the anti-Jewish legislation, barring Jews from the Italian Fascist Party, government, and the professions, which Mussolini pushed through in 1938, revealed an equally dramatic about-face. Until the late thirties, Mussolini enjoyed the friendship of European Jewish leaders, not least because, as a staunch opponent of Nazi anti-Semitism, he provided Italian bases for Zionist military training. For Jewish and black nationalists like Zev Jabotinsky and Marcus Garvey, he was the paradigm of a successful nationalist revolutionary, one who showered attention on imitators outside of his own Latin nation.[9]

Although Mussolini was obviously to blame for his own disastrous decisions, it is possible to imagine a fascist international without the bloody German contribution and those collaborators in German-occupied lands. This milder fascism would have been authoritarian and corporatist, and it would have ranged from neopagan modernizing variants in Italy and elsewhere to clericalist regimes in Austria and Portugal. It would have tried to win working-class support with guarded welfare measures but without upsetting its bourgeois base, and it would have eventually yielded to more conventional national democratic governments after the effects of interwar economic crises, particularly the Depression, were over. Fascism in the twenty-first century may no longer be possible. To the extent that fear of Communist upheaval fueled fascist loyalties, the disintegration of the Soviet empire and the vanishing of its subversive apparatus might have removed one argument for anti-Communist authoritarian government. Most importantly, looking at the social base of Mussolini's movement, a

traditional and threatened bourgeoisie alongside a by now antiquated working class, it is hard to see how the social foundation
for an authoritarian national movement could have remained
intact in any Western country. The social foundations of Mussolini's regime were the classes of yesterday, classes that do not have
counterparts in either a modern service economy or the current
universal welfare state. Both the inherited bourgeois family, with
its gender and generational distinctions, and a cohesive working
class do not belong to the social and political picture of our own
late modernity. Two aspects of the present—a postbourgeois welfare state that accommodates a variety of unconventional lifestyle
choices and, above all, women liberated from traditional home-
making roles—might have dumbfounded interwar fascists or even
Marxists. It is hard to imagine what, if anything, fascism would
look like in today's society. Equating fascists with European or
American critics of Third World immigration is a propagandistic
ploy, when it is not simply an anachronistic exercise. It tells nothing about the nature and preconditions of interwar fascism, but it
denigrates those who do not seem sufficiently enthusiastic about
government-imposed diversity as a guiding principle.

Some aspects of Nolte's depiction of fascism are, in fact, correct. Unlike Furet, who contrasted it to "the counterrevolutionary
ideas of the nineteenth century" and saw it instead as "an idea of
the future," a form of antimodernism that "regained its charm
with Mussolini," Nolte presented his object of study as a "mere
secondary phenomenon."[10] Fascism was exactly as the Marxists
presented it: a reaction against the Left that imitated what it
opposed. And it did so by adopting democratic as well as liberal
features. Fascists employed plebiscitary techniques to confirm
actions taken at the top, a method of winning majoritarian
approval pioneered by Louis Napoleon, who reached below the
French political class to the "people" when he wished to have
himself as installed as president for life in 1852 and as emperor in
1853. Throughout the late nineteenth century, as both Furet and
Nolte have observed, sworn enemies of bourgeois republican government from the monarchist Right toyed with idea of building
alliances with the working class. It was a desperate version of
Benjamin Disraeli's Tory democracy or of Otto von Bismarck's
efforts in the 1880s to identify the German Second Empire with
workers' pensions and universal manhood suffrage. In the radicalized counterrevolutionary version, which fascism developed, the
national leader was to cultivate a special relation with the masses,

who were seen as the repository of national virtue. He would operate independently of parliamentary parties and all interest-wielding cliques that might interfere with the unmediated relation between him and his people.

Another related feature of this selective democracy was *homonoia* as a principle of popular consensus. From Plato and Xenophon to Jean-Jacques Rousseau and Carl Schmitt, democracy, properly understood, has been about long-term agreement on basic matters among self-governing citizens. Not pluralism, but shared sentiments and opinions, have until very recently been seen as the hallmark of successful self-government.[11] The progressive disintegration of a society into competing individual wills and interests weakens democratic commonality in proportion to how far this development proceeds. The danger is exacerbated by "pluralistic democracy," which its critics have considered a contradiction in terms. In the historic democratic tradition, equality has far less to do with combating discrimination or even redistributing incomes than it does with knowing and carrying out the general will. Democratic practice, to whatever extent it is democratic, is about like-mindedness among those who accept one another as members of the same polity.

Having written in defense of such a conception of self-government, particularly as practiced at the local level, I would distinguish between democracy as the practice of a historical community—one guided by custom—and democracy as the imposition of consensus by fascists, global democrats, and the enforcers of political correctness. The first sort of democracy tries to preserve past elements that remain integral to the shared lives of its people; the second is constructivist and manufactures a consensus by which others are made to live. In any case, the identification of democracy with continuing consensus is the long-established view of democratic life that interwar fascists took over to produce their own form of popular government. This version was a strictly guided democracy in which, despite radical rhetoric, there was little evidence of radical changes in the socioeconomic structure. There thus took root during the interwar period a regime that, according to Nolte, incorporated a reaction to Communism and to other movements of the radical Left. As the frightened bourgeoisie rallied to and even joined the fascists, they found a haven that became the major competitor of the internationalist Left and the beholden defender of property-holders. Although fascism rarely fell into the hands of big business, contrary to the conventional

Marxist view, and while in Germany the Nazis were far from the first choice of industrialists and bankers, the nationalist or corpo-ratist Right scared those interests far less than did the radicals on the other side. And Nolte has a point that the Soviet experiment, widely celebrated in Marxist rhetoric, was a ghastly nightmare to the European middle class.

Equally relevant, Nolte stresses the interwar context as neces-sary for understanding fascism. That movement took shape as one of the two contending sides in the "European civil war" that raged in the twenties and even more in the thirties in central and eastern Europe.[12] Although there were arguably less violent alternatives available than those chosen, to partisans on both sides, Nolte rec-ognized that two conditioning factors determined the European civil war. One factor was that those who took meaningful political posi-tions often landed in one of the two polarized camps, regardless of where they had started. A second factor was that partisans picked political-existential positions only from among the significant choices that they discerned. The second point reminds me of a question that a relative once asked about why Jews in eastern Europe became Zionists or Marxists or lived under Orthodox Rabbinic control. Couldn't these people be like German Jews, my relative wondered, who came to America in the nineteenth century and then became steadfast Republicans, who imitated Episcopalians? The answer to this query is this: not everyone perceives the same historical choices or has the opportunity to make the same choice.

THE CHANGING RIGHT

The particular polarity that Nolte explored was time-bound. Fascists exerted influence and ran governments but did so in "their epoch," as readers learn from the original German title of Nolte's magnum opus. True fascists have not survived as Flemish opponents of Muslim immigration or as those types referred to journalistically as "Islamofascists." More useful than sticking our contemporaries into archaic categories, perhaps as a way to express displeasure, is to acknowledge this obvious fact: fascists belonged to the Right as it existed in a particular time and place, and while the fascist Right is no longer around, another Right may be. Making the Right what it is comes down to its mobilization against the Left, although what that Left is will differ from one generation to the next.

A look at the French Communists since the end of the Second World War illustrates the sea change undergone by the European Left in general. The Communist Party of France in 1946 polled 28.6 percent of the vote in national elections, and as late as 1956, could garner about 26 percent; by 2002, however, its electoral share had fallen to about 3 percent. As late as 1979, 46.5 percent of the French Communist vote came from industrial workers, who made up 36 percent of the French work force. But such workers' votes by 1997 accounted for only 31 percent of Communist support, extracted from a once formidable class that had shrunk to 29 percent of French wage earners.[13] The majority of French Communists were by then white-collar employees, including large numbers of government functionaries. Moreover, the old issues that had distinguished the French far Left—that is, nationalization of productive forces and support for existing Communist regimes—had given way to other, more fashionable concerns, which the Communists now share with their coalition partners in the Socialist Party. Feminism, gay rights, multiculturalism, and mobilization against "fascism," henceforth defined as insensitivity to Third World cultures and opposition to Muslim immigration, have become salient issues on the transformed French and European Left. For such as there remains of a working class vote, the French, Italian, Flemish, and Dutch Lefts are now forced to divide with anti-immigration parties on the Right. In the cases of Front National in France and the Vlaams Belang in Flanders, the Right has sometimes done far better than the Left in picking up disgruntled workers.

Although the Left's projects have changed over time, there are also overlaps between its past and current interests. An antipathy to bourgeois society, formerly associated with capitalist exploitation and more recently with sexism, xenophobia, and homophobia, has been a constant Leftist feature in the twentieth century, as also has been an obsession with secularizing public institutions seen as languishing under reactionary Christian influence. Such proclivities complement a Leftist vision of progress, understood as a gradual or revolutionary advance toward a universal society based on secularism, equality, and scientific planning. The Left, particularly in Europe, usually has indulged Soviet tyranny far more than oppression inflicted by governments perceived as being on the Right. This double standard in contemporary Europe has taken the form of a noisy crusade against "fascism"; it typically treats Stalinist and Maoist mass murder as a mere faux pas, something that progressive antifascists are not supposed to notice. This posturing has resulted in a steady stream of invectives in the French and German press, as Furet documents, against those who have focused attention on Communist crimes. Such publicists have been accused of trying to turn our minds away from fascist atrocities by exaggerating less reprehensible Communist misdeeds. At the same time, parties of the Left in Germany have honored dead Marxist revolutionaries by naming or renaming public places and streets for Rosa Luxemburg and Karl Marx and by re-erecting statues of Lenin in Berlin.[14]

What makes the Right a "secondary phenomenon" is its opposition to the Left, regardless of how that side expresses itself at any particular time. The current Right, allowing for isolated exceptions, does not treat interwar fascism as a useful model for reform; today's racial nationalists in the United States typically are libertarians who do not speak about a corporate economy or rein-troducing legal segregation. Such Rightists, exemplified by the contributors to *American Renaissance* and *The Occidental Quarterly*, have no hope of reclaiming public administration from the Left and would be delighted if government were to abandon social policy and disentangle itself from an already value-laden public form of education. It is hard to find groups on the present American Right calling for a Mussolinian state or who, in contrast to the neoconservatives, associate "national greatness" with an expanded central government. Characterizing all manifestations of the Right in the United States is a distaste for the administrative state as a promoter of a multicultural, egalitarian vision. Against this global vision, the far Right offers an identitarian or explicitly racialist defense of the majority white Christian population, whose culture and self-respect the Right sees as under attack. The Right loathes "managerial multiculturalism" and complains that the wel-fare state has become a prime instrument of cultural-social trans-formation through its socialization of the young, immigration policies, and preferential treatment of minorities.[15]

A widely used textbook with an unmistakably Leftist tilt, *Political Ideologies* by Leon P. Baradat (now in its ninth edition) vilifies Americans of "the extreme Right." In a chapter featuring a painting of emaciated inmates at Auschwitz (it is noteworthy that no Gulag art accompanies the book's generally empathetic descriptions of Communism), Baradat portrays the Right as being irrationally opposed to government: "Rightwing extremism is gaining popularity in the United States. The collapse of the Soviet Union has eliminated a traditional negative focal point of the extreme Right. With that external danger removed, those Americans who tend to look for sources of great evil in their midst have come to see the federal government as an oppressive and threatening force that must be resisted—violently, if necessary."[16] Looking beyond Baradat's unproved premises—that the Posse Comitatus, neo-Confederates, and libertarian Rights are all growing by leaps and bounds; that anxiety about government overreach is exclusively rightwing or indicative of paranoia; and that those who feel such anxiety are violence-prone—one may acknowledge that this passage makes at least one true statement. The far Right, and even the less extreme Right, holds no brief for the administrative state and, unlike the interwar fascist Right, resembles anarchists or critics of the New Deal more than followers of Mussolini or, a fortiori, Hitler.

The mainstream version of the Right that now exists here and in Europe opposes the initiatives undertaken by the media, courts, and public administration to promote the kinds of significant social change that have altered Western societies since the 1960s. Representative of this position is the activist Phyllis Schlafly, who has devoted her journalistic and legal career to fighting the social Left. A recent biography of Schlafly by Donald T. Critchlow depicts her as a relentless combatant against Leftist reforms that affect the family and the workplace. Offensive to Schlafly are such developments as the diminution of the traditional domestic role of women, the removal of Christian symbols from public places, the implementation of minority-targeted preferential hiring and admissions, gay rights, and the expansion of Third World immigration. Although her stands do not necessarily remind one of interwar fascism, and though Schlafly, moreover, has no discernible interest in racial nationalism, she is on the Right by virtue of her reaction against the social Left. Her Rightist orientation notwithstanding, her biographer might have erred by using "rightwing" too freely and associating Schlafly with Ronald Reagan in a collective "counterrevolution" carried out by "conservative rightwingers." Such a description makes this reader wonder whether Critchlow's terminology fits his subject. Should one apply to Reagan epithets that belong to Count Metternich, who worked to subdue the forces of the French Revolution, and other nineteenth-century counterrevolutionaries?

More meaningful is Critchlow's explanation about how
Schlafly understands the "people" and her place among them:
"Any characterization of Schlafly must be qualified with the recognition that she, and other grassroots conservatives who joined her,
opposed the political status quo. They waged a protracted struggle
against the liberal welfare state, with its reliance on centralized
government, bureaucratic expertise, judicial activism, and distrust
of popular democracy, traditional values, and patriotism."[17]
Critchlow convincingly shows that his subject, a Catholic Republican from St. Louis who, like her husband, is a well-trained
and articulate lawyer, brought out of her childhood the image of a
virtuous American nation that needed to be re-empowered. Her
"grassroots conservatism," as Critchlow calls it, is a tendency that
Schlafly eloquently exemplifies. It is a defining rightwing phenomenon, which distinguishes the Right, particularly since the middle
of the twentieth century, from any classical conservative tradition.
Others beside Schlafly on the postwar Right, from Pierre Poujade
and Jean-Marie Le Pen in France to George Wallace and Pat
Buchanan in the United States, have appealed to the "people" over
the heads of political elites in the name of betrayed popular virtues.

Although Critchlow draws parallels between Schlafly and
another self-assertive midwestern woman, the protofeminist Betty
Friedan, his comparison cannot be successfully extended beyond a
few personal traits to any specific populist belief.[18] Feminists and
the social Left do not call for the overthrow of political elites but
wish to work through them to reconstruct human behavior. They
certainly do not idolize the "common" man, whom they view as a
sexist and a bigot, but they are amenable to entrusting him to progressive administrators. The populist Right, by contrast, expresses a passionate and almost mystical belief in the demos,
whose instincts and natural goodness must be released in order
to restore the nation and its freedom. Willmoore Kendall, the
unvarnished populist in the early *National Review* circle, lavished
praise on those "who think in their hips" and who rallied to anti-
Communism as an expression of their outraged sense of virtue.[19]

Although the Right and the social Left exhibit a comparable
enthusiasm for electoral displays—for example, the Left calls for
extending the electorate to the hidden disadvantaged and the Right
hopes to submit every decision to plebiscites—their aims are
entirely different. One side wishes to create a broader consensus
for managerial governance, while the other seeks to mobilize the
masses for a counterrevolution. These observations lend support to

Baradat's point without imputing the stigma of the Third Reich to the entire Right. Presumably the demos, which the Right seeks to let have its way, is not any random collection of individuals; it is, or so Rightists hope, sufficiently cohesive to rule itself. And the more internally unified it is, as a nation or as a people, the more effectively it will be able to assert itself against the Left, which enjoys the support of public administration and the media.

VALUE CONSERVATISM VS. THE RIGHT

The Right is not, and perhaps never can be, coextensive with conservatism. Therefore, the term "grassroots conservative," when applied to those who believe in nonmanagerial democracy, is a problematic usage. Neither Schlafly nor Buchanan seeks to bring back a society of degrees and orders; in fact, much of what they say, as illustrated by Buchanan's taunting reference to George H. W. Bush in the presidential primary in 1992 as "King George," is ferociously anti-elitist and intended to arouse egalitarian passions. Like the Left, the populist Right makes its own appeal to equality. The confrontation between Left and Right in 2005 does not, however, replicate the nineteenth-century battle between conservatives and liberals. Different social classes, armed with different political goals, are waging a quite dissimilar struggle.

Even less than the Right equals conservatism does it mean trying to sell packages of "conservative values." A Rightist takes an adversarial position in relation to the Left; a "value conservative," by contrast, seeks to cobble together views for a TV presentation or an electoral debate. But in either case, it is a mere performance by someone who is trying to appear to have convictions but who hopes to avoid spooking his listeners. The bearers of conservative values are often experts in dealing with the establishment Left from which they are not far removed, and they are also inclined to clothe their stands in the language of self-evident truths and permanent things. One illustration of this practice is David Brooks's series of expositions of "conservative" views for the *New York Times*. In 2003, Brooks defended gay marriage as a conservative concerned about "family values"; in August 2005, he sang the praises of a "virtue of virtues" that had become manifest over the last ten years and reached a new peak in "family virtue."[20] The reason for this praise was that the incidence of spousal violence had dropped over the last ten years to its lowest point in thirty years. The

columnist tips his hat to feminist groups for involving the government more fully in family life and for working for stiffer laws to
punish male violence. In his zeal to celebrate a feminist-influenced
America, Brooks fails to notice other explanations for what he
attributed to unparalleled virtue, explanations such as the building
of more prisons to incarcerate more young men, who might otherwise be beating their hapless significant others, and demo-
graphic shifts that keep raising the median average age throughout
the Western world. Brooks talks up the social Left by attaching a
conservative-sounding value to its presumed accomplishment.

This kind of gesture has become predictable in American conservatism. The unfurling of conservative values or the renaming of
Leftist values as conservative ones has accompanied a general
retreat from "extremism" undertaken by those seeking social and
professional acceptability. The practitioners of this retreat move
closer to the Left while at the same time reassuring their followers
on the Right that they are not abandoning substantive stands.
Such activists claim to be upholding values, which they call "conservative" and which, for as long as they speak about them in the
context of public policy, can be made to seem different by virtue
of wearing a different label from what "liberals" advocate.

In December 1970, in a review of William Buckley's anthology *The Governor Listeth* in the *New York Times*, Margot Hentoff
calls attention to the value and issue realignment undergone by an
erstwhile rightwing enfant terrible: "Mr. Buckley, looking for new
ground in shifting sand, now writes of the 'new conservatism'
which concerns itself with such things as: the *democratic process*
('the rights of authorities of Harvard over against the mobocratic
demands of students and faculty'); *due process* ("how valuable due
process becomes up against the Marcusean furies"); *upward
mobility* ('for which purpose the new conservatives are giving the
free market something of a hand—for instance, by preferential hiring of Negroes')."[21]

Hentoff notes approvingly that Buckley has "taken on the
weight of middle-aged responsibility" by moving toward the political center and by swerving leftward in the preceding several years
on questions of race. This putative maturation reflected the force
of nonintellectual as well as intellectual factors, including Buckley's
known close relations with several New York Jewish liberals and
neoconservatives: Abe Rosenthal at the *New York Times*, Irving
Kristol, and Norman Podhoretz.[22] But more striking than Buckley's
application of the maxim *d'autres temps, d'autres moeurs* was his

discovery or invention of corresponding values for a "new conservatism," a centrist position he had been moving toward even before his publicized appreciation of Harry Jaffa's defense of democratic equality. Those who thereafter would not fall into line by making the required value and issue adjustment would become rightwing extremists in the eyes of Buckley and his followers. Presumably those who tacked sufficiently leftward remained conservative, because they espoused what were, at least for the moment, "conservative values." Such examples are not meant to question the journalistic privileges to change one's mind and to snub those who refuse to follow one's course. My point is to underscore the gulf between tailored "conservative values" and those features common to the historical Right that have been identifiable as such until the present day.

A final illustration of this difference is a speech given on August 27, 2005, by Angela Merkel, the chief of Germany's Christian Democratic-Christian Social Union, in the northwestern German city of Dortmund. At her party's rally, scheduled three weeks before the federal elections that her Center-Right coalition hoped to win, Merkel faced the challenge of articulating the "Christian values" said to be embedded in her party. In recent years, union leaders have gingerly sidestepped any social issue that might evoke the anger of the Left-Center media, and this has irritated Catholic bishops and some Evangelical clergy, who claim that the union has cynically exploited the "Christian" label. Although Merkel, a technician from East Germany with feminist leanings, was initially disposed to find something vaguely Christian to say, her advisors, drawn from former chancellor Helmut Kohl, rewrote her remarks to remove anything that might rattle those whom they hoped to win over to their side. Merkel thus spoke in praise of "the freedom which is due to everyone, whether man or woman, no matter what one's religion or from whither one comes." Such freedom entails "the right of women to leave the house, to choose a career, and to pick one's own partner." Merkel also stressed her concern about removing any barrier that might stand in the way of someone pursuing this vision.[23]

When she and her advisors (*Referenten*) were asked where in her speech any "Christian values" could be found, they responded that they were implicit in Merkel's words. The party chief's priority was to win the electoral campaign in which she was engaged, and then she could focus on the presentation and implementation of values. A former party chief, Edmund Stoiber, had taken care of values for the time being when he addressed the rally and mocked the opposition Social Democratic Party for wanting to "abolish German unification day while introducing Mohammed's birthday."[24] This is how the party of "value-conservatism" in Germany deals with its foundational truths while keeping the German Right at a distance. The union has tried to exclude acceptable political debate from such parties of the Right as the National Democrats and even the more moderately Rightist Republicans, and it has done so to capture votes that might otherwise go to its competitors. In Bavaria, Stoiber's home base, he and his Christian Social provincial government have been prodding federal courts to ban parties on their Right as a "danger to the German democratic order."

Such tactics, according to their critics, are detrimental to political pluralism. Even Right-Center parties use the courts to go after opposition parties on their Right. Under Article 21-2 of the German Basic Law banning parties that threaten the survival of the German Republic, this procedure is simple and effective.[25] It achieves the desired effect of marginalizing the union's rivals on the Right, who raise serious criticisms about Third World immigration and multiculturalism and who call for slashing the costly German welfare state. Whether or not these rivals are correct in their stands, they represent a modern Right, which the value conservatives in the centrist union have tried to discredit. Not surprisingly, those who campaign under the banner of "Christian values" have not only diluted their value commitment to make it indistinguishable from that of the Left; they have also contributed to a situation in which the Right, as the real counterpoint to the regnant Left, cannot hope to become a respectable political player. Although not the sole function that value conservatism has performed in either Europe or the United States, its role in stripping respectability from an explicit Right deserves attention. Some spokesmen for the American Right, like the lately deceased Samuel Francis, have ridiculed "conservative" as a term whereby their side accepts the fate of having been driven out of the mainstream political debate.[26] For those who find such an outcome devoutly to be desired, it is advantageous to go on preaching "conservative values." But there is absolutely no good reason to pretend that this concept has driven political discussion toward the Right. Its effects and sometimes even its explicit purpose have been exactly the opposite.

CHAPTER 5

THE VALUE GAME REVISITED

MOVEMENT CONSERVATIVE VALUES

One should not cynically dismiss all value conservatism as an accommodation of political fashions; nonetheless, this seems to be the path that most enthusiasts of that persuasion have taken. Not every proponent of value conservatism, however, has been deceitful or manipulative. For example, social theorist Robert A. Nisbet, whose *The Sociological Tradition* revived the thought of European counterrevolutionaries and whose later writings inveighed against the "sovereignty of the state," including its liberal democratic form, appealed to "conservative values" on at least one occasion. Whether this term is one that Nisbet would have preferred to apply in his defense of traditional moral beliefs is open to question, but the fact remains that he did use it in his now famous essay "Moral Values and Community" in 1966.[1]

The occasional appearance of the "v word" in nonpartisan polemics does not negate my general argument. Indeed, the direction in which value conservatism has traveled reflects the fact that value conservatives usually are political activists who have wedded themselves to the Republican Party. Because of their allegiance, they provide decorative language for Republican politicians and a specious moral claim that dignifies Republican programs. Although such "conservative" partisans may boast that they have influenced their party and its standard bearers, more often than not they have simply gone along with the party and its candidates. Self-proclaimed value conservatives, taking the term broadly enough to include such media celebrities as David Brooks, Sean

Hannity, and Rush Limbaugh, are Bush Republicans or neoconservatives who by now stand well to the Left of the postwar American Right.

The party's changing socioeconomic base is essential to an analysis of the symbiosis between value conservatism and the Republican Party, as Noam Scheiber of *The New Republic* observed. Less and less of the Republicans' electoral support comes from the party's "relatively affluent constituents," whereas more and more of it derives from "working-class whites." Consequently, Republicans, while talking about reducing taxes and government, "must also spend lavishly to appeal to the working class." Scheiber wrote as a social liberal and exaggerated the culturally conservative stands that Bush has taken to appeal to his base on immigration, gay rights, and affirmative action. For example, it is hard to see how Bush has veered to the right of Bill Clinton, but Scheiber is quite correct to stress the president's willingness "to shower working-class people with goodies."[2]

Bush's policies have appealed to a large segment of the electorate because American voters, like those of most Western countries, have moved to the Left on social issues over the last few decades. Republicans have responded, just like their Center-Right counterparts elsewhere, by scurrying in the same direction, albeit not as far to the Left as their electoral rivals. For example, any national Republican appeal to "family values" cannot be so unambiguous as to make feminist or gay voters, or their supporters in the media, feel excluded. Thus while former Pennsylvania Senator Rick Santorum promoted *It Takes A Family*, a book on family values that he supposedly had some role in writing, he gave TV interviews in which he greatly toned down views taken or implied in that work. Not in the least, he assured his listeners, does he encourage women to resume their gender's roles of the mid–twentieth century, before they were liberated from their socioeconomic oppression. Santorum's book featured a cover with an apparently multiracial family, lest anyone believe that the senator advocated any specifically white or Euro-American values.[3] Santorum lavished praise on the "conservative moral appeal" of Martin Luther King Jr. and on leading neoconservative journalists, but he made no more than fleeting references to postwar conservatism's founding fathers.[4]

Although a vocal Catholic and an emphatic opponent of abortion, Santorum went out of his way in 2004 to identify his values with those of his fellow Republican, the very pro-choice Senator

Arlen Specter, during Specter's primary battle against antiabortion Catholic Pat Toomey.[5] The Republican junior senator from Pennsylvania illustrates the Republican use of "conservative values," even though he remains or has positioned himself a bit to the Right of his advisors in the National Republican Committee. These Republican values have helped shore up an electoral base through largely rhetorical gestures without sounding sufficiently extreme to lose potential votes in the hypothetical center. Of course, Santorum could vote against the public funding of abortion without building his career on "conservative values," a phrase that he generously loans out to social liberals in his own party but not to those in the other.

The partisan use to which value conservatives have lent themselves has created a peculiar situation. Even as they hasten to bring their values and the applications of these values up to date, they also assert that their convictions are a permanent reference point. Santorum in 2003 publicly opposed gay marriage, but he soon met with criticism from neoconservative columnists John Podhoretz, Jonah Goldberg, and Brooks.[6] None of these younger interpreters of the faith thought it necessary to oppose gay marriage because of a conservative devotion to "family values." Brooks subsequently found such values to be entirely compatible with the establishment of gay marriage. Note that I am not designating here anything that shows the same inherited substance as Catholic canon law or the Hebraic Decalogue. Rather, I am looking at a series of partisan stances to which a dubious permanence had been ascribed. Thus in less than a decade a conservative who stayed in the movement could move from Russell Kirk's defense of "hierarchy and degrees," grounded in Edmund Burke and classical conservatism, to "equality of opportunity but not of result." This for-the-time-being eternalized value, articulated not by Kirk but by William Bennett, Lynn Cheney, Rick Santorum, and David Horowitz, has been linked to Martin Luther King Jr., despite King's support of monetary reparations for American blacks. The fallen civil rights activist has been brought back to life counterfactually as a neoconservative opponent of affirmative action, albeit one who would have favored giving special attention to the recruiting of black students and black workers.[7]

The value game has two aspects that betray its fragility. One is that the appeal to "conservative values" does not valorize all meanings of "conservative"; it notably excludes classical conservatism and the social base out of which that movement sprang.

"Conservative values" have nothing to do with either the world defended by Burke in the *Reflections* or the mental habits described by Karl Mannheim as "conservative thinking." The values of Santorum and Brooks have little to do with bourgeois liberalism as it prevailed with the professional and commercial classes that survived into the twentieth century. Nation-states controlling immigration, well-defined gender roles, Victorian morality, and the separation of civil society from public administration were the constituent elements of the bourgeois civic idea that both value conservatives and their talking partners on the Left have excluded from their political conversations. Both sides may believe that governmentally imposed social policies dealing with the family, women's and gay rights, enforced diversity, and a global democratic foreign policy are better or more humane positions than those that aristocrats, churchmen, or the bourgeoisie offered in centuries past. They may also believe that they are saying and doing exactly what the voting public desires in a "democratic" government. But why should we accept as "conservative" that which does not meet the once regnant (at least in the Western world) definition of the term, and which now refers to something that is being steadily reconfigured?

Value conservatives expose their second weakness when they call their opponents nihilistic or relativistic. The Left does not thrive because of its refusal to take moral positions. Here and in Europe, it showcases one "value" after another, be it cultural diversity; preferential treatment for non-Western peoples and religions as the historic victims of Western injustice; social equality; or reproductive freedom for women. Why are such positions less subject to being classified as moral preferences than the electorally flexible "family values" of the Right-Center, now deemed to be "conservative"? And what evidence did the value-conservative John Hallowell have, in his much quoted *South Atlantic Quarterly* essay of 1947, "Modern Liberalism: An Invitation to Suicide," for this judgment: "Vitiated by fear and lack of conviction in the truth of his own doctrine, the modern liberal has neither the courage born of conviction nor the words to condemn despotism. That was true in 1933 and it is true in 1947. Modern liberalism is an invitation to suicide."[8] Despite Hallowell's crusade against "suicidal liberals," he supported both an American welfare state and American involvement in the Second World War, and he was in a position to notice that left-of-center intellectuals shared his commitments. He could also have observed the willingness of much of

the American Left to suspend civil liberties and pull out other
stops in order to defeat "fascism." Were these "liberals" lacking
"conviction" when they took such stands?

In his discussion about the beginnings of the post–World War II
"conservative intellectual movement," George Nash emphasizes
the crusades against "relativism" and scientific "reductionism"
that preoccupied his subjects. He talks about how Hallowell,
Richard Weaver, and other critics of a perceived moral disintegration attacked the adversaries of moral absolutes.[9] In a desperate
cry against the Zeitgeist, Hallowell, then a respected political theorist at Duke University, complained that "implicit in positivism is
a nihilism closely akin to, if not identical with, the gospel of cyni-
cism and despair that produced the mentality of fascism."[10]
Although some "intellectual conservatives" in Nash's exposition
found other enemies on the American Right, whether Jacobins or
utilitarians, these targets were less popular than the hated relativists. The attention given to these other targets only rarely went
beyond declamations and, particularly in the case of Frank Meyer,
involved judgments made in the context of political diatribes.

This assault from the Right on value disintegration came in
the wake of an intense revival, which went back into the interwar
period, of interest in Catholic natural law. Identified with, among
others, the French philosophers Jacques Maritain and Etienne
Gilson; the Nazi refugee and Georgetown University professor of
government Heinrich Rommen; and the Jesuit author John
Courtney Murray, this defense of universal moral norms struck a
chord among those who were then reacting to the totalitarian
regimes of the modern era. Authors persuaded by natural law
thinking denounced such notions as "might makes right," "laws
come from the sovereign will of the ruler," and "everything inside
and nothing outside of the state." Relativism of the kind found in
these aphorisms had supposedly led to mass acceptance of tyranny
and, at least indirectly, to the wars that arbitrary power in the
twentieth century had unleashed.[11] It was therefore necessary, as
Rommen explained in *The State in the Catholic World of Thought*
(1935), "to reach back to the ultimate and most general of legal
judgments, to the question whether the result corresponds to justice or not. The necessity for such decisions, in which the question
of concrete right or injustice cannot be answered by referring to
the will of the legislator, according to legal positivism, but must be
examined anew from individual cases; this very necessity indicates
that there must be a primordial, nonderivative source of right,

namely a 'natural' right."[12] In the fifties and afterward, belief in the need for such moral reasoning led American and other thinkers into embracing Catholicism or High Anglicanism as a repository of the natural law position. But the two were not necessarily connected.

Although Rommen and the French neo-Thomists tied the sense of a universal moral standard operating *praeter legem* (beyond the law) to a medieval Catholic metaphysic, one could make similar arguments about the nature of "right" from a less explicitly scholastic perspective. Less metaphysically grounded but still recognizably Catholic or Anglo-Catholic formulations of a natural law argument are available in the works of C. S. Lewis, John Finnis, and Robert George. Dispensing with a religious point of departure entirely, the Columbian-American ethicist Eliseo Vivas, who defined himself as an "axiological realist," devoted his energies to proving that "values are real and antecedent to our discovery of them." This enterprise, however, did not lead Vivas back to the Catholic religion of his ancestors. He remained content to argue that ethical values were the bedrock of stable social relations and, as such, were knowable to our minds.[13] Attempts to defend the concept of universal moral reason by which existing laws are to be measured has taken a variety of forms—that is, rationalistic, Aristotelian, and neo-Thomistic—and it is questionable whether appeal to such a standard indicates by itself, as maintained by some journalists, an attachment to the Catholic Right.

With only some exceptions, the conservative movement posited natural law as "values" that stood in opposition to the denial of values, the despised stance of relativism. The main target of the Catholic natural law exponents, however, was not relativism but rather positivism or else naturalism. Accordingly, one of Rommen's most hated thinkers was the English philosopher Thomas Hobbes, who had depicted society as a collection of isolated individuals held together by the will of the sovereign. "Not justice but power creates law," was one of Hobbes's best-remembered aphorisms. Thinkers rooted in the Catholic natural law tradition, like Rommen, also targeted "historicism," which interpreted moral truths in terms of the historical periods in which particular ideas had become popular. Rommen believed that the haste with which some bourgeois espoused the historicism of Friedrich Carl von Savigny reflected a nineteenth-century social development: "the bourgeoisie having achieved its political goals" lost interest in the natural rights position that had earlier aided their ascent to power.[14] Less tendentiously, Rommen distinguished the Lockean natural right position of the rising bourgeoisie, which the Marxists transformed into human rights said to be upheld by the proletariat, from "the older natural right." It was, in fact ,still an older concept of right, which is the medieval Catholic interpretation of right rooted in Greco-Roman sources, which Rommen commended to his readers. But less obvious among the errors that he engages in his work is that relativist false step that American conservatives purport to have opposed since the 1950s.

It might be helpful to draw a distinction here that should be obvious for some readers. The value terminology that runs through the discourse of such ethicists as Vivas, Max Scheler, J. N. Findlay, and the Swedish humanist Claes Ryn refers explicitly to a morally structured universe, one in which ethical choices have to be made in terms of either a supposedly recognizable order of ascending goods or a single highest good. As the German Catholic vitalist Scheler put this case, "The characteristic (as the most primordial) of what is taken for the 'highest value' is that which is less relative and therefore the 'absolute' value. All other essential connections (among values) are dependent upon it." The "highest value," according to Scheler, is one that does not depend upon another, much less a changing context, and is anchored in existence itself and ultimately "in the divine ground of all existence." Scheler, borrowing from Aristotle's ethics, constructed a hierarchy of "value modalities" running from what is agreeable through what is useful to what is beautiful.[15] However the argument is phrased, clearly it is possible to talk about "values" in a sense differing from the modern conservative sense. This latter does not relate to an ontological or axiological study presenting the nature of the "Good"; it is about subjective preferences in political life pretending to be something more.

A striking feature of the journalistic debates centering on values in the fifties and sixties was the feebleness of the responses offered by the "conservatives" against their Leftist scorners. When "value-free" sociologist Herbert J. Muller lashed out against the "neo-feudal certainties" of Weaver and others on the Right, those under attack went after their critics as "relativists" or occasionally as "positivists."[16] A more compelling response would have been to investigate the other side's values, for example, government-imposed social equality and secularism presented under the banner of "scientific" administration and education. The Right should

have underlined that the democratic Left was foisting on the public its own social vision—and not some jumble of private, supposedly relativistic moral choices. What had to take place, if the
intellectual Right were to makes its case, was a debate about con-
flicting views of the good, both of which included values. But this
debate could not be honestly waged if one side claimed to stand
on the bedrock of scientific truth while the other foolishly pretended that its opponents were "relativists."

We might distinguish relativism from two other positions that
are sometimes confused with it, namely, hedonism and subjectivism. The practice of living for pleasure, whether of a material or
of a sensual kind, and the presentation of this practice as a philosophical stance is not the same as the interpretation of all values as
being of equal worth or as being equally trivial. The former
involves the decision to embrace gratification as a life choice or
else a surrender to desire; the latter is a distinctive approach to
value judgment that specifically excludes the elevation of some values over others, save as an arbitrary choice. Relativists deny the
possibility of a valid explicit or implicit hierarchy of moral goods
that is universally applicable.

Such a position is equally far removed from subjectivism,
which refers to the view that everything that we posit as truth
derives from our individual minds. This egocentric point of reference precludes any objective knowledge or, in the philosophical
sense, objective values but by no means requires the relativistic
assumption that all moral and cultural standards are equal. Nor
does it suggest the relativistic premise that there is no valid way of
ranking moral standards. Subjectivists start from the assumption
that their own mind and consciousness provide a standard of truth
that is not relative in terms of their own judgments.

The misrepresentation of the confrontation between the
Right and the social-engineering Left, which was really a struggle
between competing worldviews, helped to prepare that revolving
door of values that became characteristic of the conservative
movement. Although the Right might have lost its struggle in any
case because of political and socioeconomic changes and a cultural
imbalance of forces, it should have identified the imposers of
Leftist values for what they were, namely, as partisans who were
enlisting the state in *their* moral crusade.

The Right's argument against "relativists" became even easier
when anticolonial and multicultural special pleaders entered the
court of public opinion. It was at that point that, according to

French social critic Pascal Bruckner, there appeared a resort to a "double sophism" among the exponents of "all cultures are equal." In this morally charged defense of relativism, Westerners are accused of being especially ethnocentric and therefore especially wicked, but paradoxically they are also especially sensitive to this charge, presumably because of their moral superiority. In both cases, argued Pascal Bruckner, who found this double sophism in the commentaries of ethnologist Claude Lévi-Strauss, the assumption of equal value for all cultures gets called into question.[17] Taking a different tack, one cannot assume that the cultural entities compared are equal unless there is a recognized standard against which they can be evaluated. "Equal in relation to what?" is the obvious response to the statement that one cannot claim that one's culture is superior to another.

Ample evidence exists that the newer, self-styled relativists, like the ones who came before and invoked "science," are also making inconsistent claims. But the depiction of them as "permissive" or "value-free" is a dubious description, even if it allows politicians and journalists to flaunt "conservative" values against the "relativist Left." Since the 1940s the same tirades have been leveled against the same foe with less and less cogency. The exercise has benefited a movement that is not averse to tinkering with the "permanent things."

The alternative to imputing amorality to one's opponent is to recognize that political positions are value-related and that politicians may disagree about the related values as well as positions. Holders of and candidates for public office are entitled to take stands that may appeal to their potential voters on the basis of shared beliefs. It is hard indeed for a candidate to seek electoral office without revealing some moral preference. But this is not the same as attributing to oneself a worldview based on universal, nonnegotiable values or treating one's cobbled-together values as unchanging "conservative" verities that define a permanent conservative essence. It is this latter pretension, or, more properly put, the difference between it and reality, that warrants critical scrutiny.

VALUES FROM HEAVEN

The ascription of universal validity to one's personal values is an even more ominous development in the "conservative" value game than positing a relativist straw man. Although it is possible to find other, equally vivid illustrations of this practice, someone who stands out because of his central importance as a value conservative is Harry Jaffa. In "The False Prophets of Conservatism," an essay that he presented in a modified form as a Claremont Institute address, Jaffa goes after "moral relativism," a now supposedly pervasive problem that prevents proper understanding of the American founding. That act of state-building was predicated on the "principles of the Declaration," which became the moral mission of the new republic: "the 'laws of nature and of nature's God' in the Declaration represent a distillation of the wisdom of a tradition of more than two thousand years." Furthermore: "they—and the American founding generally—represent the culmination of the attempt of Socrates, described by Cicero, to bring philosophy down from the heavens. They also represent the agreement of reason and revelation—of Athens and Jerusalem—on the moral ground of human government."[18]

Almost explicit in Jaffa's past and present oratory is his conviction that all decent people, including Pope John Paul II, Ronald Reagan, and the pre–affirmative action American civil rights leaders, would have agreed with his rendering of "political philosophy." The holdouts against his view are the still unenlightened moral relativists, for example, Justices Antonin Scalia and William Rehnquist; Judge Robert Bork; the nostalgic reactionary Kirk; and such black critics of the American founding as Thurgood Marshall and John Hope Franklin. These recalcitrants shrouded by darkness have questioned, or may not have heard of, "the constitutional standing of the doctrine of natural rights enunciated in the Declaration of Independence and expounded by Lincoln."[19] The United States supposedly from its beginnings was intended to exemplify the "all men are created equal" phrase of the Declaration, which, as fate would have it, was the "bringing of philosophy down from heaven."

Out of courtesy, I spare my reader a detailed account of the exegetical marvels by which Jaffa arrived at his political-theological conclusion. A selective reading of such sources as Aristotle, Plato, John Locke, Martin Luther King Jr., James Madison, Leo Strauss, and the idolized Abraham Lincoln is made to show that "democratic equality" is the most vital and most essential Western moral teaching. Supposedly it is the core of the Declaration, which yields the hermeneutic key to understanding the Constitution. What makes Scalia and Rehnquist (though not Clarence Thomas, who was an avowed Jaffaite before becoming a Supreme Court justice) the slaves of "unadorned positivism, relativism, and nihilism"—in short, a microcosm of "the crisis at the heart of present-day conservatism" and of "the crisis of the West"—is that they have dared to substitute "majority rule" for Jaffa's teaching. Such judges believe that "the only rights that the people have are the rights that the people themselves have decreed." In place of his "political philosophy," these jurists wish to put the majority will, which Jaffa equates with both "moral relativism, which denies any intrinsic worth to human freedom," and the electoral practices of Hitler and Stalin, whose "legitimacy was ratified by plebiscite."

It is hard to imagine how a Supreme Court would operate if it were made to appeal to Jaffa's standards each time that it decided a case. The "living constitution" proposed by the judicial Left may be a paragon of stability compared to what Jaffa and his numerous disciples are demanding as their moral agenda. Contrary to Jaffa's statements or their implications, the Declaration contains far more than the phrase that Jefferson borrowed from Locke, which only broadly understood suggests a duty to enforce democratic equality. Locke was asserting a natural right to equality in liberty but not universal political equality, much less universal social equality. But why should the list of abuses seen to violate the rights of Englishmen, to which the Declaration devotes far more space than to Lockean phraseology, be less relevant for understanding the reasons for the revolt against England than the passages that Jaffa highlights? While his interpretation may, in fact, follow Lincoln's tropes during the Civil War, Jaffa has not thereby created an American superlegality to which our written law must be subordinated. Lincoln may have been morally justified to oppose slavery, and he certainly found a usable text from which he could argue slavery's incompatibility with the American founding. His citation of that text, however, did not preempt the authority of the document by which Americans in the 1780s agreed to be ruled as a political society. And even less did they agree to be governed by Jaffa's reading of the passage in question.

The Constitution, under which Americans did consent to live, does not incorporate the Declaration, a fact that Jaffa seems to have acknowledged in some of his earlier writings but later ignored. While Blackstone's *Commentaries* and the English common law clearly shaped the legal traditions out of which our governing framework came, the Declaration had far less importance for clarifying that framework. Although personally I might choose for edification Deutero-Isaiah, Paul's Letter to the Romans, and Plato's

Phaedo over the paraphrase from Locke in the Declaration, Jaffa, Charles Kesler, and Bennett surely are entitled to their inspirational readings. But *their* choices and *their* interpretations of selected readings should not determine how American citizens are to be legally governed.

Finally, there is no evidence that Bork, Scalia, and Rehnquist believe in "plebiscitary" government or the unbridled popular will on the grounds that they disagree with Jaffa's jurisprudence. Whether they are arguing for a strict construction of the Constitution or for the continued rights of the states in relation to the central government, such men are not inciting majoritarian terror or throwing their support behind totalitarian leaders. These jurists are all devout Christians, a term that does not cease to apply to them because they fail to interpret constitutional law through Jaffa's moral lenses. It is hard to see how Justice Scalia, who is a fervent practicing Catholic and whose son is a traditionalist priest, can be turned into a nihilist because of his deviation from Jaffa's political philosophy. Nor does the fact that Scalia reads the document that he had sworn to uphold differently from Jaffa and the Jaffaites make him part of the "crisis of the West."

While Jaffa considers the natural equality of humankind, which he believes requires democratic governance, as a kind of divine revelation, he does not infer from this premise the need for policies that other more explicitly Leftist egalitarian thinkers propose. Unlike Michael Walzer, Jeffrey Stout, or John Rawles, to name three representatives of this persuasion, Jaffa does not advocate socialism or more extensive social projects than those already in place to insure equality. His attempt at implementing his egalitarian doctrine is distinctive and based on educational outreach. On the international plane, this outreach requires the assistance of groups like the National Endowment for Democracy and the prosecution of an international crusade, including military intervention, to propagate the American democratic creed globally.

Jaffa's Claremont Institute, its affiliated publications, and Michigan's Hillsdale College, which has come under the presidency of Jaffa's longtime disciple Larry P. Arnn, feature studies and conferences on the statesmanship of Winston Churchill and Lincoln, both seen as model "democratic" national leaders.[20] Arnn serves as vice chairman of the Claremont Institute, which is closely connected to Beltway "conservative" foundations, particularly Heritage. An ardent exponent of the Jaffaite creed, Arnn is also currently establishing a graduate program in statesmanship, which will likely implant Jaffa's opinions and interpretations even more firmly in the conservative movement. In sharp contrast to the interwar Right that had eschewed foreign military entanglements, the Jaffaites are conspicuously fond of America's war presidents, especially Lincoln and those who had rallied to "democratic" England in the two world wars. Given Jaffa's outspoken Zionism, which he shares with the other neoconservatives, it is also not surprising that he includes Israel among the premiere liberal democracies of the world. Those who fail to take his side on these matters are attacked not only as anti-Jewish but also as insufficiently supportive of democratic fraternity.

These opinions are not the mutterings of an isolated eccentric. No less a figure than President Bush wore a Jaffaite mantle when, in his second inaugural address, he affirmed America's unconditional duty to spread democracy. The president's speech sounded as if Jaffa or his acolytes had scripted it. Along with Bush and lesser politicians, members of the private sector also have responded to Jaffa' rhetoric. The financial assistance his benefactors showered on the Claremount Institute and now on its Hillsdale satellite indicates that his views have attracted rich, influential supporters.

The historical picture drawn by Jaffa, however, is by no means original and is available in the works of mainstream liberal, pro–New Deal historians like Arthur Schlesinger and James MacGregor Burns. Jaffa's emphasis on activist presidents who advance the idea of equality domestically while waging wars against "anti-democratic" enemies abroad or against the slave-holding South comes straight out of the conventional historiography that many of my generation had to digest in high school and college.[21] Jaffa clearly is not disseminating a storyline that today's mainstream media or academic authorities would find strange or repulsive. If anything, he sharpens that storyline by investing it with universal moral significance while decrying those on the Right or Left who challenge it as "relativists." These gestures do not raise his "values" into transcendent truths—and even less into conservative ones.

But they do show how his political rhetoric has become a political religion. His presentation of his democratic values and his crusade for its implementation elsewhere call to mind the attacks made by the current Pope on "relativism" as the great moral evil. According to Pope Benedict XVI, while he was still called Cardinal Josef Ratzinger and speaking at the Lateran University in May

2004, relativists had fashioned a "super-confession" that was threatening all traditional religion in the West. The only way to combat this danger, according to Ratzinger, was for Christians to assert their own beliefs as a paramount truth that stood in opposition to those who were breaking down moral distinctions.[22] Whether or not the enemies of traditional Christian ethics are relativists or upholders of their own value system is not a question that need be addressed here. More to the point is the borrowing, by Jaffa and his disciples and by neoconservatives generally, of ecclesiastical homiletics that are consistent with their political agenda. It is no longer Christianity but global democracy and its fevered propagation that are the favored answer to relativism. During Christmas in 1988, neoconservative Catholic theologian Michael Novak made this point explicit when he described the present American regime as an epiphany "that will be remembered like the babe in the manger in Bethlehem."[23]

The positing of democratic equality as the highest value by the Jaffaites has certain advantages vis-à-vis other values put forth by the conservative movement. Democratic equality is a value that originated and has flourished on the Left, and one to which American educators and the media have long been sympathetic in principle. Having embraced this highest value enables its "conservative" bearers to avoid being ostracized as "extremists." Although they may argue with partisans on the Left over what exactly Lincoln or King meant by it or about how equality in a democracy should be implemented, they and almost all others but the hated paleoconservatives can be brought inside the tent of universal equality. Moreover, Jaffa's highest value is more than a simple slogan suitable for insertion into a Republican campaign. It is an ideal in the name of which young people are sent to war. Like Marxist-Leninism and Jacobinism, democratic equality is a revolutionary ideal that requires violent struggle to promote it. While the now reviled antiwar Right since the 1930s has mocked the interventionist Left for wanting to "wage perpetual war for perpetual peace," Leftist militarists under powerful presidents, much admired in neoconservative circles, have been able to mobilize the masses. This is a facet of modern history that Nisbet, in *The Twilight of Authority* and in *The Present Age*, developed with deep insight. Wars have not only been the "life of the state"; they have also strengthened the centrality of national administrations in the lives of their subjects.[24]

THE TYRANNY OF VALUES

Early twentieth century German scholars, most notably Max Weber, Nicolai Hartmann, and Carl Schmitt, constructed a "value theory [*Wertlehre*]" that would explain a concept that had moved from economics to culture and morality. Prior to that time, "value" had referred primarily to determinations of material worth, a term that was later extended to other classificatory and investigative endeavors. This process occurred in tandem with the rising importance of individual judgment. Value judgments (*Werturteile*) entered into language in proportion to the growing emphasis placed on individuals' forming opinions and then rating the opinions of others on the basis of their own. Although "elite" values also exist in our society, they belong to an ever more nontraditional culture. They are the things valued by those individuals who have risen to high status in a late-modern, consumerist society.

In an essay produced in 1917 during the First World War, "The Meaning of Value-Freedom and Economic Sciences," Weber lamented the "unavoidable" tendency among German professors to engage in "personal judgments from the lectern." As Weber explained, "It is indeed an unprecedented situation, in which numerous, state-accredited prophets are preaching not in the street or in churches or else in public or in congregations of believers that profess themselves as such, but do so in the supposedly objective setting of a state-protected lecture hall secured against opposition in the name of 'science.' Here they dare to toss around authoritative opinions from the podium about questions relating to their world views." For Weber, this grandstanding typically occurred among professors who were exhibiting their wartime patriotism, but his critique applied equally to a more general situation in which the professor's "right to personality" or "cultural judgments" has appeared as a form of scientific knowledge.

Contrary to the picture of a valueless landscape that today's conservatives have sometimes drawn, Weber depicted fierce struggles among values and value advocates that continue to convulse modern society. He complained about the "glaring misunderstanding" that has led "to the attribution of a relativistic intention to those who show this collision of values." A detached interpreter might well seek to understand the "relation of spheres of values to each other"—and might even pursue this end "by means of an organic metaphysic broad enough to embrace contradictions."[25]

Weber took it upon himself to prove that most of what is conventionally considered "rational," and unattached to cultural or personal value judgments, is based on definite value opinions.

In the matter of ends sought, such judgments affect personal assessments, and Weber pointed to the example of a free enterprise economy taken as an "exhaustive representation of natural reality that is undistorted by human folly," that is, as a pure fantasy. This fantasy that Weber brought up is "an ought, a value-fraught ideal" that has not been put into practice. He therefore questioned the view that the pursuit of commercial profit is a value-free activity driven by a universal passion for gain. Having earlier and famously examined the relation between Calvinist moral theology and the spirit of capitalism, Weber explicitly denied in 1917 that the systematic pursuit of profit could operate independently of a cultural context. "One would only be inclined," Weber noted, "to take a commercial article off the market in a society that emphasizes profit more than or to the exclusion of other cultural values."[26]

Weber did not treat all values in a uniform way. There are some, he acknowledges, that are appropriate to particular activities and relations and that amount to more than "personal claims." The "rationality" displayed in scientific research differs from the nationalist or revolutionary grandstanding so deplorable in Weber's fellow professors. Especially with regard to scholarship, Weber insisted on the need for empathy (*Verstehen*) in the study of attitudes and beliefs that are clearly not one's own but that imprint social and historical contexts. Despite his greater interest in historically rooted structures of authority, Weber did concede the possibility that a social-political order could be based, comparable to science, on substantive rationality, the appeal to which "typically takes the form of natural right." As he explained, "However limited such a concept of right would appear to be given its ideal claims, one can not dispute the considerable influence its logically revealed suppositions have had on some human activities." Such "natural right," he observed in passing, "is distinctly different from both positive and traditional notions of right."[27]

Although Weber did not sneer at substantive rationality as a social and political principle, he recognized problems that its application would likely engender. Such rationalist undertakings did not have behind them the benefit of custom and habituation that render traditional orders stable. In brief: "They are far more precarious than social orders, which provide a binding character, which is 'legitimacy.'" Weber's emphasis on the "affective" aspects of traditional and customary ties indicates his view of the sources of ordinary moral conduct. In some instances, substantive rationality could supply the basis for a long-standing structure of human relations, but Weber continued to express doubts about the widespread applicability of this model. He also tried to distinguish rationally based government from merely personal, partisan claims masquerading as "science." Weber's concern in these matters led him to clarify two distinctive realms of activity in a pair of widely read essays, "Politics as Calling" and "Science as Calling."[28]

A younger contemporary of Weber, Schmitt, who attended Weber's lectures at Munich in 1919, carried the critical assessment of values toward further insights. In "The Tyranny of Values," Schmitt read his own provocative conclusions into Weber's critique of "personal values." From the philosopher of ethics Hartmann, as well as from Weber, Schmitt constructed a picture of values as a source of seething conflict and as a characteristically modern phenomenon. According to Schmitt, values work as *Angriffspunkte*, points of attack by which individuals try to impose their wills on each other. Unlike the inhabitants of Weber's traditional order, who respect custom and status, value-asserters are engaged in improvisation. They are expressing *their* judgments about what they consider the highest good, which they then wish to make binding on others.[29] By legislating their value preferences, or by otherwise projecting them outward, they hope to give these preferences wider scope. Schmitt cited the example of Kant, whose *Critique of Practical Reason* presents the universal character of moral precepts, the "categorical imperative," as an indispensable vehicle of validation. Like the Kantian ethicist, the asserter of a value desires universal validation for his belief. His "highest value" can be rendered valid only in proportion to how widely he can apply it by winning or forcing its acceptance.[30]

The critique of *Höchstwertsetzung* (the assertion of a highest value) constructed by Schmitt is not about ego validation of the kind addressed by contemporary psychology. Schmitt and Hartmann before him were not discussing people who threw their weight around in order to feel self-important; they were examining the way value claims are advanced because of the need to validate subjective preferences, which require that one's values be made to appear universally valid. And this practice derives from the fact that, according to Weber, modern society is a "battlefield of competing values," from which all traditional authority is departing.

THE IMPLEMENTATION OF THE HIGHEST VALUE

I am not arguing that moral reasoning necessarily is tainted by subjectivity and in consequence deserving of rejection as the product of purely individual judgment. My target is the style of value assertion that characterizes contemporary and at least putatively individualistic society. This style is one in which value clarification leads to the privileging of one's "own values," which may, in fact, be those of one's peer group or the national media. These values are then elevated until they become a universal good to which humankind is expected to commit itself with varying degrees of intensity. Once values have been posited, a dispute must follow to determine how the "highest value" among them should be implemented. Presumably it is not enough, to get back to the case at hand, to acknowledge democratic equality as the distillation of human and divine moral knowledge through the ages. It is also necessary to find the suitable "policy" by which the state can implement this highest value.

This value application is now the subject of a heated debate among Jaffaites and neoconservatives about how the United States government should bestow—or impose—on other parts of the world the only morally allowable regime. In a signature Claremont Institute statement, Kesler, the director of the Henry Salvatori Center at Claremont and the editor of the *Claremont Review of Books*, explained how the Reagan notion of "regime change" had given way to the "Bush Doctrine," which calls for the "planting of democracy and freedom" worldwide. Kesler underlined that "the Bush Doctrine puts the democratization of once totalitarian, quondam authoritarian, and persistently tribal societies at the center of its objectives" and therefore represents an advance over the less bold approach to nation-building practiced by earlier Republican administrations.[31] Although Kesler extolled a value that his movement had elevated, he wondered how far the government should go in support of "the duty, as a result of our respect for human rights, to help the Iraqis and others realize their democratic entitlement and destiny."[32]

Kesler quoted James W. Ceasar and Daniel DiSalvol, two like-minded political theorists writing in *Public Interest*, who judged Bush's appeal to the "'universality of democracy and human rights" to be "a watershed moment in the history of American politics, with enormous significance for the Republican Party and the conservative movement." Ceasar and DiSalvol tried to ground their global democratic commitment in Madison's praise in *The Federalist* for "that honorable determination which animates every votary of freedom to rest all of our political experiments on the capacity of mankind for self-government."[33] This determination in favor of freedom depends for its success on "potential needs [being] made actual." Such a process of satisfying the yearning for freedom depends on "needs to be awakened by practice and habit."

While Bush tried to ground his mission, as he stated in his State of the Union Address in 2002, in a universal concern shared by "fathers and mothers in all societies" who "want their children to be educated and live free from poverty and violence," Kesler insists that this is not enough to build democracy, as the founders and Lincoln hoped to do, on "the mutual recognition of rights and duties, grounded in an objective natural order that is independent of human will." From his Jaffaite reading of America's foundational documents, Kesler concludes that we must urge the American executive, whom he generally applauds as a global democrat, to show caution. Although "it is a wonderful thing to hear President Bush reassert the natural rights basis of just government," he may be carrying a good thing too far: "The worry is that in tracing he individual right to be free to ordinary human compassion or fellow-feeling and then confounding that right with an entitlement to live in a fully democratic regime."[34] More specifically, Kesler warns against overreaching in Iraq: "By raising expectations—by making democracy appear as an easier conversion and way of life than it really is—Bush risks not only the erosion of liberal and pro-democratic support within Iraq, but also a loss of public confidence in the whole war effort."[35]

Kesler's warning reflects his awareness that at least part of the movement conservative community intends to carry on the democratic mission with even more military vigor. Bill Kristol, David Frum, Victor Davis Hanson, Robert Kagan, Michael Ledeen, and Charles Krauthammer all share Kesler's highest value but advocate additional initiatives by the U.S. government in Iraq and elsewhere, well beyond the point that Kesler deemed such outreach prudent. He correctly noted how the democratic education that neoconservatives wrongly imagine had succeeded in postwar Germany and Japan in the absence of democratic traditions succeeded for precisely the opposite reasons: both Germany and

Japan had been industrialized countries, with sizable middle classes and histories of parliamentary experience, before they had succumbed to expansionist dictatorships during the Depression.

The question, then, is how far the current conservative movement can accept deviations among its members in the implementation of those values that its most influential spokesmen have proclaimed. Whereas today's conservative movement will not likely re-embrace the values of the first edition of *The Conservative Mind*, some disagreement may be allowed (or so it might appear) in the prescriptions offered for bringing democracy and equality to other parts of the globe. Such debate will have to be delimited, however, lest the discussion moves in a direction that is contrary to the wishes of neoconservative leaders. For example, those who reject a hard line against the Palestinians or who come out explicitly against the war in Iraq may be unacceptable as "conservatives," even if they also affirm today's democratic-egalitarian-universalist conservative creed.

One reason for the limiting of permissible policy differences is that the present movement conservative creed and its icons incorporate features that, until recently, could be found on the Left-Center. And the overlap between these sides as long becomes especially apparent when "conservative" partisans stick to the enunciation of values. Thus when *New York Times* (designated conservative) columnist Brooks, in a speech on August 25, 2005, before a largely Republican-friendly audience at the American Political Science Association, demanded that Republicans stress social equality to a greater degree, in the manner of Hillary Clinton, his opinion did not seem to disconcert his listeners.[36] But if Brooks had argued for the immediate withdrawal of American troops from Iraq or for a more sympathetic attitude toward the Palestinians, he would undoubtedly have lost his movement conservative standing. Let us assume, however, a different scenario. If Brooks had spoken in favor of a neoconservative foreign policy (which he did not) but, instead of deploring American underclass poverty and instead of calling for income redistribution, had challenged the current preoccupation with the ideal of equality, his listeners would have reacted, at best, with stunned silence. And if he had then gone on to praise Kirk's nonrevised conservative principles of 1953, his audience would have likely responded with open hostility. If it were not assumed that he had taken leave of his senses and should be put under psychiatric care, his erstwhile admirers most certainly would have withheld the hearty applause that he did receive at the end of his remarks.

Those who now embrace the conservative label have tied their own highest values to a particular agenda and to a particular manner of implementing it. With a claim to the permanence of these values, "conservatives" differentiate themselves from their opponents on the Left. The latter present their ideology as a march toward a progressive future that will rescind the past. This approach differs from the way in which "conservatives" dress up their preferences by attributing constancy to mutating beliefs supposedly based on the funded wisdom of the ages.

This value conservatism has little to do with what its journalistic exponents would have the public believe that it is. Its vision of the good has much in common with what it supposedly opposes—and amounts to a restatement of ideals that the Left held yesterday or may even hold again tomorrow. This "conservative" point of reference does not correspond to those principles and understandings that American conservatives considered essential only fifty years ago. As the early chapters of this book show, that older worldview was devised to meet a particular foreign threat. It came to prevail during the cold war and eventually replaced the small-government Right, whose spokesmen (and spokeswomen) often fell afoul of the new alliance. The winners in that older ideological contest would also come to new forks in the road, at which point new choices would be made. Those who did not side with the leaders, who enjoyed media acceptance, would then fall under the ban of the reorganized empire. That is how we reached the present state of affairs, with the heirs of postwar conservatism enjoying, at least for the time being, an appearance of permanent dominance based on wealth, media access, and the opportunity to push all opposition "off the bus."[37] The establishment Right now thrives, benefiting from the complementary advantages of continued dialogue with conversation partners drawn from the Left-Center and an alliance with the Republican Party searching for an electoral vision. Individual Rightist intellectuals are permitted supernumerary roles in this respectable Right—until the neoconservative media decide to replace them with new expendable casting.

CHAPTER 6

———•———

OFF THE BUS

In October of 2005 the national press celebrated the fiftieth anniversary of the founding of *National Review* and the eightieth birthday of its creator, William F. Buckley. Publications normally not in sync with one another seemed univocal as they bestowed accolades on Buckley for his role in building the postwar conservative movement. Two of these tributes, by E. J. Dionne in the *Washington Post* and by Jonah Goldberg on the *National Review* Web site, deserve mention because of their reliance on what has become received history after fifty years. For Dionne, Buckley was "the Right's practical intellectual," who had been "challenging liberal elites on their own ground." He "pioneered the most effective form of conservative jujitsu," constructing a movement "devoted to the interests of the wealthy and powerful casting itself as a collection of populists challenging liberal snobbery." Dionne then admits, "I am now and have been almost all my life an admirer of William F. Buckley, Jr.," despite the fact that Buckley "was far too effective on behalf of a movement that I think should be driven from power."[1]

Dionne dwelt on what he called his "illicit love" for Buckley because of this figure's putative achievement: "Buckley was determined to rid the right of the wing nuts. He was to his everlasting credit the scourge of anti-Semitism that once had a hold on significant parts of the right. He also blasted the strange conspiracy theories of the John Birch Society. But most important were Buckley's efforts during the 1950s to resolve conservatism's contradictions. These exertions made it possible for Barry Goldwater and then Ronald Reagan to turn the remnant into a mighty political force."

A similar but more elaborate judgment about the conservative movement and its alleged founder appeared in Goldberg's

summing up of the "golden years" when Buckley rose to prominence and his ideas became prevalent on the moderate Right.
Goldberg observed that American conservatism "is the youngest
ideology on the block" and that it "begins in the 1950s with
National Review." We are also told "it would be an exaggeration
to say the 'Old Right' is a myth, but that term is really more of a
label imposed on a eclectic collection of 'superfluous men' who
stood outside of the historical currents, lamenting the rush and
foam of the Progressive tide. But they belonged to no movement,
shared little that could be called a political program and, as a
group, if they voted at all, they did so the way a man in a blindfold
shoots a crowd."[2] Goldberg makes clear that he is not speaking
about "small-c conservatives," who have existed in every society
and are simply people averse to experimentation. He is describing
that movement that Buckley forged. As Goldberg explained, "the
core of American conservatism—which is Buckleyite conservatism—
is traditional Anglo-American liberalism." Seeing modern Libertarians as the embodiment of this tradition, Goldberg praised
them for their role in the creation of a conservative movement
that "crafted a new ideology which stood up to Hegel's historicist
state." Buckley was apparently nothing less than the American
protector against this invasion of Teutonic influence: "Indeed had
not Hegel proclaimed that the state was the 'march of God on
earth'? That is the History *National Review* was founded to stand
athwart and yell 'Stop' to."[3]

From this anti-Hegelian statement, Goldberg segued into an
attack on "uninformed or disingenuous people" who "seem to
think that neoconservatism is warmed-over Trotskyism while the
original *National Review* represented real and American conservatives." The only proof Goldberg can marshal against this apparently defective belief is that "the titans who founded *National
Review* were the all-star team of ex-Communists while the neoconservatives were at best the equivalents of gophers and interns
in the Communist Party."

Goldberg ignores the critical difference between former
Communists, who moved decisively to the Right, and Trotskyists
or former democratic socialists, who did not make a comparable
sea change. One's status in a Marxist-Leninist organization does
not determine whether a change that one resolves to make at a
later point is genuine. For example, having been a Catholic bishop
before one converts to Lutheranism does not render one's conversion more suspect than that of a Catholic layman who takes the

same action. Another point may be equally relevant here: those who leave one persuasion for another do not always take along the same object lessons. Former revolutionaries who extract from their Marxist experience an understanding of the importance of social history differ from those who continue to believe in world revolution albeit without a Soviet sponsor. That is to say, the past works differently on different people. Finally, there is no evidence that Buckley's intention, voiced in the first issue of *National Review*, to stand athwart the times was aimed expressly at Hegel. A journalist in a hurry, Goldberg never proves his assertion.[4]

Having finished his disconnected thoughts on conservatism and liberalism, Goldberg then came to the heart of his tribute to Buckley. The founder first established the conservative movement and then supposedly preserved it against those who were threatening conservative solidarity:

> Buckley employed intellectual ruthlessness and relentless personal charm to keep that which is good about libertarianism, what we have come to call 'social conservatism,' and what was necessary about anti-Communism in the movement. This meant throwing friends and allies off the bus from time to time. The Randians, the Rothbardian anarchists and isolationists, the Birchers, the anti-Semites, the me too Republicans: All of these groups in various combinations were purged from the movement and masthead, sometimes painfully, sometimes easily, but always with the ideal of keeping the cause honest and pointed north to the ideal in his compass.[5]

The "ideal in the compass" that justified these expulsions "has come to be called 'fusionism,' which seeks to bind the imperatives of virtue and freedom." Although a few lines further readers learn that these two principles can be only fused "on paper" and that "conservative dogma remains unsettled, conservatism remains cleaved ideologically," Goldberg exalted the architect of an accomplishment hailed as a political and theoretical success. This achievement continues to command respect, despite the fact that Buckley and his associates have been hurling former friends off the bus, presumably in order to make a theory that can work only on paper provide a justification for their mission.

It would take entire volumes to refute with any thoroughness the flawed generalizations that Dionne and Goldberg bring forth while extolling Buckley and his influence. Such apparently self-evident truths are summed up in the assertions that the Reagan administration owed its policies to the movement that Buckley had constructed decades before (the lack of evidence for this allegation notwithstanding); that there was a direct link between the Reagan presidency and the markedly rightwing ideas that abounded in *National Review* thirty years earlier; that conservatism in its current form stands well to the Right of mainstream American political ideas in the 1950s; and that the anti–New Deal Right that existed before Buckley came on the scene lacked any semblance of intellectual and ideological coherence.[6]

It is hard to believe that the conservative movement, which now stands weakly opposed to the social Left in the United States, would look any different had Buckley never lifted a pen. One would still likely encounter religious traditionalists and advocates of small government in an uneasy alliance while a Right-Center dominated by commercial interests and cold war liberals—the latter reincarnated as neoconservatives—might still be jockeying for power in the Republican Party. Neither Buckley nor the movement that his friends in journalism credit him with building, but which he has influenced only minimally for years, need be posited as a precondition for either this development or another, namely the character of the Right-Center coalition that now exists in the United States. This kind of coalition is by no means unique. The same kind of alignment can be found in Western Europe, where the media and public educators set identifiable ideological limits on the permitted political conversation. The debate that then ensues has a certain institutional value, even though arguments that are deemed too insensitive to some groups to be aired are kept out as "extremist." This debate can be cited as proof that parliamentary democracy, as a form of government marked by contending parties or party blocs, continues to work.

With some slight differences, all Right-Center parties in industrial Western countries have the same general outlook. All, or most of them, following the media have moved leftward on social issues since the middle of the last century. Although favoring "equality of opportunity but not of result" and quoting Martin Luther King to this effect used to be Left-Center positions in the United States, they are now identified with the respectable Right. There is, in fact, very little that can be found now in establishment conservative magazines that would have offended the post-World War II anti-Communist moderate Left. An exception is the more

up-to-date feminist position that today's "conservative" magazines hold in comparison to the beliefs of women's rights advocates in the past. Eleanor Roosevelt, Frances Perkins, and other
concerned women reformers of the 1930s stressed the dignity of
women as mothers and homemakers. To preempt an assault on
that dignity, the prewar reformers opposed any weakening of the
"single-family wage." Least of all did they want women torn away
from their children and thrust onto the job market.[7] These positions, which seem almost quaint by today's standards, were taken
by those who never claimed to stand anywhere near the Right. In
sharp contrast, the respectable Right in the twenty-first century
hardly questions either the liberating value of the professional turn
taken by women since the 1950s or the value of at least some governmental intervention to achieve their personal empowerment.[8]
But the relevant question is whether Buckley and those who
helped set up his magazine have stood "athwart the times" in the
way that they had initially intended. Did they dismantle the welfare state by rolling back the New Deal while also prosecuting the
cold war? And did they seriously impede the progress of the ideal
of equality, as Buckley had sought to do fifty years ago? The
answer to both questions is plainly no.

Other questions arise about those phantoms out of the past
who were thrown from the bus, those whom Dionne pungently
called "wing nuts." Were they typically "anti-Semites," as Dionne
suggests, or those whose conspiracy theories needed "blasting"?
Neither description does justice to a historical reality that often
gets oversimplified. *National Review* in October 1965 devoted
most of an especially revealing issue to denouncing the John Birch
Society (which had an advertised but never confirmed list of
80,000 members). The reason for *National Review*'s hostility, as
can still be discerned from the dated diatribes of Burnham and
Frank S. Meyer, was the failure of the Birchers and their magazine,
American Opinion, to endorse the Vietnam War. It was not their
conspiratorial theory about Communist infiltration or their alleged
anti-Semitism that caused the irreversible expulsion from
Buckley's movement. Their apostasy was their declared isolationism, which emerged or re-emerged during the war.[9] Furthermore,
the banality that Buckley saved the conservative movement by
ousting anti-Semites inherited from the Old Right is a glaring
exaggeration. His bitterest wars were with such Jewish Libertarians as Murray Rothbard, Ayn Rand, and Ronald Hamowy, even
as he allowed the neo-Nazi and brilliant classicist Revilo P. Oliver,

who was in Buckley's wedding party, to publish in *National Review* for years after the troublesome Jews were forced to depart his conservative communion.[10]

Even more inconsistent with the established image of Buckley as a fierce opponent of anything that carried even a trace of anti-Semitism is the statement published in his magazine (and possibly written by him) in April 1961 about the forthcoming trial of Nazi war criminal Adolf Eichmann in Israel:

> We are in for a great deal of Eichmann in the weeks ahead—We predict the country will tire of it, and for perfectly healthy reasons. The Christian Church focuses hard on the crucifixion of Jesus Christ for only one week out of the year. Three months—that is the minimum estimate made by the Israeli Government for the duration of the trial—is too long. . . . Everyone knows the facts, and has known them for years. There is no more drama or suspense in store for us. . . . Beyond that there are the luridities. . . . The counting of corpses, and gas ovens, and kilos of gold wrenched out of dead men's teeth.
>
> There is under way a studied attempt to cast suspicion upon Germany. . . . It is all there: bitterness, distrust, the refusal to forgive, the advancement of Communist aims.[11]

More pertinent for our purposes than *National Review*'s warning about a "hate Germany movement" instigated by Jews is the fact that Dionne, Goldberg, and other Buckley celebrants have steadily ignored it. This testifies to the success of the role reversal that Buckley devised for himself and his movement during the next two decades. By the 1980s, he and his magazine had moved into a predominantly Jewish-Zionist and, from all appearances, Teutonophobic neoconservative camp, which graciously allowed him to revise both his past and, by implication, that of his movement. But this fact does not change the reality of what transpired. The movement's expulsions, usually marked by a definitive verdict of excommunication and then periodic reminders of this judgment, are the most significant defining characteristic of postwar conservatism. They facilitated cooperation among those who had put themselves in charge, and they provided the modus operandi for an anti-Communist group often led by former Communist organizers. Thus about fifty years after the first expulsions, Dionne's tribute repeated Buckley's self-justificatory maxim that "cranks were bad for the movement."

The problem is that the reasons now given for who were "cranks" were constructed to please a later generation and to corroborate the movement's transformation into what Buckley himself had arranged for it to become. Such retrospective justifications differ from the original motivations, which were usually the perceived demands of the fight against international Communism. Although one encounters a comparable monomania when the intellectual Left talks about sexism, racism, and homophobia, historian Walter Karp in 1968 discerned the peculiar intensity of Buckley's idée fixe in a review of his anthology *The Jeweler's Eye*:

> For Buckley, Communism is not merely a pernicious doctrine or a vile social system—the two meanings are not even distinguished in his essays. It is nothing less than an individual, absolute, moral evil. It is so evil that its evilness is beyond comment, so evil that it ought to be extirpated even at the risk of nuclear war, even, as Buckley will argue, at the expense of the nuclear war. Note the point: Communism, for Buckley, is not evil because it endangers us; it endangers us because it is evil.[12]

Recognizing Buckley's past fervor is not the same as accusing him of being wrong to see in Communist totalitarians the same degree of evil that Leftist intellectuals still attach to an ill-defined "fascist" menace. My point here is merely to note Buckley's preoccupation with a single issue, which, consistent with the evidence available, was the reason for his break with ambivalent defenders of the cold war. Remaining Old Rightists and Taft Republicans had to be jollied into supporting "victory against Communism" or else they were to be escorted out of the new movement.

George H. Nash devoted an entire chapter in his study of American conservatism to the "red nightmare" that formed the mentality of the postwar conservative movement, while John P. Diggins titled his study of four of its leading personalities *Up From Communism*.[13] In line with this preoccupation, Meyer wrote a column for *National Review* called "Principles and Heresies" for fifteen years and in 1961 revisited his own revolutionary past in *The Moulding of Communists: The Training of the Communist Cadre*.[14] The postwar American Right even carried out its own distinctive "counterrevolutionary imitation of the Left" by promulgating the foundational beliefs for what Burnham called "the protracted struggle." An inevitable byproduct was the development of its own rank-and-file followers and ruling cadres, a structure that mimicked the organization of the Communist enemy. The final turn of Meyer and many others in the movement toward the Catholic Church has been interpreted, fairly in my opinion, as an expression of their need for institutional authority that could take the place of their failed Communist faith. Regardless of that interpretation's validity, the revamped conservative movement filled a similar need. The movement's organizers fashioned a structure bearing a striking resemblance to the American Communist Party and some of its European counterparts.

THE COMMUNIST PARALLEL

A number of informative books have appeared in the last thirty years—for example, Annie Kriegel's work on the French Communists, Andrea Ragusa's writing on the Italian Communist Party, and Aileen S. Kraditor's detailed analysis of American rank-and-file Communists—that throw light on the mentality of ordinary CP members in various Western countries.[15] Apparent from these studies by former party members is the insulated world in which the *membres de base* functioned throughout their lives. Whether or not one accepts Kraditor's notion, which she borrowed from Eric Voegelin, about the "second reality" in which Communists lived, the impression one obtains from her research is that rank-and-file loyalists acted on the basis of a filtered reality that reflected certain constant variables. It denied or seriously challenged the reports of the "bourgeois" press and political class about what was transpiring domestically and internationally. Nothing emanating from the active enemies of the working class could be trusted. To learn the countertruth, which was presumably the real truth, of the mainstream reporting, the Party's members had to read Communist newspapers and attend its meetings. There the Party cadre instructed compliant members, whose network of associations was mostly with each other, on what it behooved them to believe about the outside world. And the cadre appealed to the established Party hagiography, which traditionally placed Lenin and, even more conspicuously, Stalin ahead of Marx and Engels as the "fathers of Communism."[16] Such indoctrination ossified beliefs that the party later sometimes had to discard, for example, when it publicized the diminished status of Stalin after the Soviet leadership admitted to the evils of the dead dictator's "cult of personality" in 1956, or when it dealt with the reluctance of French Communists over the age of sixty to accept the abandonment of revolutionary language and the references to "the commanding role of the working class" after these were dropped from the statutes of the French Communist Party in 1994.[17]

On the whole, the rank-and-file accepted what the Party told them because it was their social and ideological point of reference and because it helped to explain whatever was occurring around them. Thus, according to Kraditor, CP members held an idealized view of life in the Soviet Union under Stalin, and those who traveled there came back believing that they had witnessed a society a thousand times better than the socially unjust America they had temporarily left behind.[18] The damning errors of heresiarchs were cited to enhance the loyalty of the faithful and, even more, the wavering. In American Communist Party publications, it was customary to contrast the merits of Lenin and Stalin to the heresies of Stalin's fallen enemy, Leon Trotsky. Such propagandizing evinced a Marxist-Leninist dualism equivalent to the Christian one between Christ and Satan. This theme recurred in the publications of national parties that had lost prominent defectors, like Pietro Nenni, who became the Socialist leader in Italy. The Communist press treated these disloyal members as agents of international capitalism or else as fomenters of the cold war.[19] They were reminders of where unguided thinking or insufficient attention to party instruction might lead wavering members. And because socially and cognitively the ecclesiastical formula "nulla salus extra ecclesiam" (no salvation outside the church) applied, rank-and-file members generally avoided thinking outside the box.

Without pushing a point too far, it is possible to note overlaps between this rank-and-file Communist behavior and the mentality of movement conservatives in the second half of the twentieth century. Such a parallel should not surprise anyone since the movement's architects, starting with Buckley and Meyer, were seeking to fight international Communism with a counterorganization that would be tightly disciplined and exhibit a common mindset. The conservative movement's purges were attempts to deal with unwelcome dissent and concurrently to foster a compliant attitude toward those who were doing the disciplining. Once the neoconservatives took over in the eighties, the excommunications became considerably more painful. Unlike the older *National*

Review Right, with the exception of Buckley, the new authority figures had well-placed friends in the journalistic community, and these friends would happily second their outings of "anti-Semites" or of those "flirting with fascism." It was more useful for leaders to feature these charges than to call dissenters "soft on Communism." The more fashionable charges had the effect of professionally ruining someone they targeted: any association with Hitler, the ultimate evildoer, however distant or arbitrary, could hurt a journalist or foundation "policy expert" more grievously than an imputation of indecisiveness about waging the cold war. What Pat Buchanan and Murray Rothbard in the late eighties called the "branding iron of anti-Semitism" was a better instrument of control than the weapon that *National Review*'s editors had had at their disposal thirty years earlier.[20] In the revisionist history dealing with Buckley's role in the American conservative movement, moreover, he and his apologists would be allowed to apply the same "branding iron" long after the fact.

It is essential to underline the difference between the estimable advantages that the neoconservatives brought to the movement and the receptive followers that were already there. A magazine editor who works for a conservative institute tried to explain the thoroughness with which the neoconservatives marched through the establishment Right in this way: "they had so much money and played the patriotic card, while the older Right had been too pessimistic." All of this is, of course, true. From gaining access to formerly Old Right philanthropic foundations and then consolidating the distribution of collected funds through a central clearing house in Washington, the Philanthropic Roundtable; to funding and staffing the Heritage Foundation, the American Enterprise Institute, the Manhattan Institute, and other think tanks; to taking over newspapers, magazines, and presses, the neoconservatives were relentless, methodical empire-builders.[21] They also eventually managed to make their weight felt in two Republican administrations while keeping some of their troops around the Democratic camp as a fallback strategy. But it is factually wrong to treat their ascent as either an act of God or, no less inaccurately, the result of those whom the neoconservatives took over being simply overwhelmed.

The new master class benefited from the active collaboration of movement conservatives, who ran to greet them when they came and who happily accepted their guidance. Some of those who submitted to the new order went beyond quiet obedience and broke from friends who failed to meet the changing tests of moderate conservative orthodoxy. This eager surrender did not occur because the preponderant group of movement conservatives had all been sliding leftward, although some had, in the direction of cold war liberalism, global democracy, and admiration for Martin Luther King Jr. and the American welfare state. They assumed these positions primarily because the movement to which they belonged required them to comply, for example, when that movement's leaders enthusiastically endorsed the compulsory national celebration of Martin Luther King Jr.'s birthday despite the unequivocal record of movement publications and movement celebrities having held for decades that King was a Communist tool and a dangerous rabble-rouser. New interpretations would duly follow about FDR, Harry Truman, Joe McCarthy, and other historical figures; and movement conservatives would hear the call to approach the American past and its heritage in a way that differed from what they had been taught to believe up until then. Whole segments of the movement, especially the Southern conservatives, were made to feel superfluous and finally unwanted, since they were the bearers of the prejudiced Confederate past, which the revised edition of "conservatism" never hesitated to equate with the Klan or even more sinister organizations.[22]

That the vast majority of movement conservatives meekly accepted these changes and incorporated them into their worldview suggests attitudes that were not dissimilar to those of rank-and-file Communists. Analogous to the latter's total identification with their movement, these other rank-and-filers took employment with their own corresponding organizations and publications, where they internalized an utterly prescribed understanding of recent history. This was the impression that I took away from interviewing hundreds of movement conservatives in preparation for an earlier study and discovering the degree to which they read the same magazines and newspapers and frequented like-minded company. That the subscription list of *National Review* has swelled from about 50,000 in the 1980s to over 170,000 in 2005 has more to do with the need for a constant guide among the movement faithful than with any evidence of an improved content.[23] Movement conservatives may prefer to take their bearings from this fortnightly rather than from, say, *Commentary* or even *Weekly Standard*, both of which include more ideational articles but are also, particularly *Commentary*, more ethnically Jewish. More recently, movement conservatives have turned into steady viewers of FOX News and can be counted on to recall what Ann Coulter, Sean Hannity, Bill O'Reilly, and Brit Hume think about the latest tiff between Republicans and Democrats. These movement types discovered the threat of "Islamofascism" just after their publications of choice had unveiled that term, but they usually have trouble explaining the character of European fascism, except that it was anti-Semitic and nowadays would be opposed to both Israel and global democracy.[24]

Partisans of the American Left-Center arguably behave in an equally ritualistic and intolerant manner, stubbornly defending their ideologically driven take on the world. But there is one noteworthy distinction. Those on the Left side of the spectrum inhabit a much broader culture, which is that of the establishment Left, and it includes universities and high society. Engaged conservatives live in a narrow world of activists, who are very often embedded in their movement socially and professionally. For them, their ideological allegiances set the parameters of daily existence, not least because it commonly intersects with family and religious connections. The prospect of being "thrown off the bus" would have been as shattering an experience for a movement conservative in 1985, or in 2006, as it would have been for a French Communist who in 1950 had been forced to leave the "party of the workers' revolution." This comparison is entirely deliberate: the remnants of the conservative movement that existed when the neoconservatives swallowed it up were an antiquated anti-Communist organization. And it took its manners and treatment of dissent from its enemy. By the 1980s, those who would not follow orders and tailor their opinions accordingly did not fit into a movement that often employed as well as instructed its members. The undesirables in fact had begun to be pushed out quite unceremoniously thirty years earlier.

This situation did not mean that the conservative movement has sponsored no worthwhile scholarship, for there is considerable evidence to the contrary. Impressive researchers like Charles Murray, Richard Herrenstein, and James Wilson have received over many years funding and favors from neoconservative-run foundations, and since the fifties, the Intercollegiate Studies Institute and its magazines, which now benefit from neoconservative contacts, have fostered and publicized humanistic learning. There are also neoconservative magazines allegedly devoted to art and culture, for example, *New Criterion*, and one can find there an unexpectedly thoughtful essay on the violin concertos of Saint-Saen or another on twelve-tone musicology. But like the Italian Communist Party, which served, among other functions, as a meeting place for social and economic theorists, the American conservative movement advances its political agendas behind costly window dressing. Despite its relative strategic insignificance, this window dressing may be the movement's only product with more than transitory merit. If so, this also would be reminiscent of the postwar Italian Communist Party. In the sixties and seventies, Italian Communist leaders provided outlets for serious academic debate in their weekly *Riunita*, as well as in the books published by Editori Uniti press, and in their periodical *Studi Storici*.[25] But such occasional generosity in neither case should be mistaken for the willingness to engage dissenters openly and honorably.

Like Communist parties, the conservative movement features an organizational hierarchy going from command positions through the cadres and then the rank and file, with fellow travelers at the bottom. The heads of foundations and magazines, who depend on neoconservative funding and good will, have risen to become the cadre, and those who are under them within a subinfeudated structure of command carry out the instructions that go from the top down through the cadres, or else originate directly from the cadres. The enormous salary disparities that persist in conservative foundations between those in administrative posts and those who do "research" on policy issues are on a scale of at least ten to one. The same type of inequality can be found in magazines and newspapers, where the scions of neoconservative magnates earn typically half a million dollars or more, while those of less illustrious parentage, who do not enter from the top, earn considerably less.[26] Oligarchic disparities are simply taken for granted in this closed world of conservative journalism and policy production.

The fellow traveler is located one remove farther from the sources of power and opinion making. While this enthusiast may never work directly for a foundation, magazine, or even possibly the Republican Party, he devotes his energies to "representing" the conservative side. He (but hardly ever she) presents to his social group those opinions most recently heard on FOX; he may also make special trips to attend Rush Limbaugh's radio programs, and he fills his shelves with books authored by or ghostwritten for movement conservative celebrities. His importance is enormous. Without this fellow traveler, who usually shows an even shorter memory span than the rank-and-file about where the movement had stood in the past, it would have been difficult for the conservative movement to reach its current level of popular support. The fact that FOX is the most widely viewed TV news channel stems at least partly from the size of the following that its largely neoconservative reporters and commentators have been able to cultivate. Of course, this success also results from the prudent practice of keeping off the screen any journalist, with the occasional exception of Buchanan, who stands to the Right of where the movement has situated itself. Viewers get the impression, which the network's staff works steadily to sustain, that FOX and its allies constitute the respectable Right. Its main job seems to be resisting the Democrats who are brought on screen to debate the forces of patriotism and courage.

The history of the struggle against rightwing dissenters that the movement's leaders waged in the late eighties and early nineties illustrates the movement's chain of command functions. This campaign would have been little more than a mopping-up operation, save for the inconvenient fact that Buchanan had tried to capture the Republican presidential nomination from a faltering George H. W. Bush in 1992. Also fueling the war was the perception among neoconservatives that their takeover had been too easy. Lurking behind the appearance of a docile army of followers, they feared, were ferociously anti-Semitic and intransigently rightwing forces whose advance guard they encountered in the fight against Buchanan.

The soon-to-escalate ideological crisis began on May 5, 1989, with the firing of neoconservative ally Rev. Richard John Neuhaus by the Rockford Institute, a heavily paleoconservative think tank in northern Illinois, when it became apparent that Neuhaus had warned potential donors against "the extremist politics" of his employer. Since Neuhaus had been hired to oversee the institute's New York branch because of his known contacts with philanthropic organizations, his dismissal brought swift repercussions for the institute.[27] The neoconservatives scolded its staff for discharging one of their allies, and they also amplified Neuhaus's warnings against the holders of "extremist" positions. By "extremist," they meant those who flaunted opposition to the movement's new direction and published the work of southern conservatives who were scornful of the civil rights movement.

Fueling this incident were several events that occurred in the next two years, starting with the formation of a Buchanan-led rightwing opposition to the first Gulf War in 1990. Buchanan was a spirited journalist who had served in the Nixon administration and had already spoken out against the American Israeli Political Action Committee and had used one of his syndicated columns to call the neoconservatives "fleas on the conservative dog."[28] When Buchanan at the National Press Club in November 1990 specifically named the neoconservatives as the enemies of the Right, he may still have had in mind an invective that Joshua Muravchik had hurled at him the year before in a feature article in *Commentary*. Muravchik attacked Buchanan and his fans as anti-Semites with detectable Nazi proclivities. Buchanan's savaging of the Zionist lobby, his obstinate opposition to immigration, and his call for protectionism were all cited as evidence of rightwing extremism.[29] The attack on Buchanan may have been timed as a countermove to an event for which the *Commentary* circle was then preparing, namely, Buchanan's entry into the presidential campaign, a step that he took after he had conferred with his paleoconservative advisors in December 1991. Over the next several months, not only Buchanan but also his lieutenants assaulted the neoconservatives as both unreconstructed Leftists and obnoxious "interlopers." On January 18, 1992, the exhilarated Old Right warrior Rothbard announced to a room full of cheering paleos in Washington and to the consternation of an observer from *National Review*: "With Pat Buchanan as our leader, we shall break the clock of social democracy. . . . We shall repeal the twentieth century."[30]

The neoconservatives eventually triumphed over this isolated challenge to their authority, but not before some of their cadres began to waver. In 1992, *National Review* provisionally backed Buchanan in the primaries against Bush, although Buckley had recently reprimanded Buchanan over the use of phrases that might raise the charge of anti-Semitism.[31] Moreover, at least for some liberal journalists, it seemed that the paleoconservatives were exhibiting "the vigor of youth" while "after eight years of Reaganism and one year of Bush, the neoconservatives [were] beginning to show their age."[32] Buchanan had been able to bring together antiwar libertarians with rightwing nationalists favoring protectionism and immigration controls. Winds of change could be felt.

On January 22, 1990, however, the movement's cadres under its neoconservative commanders met at New York's Union Club to discuss how best to deal with the problem at hand. Those who were targeted were not asked to come; as Paul Weyrich, president and founder of the Free Congress Foundation and a beneficiary of neocon largess, explained: "certain people were not invited because they made a career out of attacking people who were there."[33] Although the meeting did not produce an overall strategy and even brushed aside an "Agenda for the Nineties" that Buckley had brought with him, its value lay simply in the fact that it had taken place. The neoconservatives and the heads of the foundations and magazines that were becoming their empire could at least agree on enemy lists, and they planned to meet again to discuss their shared concerns sometime in the near future. One result, or certainly so it appeared, was that foundation heads went back to Washington and carried out what remained to be done by kicking out particularly enthusiastic Buchanan backers or those they found weak on Israel. Within a few years of this crackdown, the commentary section of the *Washington Times* had removed any offending columnist, that is, any who had not fully accepted the new direction. This paper, though technically owned by the Unification Church, was micromanaged by its neoconservative staff; it would be a rigidly orthodox movement publication by the late nineties.[34]

Having personally witnessed these purges, I believe that a purely material explanation for the degree of compliance with those in power does not suffice as an historical interpretation. During the Reagan presidency, movement conservatives gravitated in droves toward the nation's capital, and most went to work for good salaries in movement conservative foundations and publications and government posts. Even as they did so, however, their behavior involved more than efforts to secure income. These activists were afraid of being out of step with their movement, specifically of believing and saying things that were no longer socially acceptable. This sensitivity to a mutating party line recalls the experiences of American Communists during and after the Soviet alliance with Nazi Germany. Friends and villains were switched overnight. Those who previously had been condemned as fascists became for American Communists in the fall of 1939 the allies of the Soviet motherland. In a similar way, American movement conservatives were forced to juggle their list of heroes and heroic turning points in American history. FDR, Truman, a racially egalitarian Lincoln, and Martin Luther King Jr. were put atop the new list; Robert E. Lee, Joe McCarthy, and soon Robert Taft were erased from it. And the movement was no longer aligned against a federal welfare state or a Wilsonian foreign policy, both of which were now elevated into the preconditions for conservative policymaking.[35]

HOW THE COMMUNISTS DIFFER FROM MOVEMENT CONSERVATIVES

It is important to note the ways in which the mentalities of the two rank-and-file memberships differed, lest their overlap be exaggerated. Although Western Communists lent themselves to far worse knavery and spent years glorifying notorious mass murderers, they also displayed an intellectual seriousness that the American conservative movement has rarely approximated. Because the Communists started with a materialist theory of history and a related body of commentary, they also inherited a coherent understanding of the modern age and a standard for verifying historical conclusions. This was the case despite their reprehensible faults, including the bureaucratic manipulations of truth that Communist parties and regimes practiced and their indulgence of Procrustean conclusions that dialectical materialism once produced for Marxist scholars. In comparison to the Communist tradition, the conservative movement has been a plaything of political activists. Their value language and shrill war against relativism have been attempts to invest the movement with a deep intellectuality and moral purpose that it lacks. Its shallowness remains obvious despite its journalistic success and its occasional borrowings from Catholic ethics.

An even more notable difference between Communists and movement conservatives is the presence of a social base in one case but not in the other. The French and Italian Communist Parties, which were the largest ones in Europe outside of the Soviet bloc, were identifiably working class organizations into the late 1970s. Not only the rank and file but also the directing committees had heavy representations of workers or former workers. Therefore, when the party claimed to speak for a particular social class, it did so with credibility. The American conservative movement, by contrast, claims to be speaking for the entire human race. In a bitter analysis of Buchanan in October 1999, *National Review* senior editor Ramesh Ponnuru quite ingenuously expressed wonder that anyone could consider the populist Buchanan to be any kind of conservative: "Conservatives tend to place a lot of emphasis, maybe too much, on the idea that ideas have consequences. They hoist their ideas on flagpoles and then see who salutes. Buchanan-ism puts its idealized social base first and lets it drive everything else. For Buchanan loyalty to the tribe trumps everything else. . . . Buchananism is a form of identity politics for white people—and becomes more worrisome as it becomes wedded to collectivism."[36]

Aside from raising practical questions about Buchanan's pro-tectionist position or his ability to assemble a blue-collar con-stituency, Ponnuru moved his reader to look at the self-image of the American conservative movement. Ponnuru chided Buchan-an for failing to live up to this image. Unlike European conser-vatism and any past European Right, the movement touted by Ponnuru and his fellow editors shuns any identity with "tribal" nations or classes. But it is difficult to figure out how a movement that explicitly rejects what other conservatisms understood as an essential element of what they were can persist in labeling itself as "conservative." Ponnuru's ideal is a movement without a social core. It is also one that latches on to temporarily usable con-stituencies—or periodically tries to direct or serve the Republican Party. It is a cluster of foundations and publications, and a collec-tion of employees who serve their employers by occasionally becoming a cheering gallery. But unlike socially rooted move-ments, to which American movement conservatives would cer-tainly not want to compare themselves, this movement does not speak for anyone or anything beyond itself.

Note that this stricture is not a whitewashing of all move-ments that either grew out of or tapped into real social or national bases. Some of these groupings were far from admirable and pre-pared the ground for lawless regimes. But this fact does not make the American conservative movement look any less contrived or any less of a media phenomenon. Nineteenth-century liberals and conservatives and twentieth-century Marxists and Fascists had a definable social frameworks; today's conservatives have merely a disciplined and obedient movement that operates in the Wash-ington Beltway and frames values and policies under close scrutiny. It has a viewing public and numerous publications, which can pro-vide the Republican Party, when necessary, with PR. Whether this also renders it a popular social movement remains at the very least debatable.

CONCLUSION

The preceding text raises so many questions that my conclusion will address some of the more obvious ones. A sweeping critique of this work came from my older son, a distinguished physician and corporate attorney, who maintained that I would be wasting my time with this kind of study. While changes have undoubtedly occurred in the American conservative movement since the middle of the last century, there is no sufficient reason, he argued, to abandon the label "conservative" that both the establishment Left and the establishment Right have attached to the same positions and personalities. The public knows exactly what this label means, and so there is no need to argue from what that term used to mean that it couldn't take on a more up-to-date connotation. Virtually everyone now understands that a person who advocates restrictions on abortion, objects to homosexual marriage, and favors military intervention to achieve our government's international goals must be "conservative." Why then should one quibble about the meaning of "conservative" by resurrecting the obsolete self-image of those who once called themselves "conservatives"?

My son compared me to an elderly professor of medicine of his acquaintance who adamantly refused to call osteoarthritis by its now accepted name. This professor insisted that true arthritis was not a problem of joint pains brought on by the wear and tear of age but rather the autoimmune disease "rheumatoid arthritis." A proper terminology would limit the application of "arthritis" to its rheumatoid form. Presumably only a pedant, one as advanced in age as I am, would insist on limiting definitions beyond the point where such a practice serves any general benefit.

Another possible objection to my arguments is that I have exaggerated the originality of my insights. Leading conservatives since the 1950s have voiced some of the same protests against the "value game" as those that I raise. Indeed, no postwar thinker assailed this practice more furiously than did Russell Kirk, who still functions posthumously as a conservative icon. In *Decadence and Renewal in the Higher Learning* (1978), Kirk explains: "Values are private and frail reeds. One's man's values are charitable work; another man's value is brothel-frequenting. Who can judge which is the preferable value—dogmata lacking. A dogma is not a value preference. A dogma is a firm conviction received on authority. No one but an ass would die that his value preference might endure; while dogmatic belief sustains saints and heroes." Moreover, "dogmas grow out of the ineluctable necessity for a core of common belief, in church, in state. Private judgment, unattached to dogmas, is insufficient for the moral order or the social order."[1]

Kirk anticipated my warnings against the tendency to rely on value construction and, like his friend Robert Nisbet, treated "the moral order" as dependent on social authorities. The same propensities characterize Kirk's defense of "cultural conservatism," which, for him, referred to a Christian cultural order whose existence he sought to explain and justify.[2] Have I erred then by placing him at the beginning of a process by which the "conservative movement" steered leftward?

A related objection is that I have downplayed the continuities in the positions taken by prominent conservatives over the last fifty years. I have also focused too much attention on the limited alterations that the movement has undergone as part of a natural growth process. The result is a distorted perspective made plausible through citing the occasional journalism of certain neoconservative publicists while disregarding the movement's continuing commitment to particular stands, for example, opposing abortion on demand and the use of gender and racial quotas.

My arguments seem vulnerable to still another criticism, one that the neoconservative publicist David Frum raised in 1986 when responding to a lecture given by me on the changing American Right, that I have omitted "the question of race." While the preneoconservative American Right is said to have been profoundly racist, even when it failed to discuss the issue of race explicitly, the neoconservatives have prided themselves on having made amends for this defect. Supporting the Civil Rights Act in 1964 and the Voting Rights Act in 1965, and strongly backing the congressional legislation that created the Martin Luther King Jr. national holiday, neoconservatives have pushed the respectable Right to break with its past, by recognizing the need to integrate blacks into the American political community. Neoconservatives worked to exclude old-styled Southern conservatives because of their segregationist baggage. Even though neoconservatives have dissented from the liberal Left over affirmative action programs, they claim to have done so as antiracists without blemish. When Senator Trent Lott in December 2002 praised the states rights position once held by South Carolina Senator Strom Thurmond, no one attacked the Mississippi lawmaker more vehemently than neoconservative journalist Charles Krauthammer. Lott had shown himself deaf to "the most important political development of my [Krauthammer's] life. . .the success of the civil rights movement."[3]

Another objection to my study is that I have criticized the seemingly only possible line of defense available to the Right in its struggle against the Left. If the best is in fact the enemy of the good, any repositioning of the American conservative movement farther to the Right will thwart the efforts of moderates to keep American politics and American political discourse from becoming more radical. In presidential contests, there exists a division between the Right, the Left, and middle-of-the-road voters who may cast their votes either way. Would not a right-of-center national party influenced by a movement that took more emphatically rightwing positions than those of the current conservative movement lose the "undecided" centrist voters? Such a shift might have the effect of driving leftward those whose "conservatism" is perfectly consistent with voting for Hillary Clinton for president. Not everyone who describes himself as "conservative" is even as far to the Right as the Heritage Foundation. Moreover, a certain percentage of "liberals" eventually votes Republican, while at least some "conservatives" vote Democratic. The "conservative movement" may, therefore, be adapting itself to political trends, trends catalyzed by cultural change, that the Right cannot alter and which limit its capacity to move any farther Right of center than it has.[4]

A careful consideration of the foregoing arguments has left me convinced that my interpretation of the American conservative movement is by and large correct. This conviction has not left me in a celebratory mood but may require me to spell out the reasons for my conclusion. The media and much of the public admittedly do understand certain semantic distinctions between "conservative" and "liberal," but these terms nonetheless remain in flux. This force typically pulls movement conservatives in one of two directions, toward the social Left or toward arbitrary litmus tests. To the extent that we in the West are moving into a post-Christian and multicultural society and polity, political labeling will certainly reflect this process of change. Persons on the Right who wish to be elected to national office must be extremely careful not to offend gays, feminists, the civil rights lobby, and other highly visible pressure groups who enjoy favor with the media and among entertainers and educators. Accordingly, celebrities who take "conservative" labels must signal their "values" discreetly or else learn to make noise without bringing down the full wrath of the liberal establishment. Others, particularly of the younger generation, who wear the "conservative" label are often at least partly sympathetic to the progressive social agenda. This is particularly true of younger conservative journalists who express sympathy with gays seeking to marry. Lastly, there are the talk show hosts, who, in addition to their skill at rattling liberals, have developed a strategy for diverting social protest on the Right, by channeling it into the Republican Party—and usually toward candidates of the center reaching Left as well as Right. Whatever the complaints against the hated "liberals" one hears from Rush Limbaugh, Ann Coulter, and Sean Hannity, the solution is always at hand: go out on election day and vote Republican.

The use of shifting tests for defining "conservative" is another characteristic of the establishment Right. Exemplifying these fashionable tests are vouchers for students to attend schools of their choice, a campaign to spread something like American democracy throughout the world, and in the seventies and eighties the establishment of urban "enterprise zones" in which black entrepreneurial skills would supposedly unfold under the stimulant of reduced taxes. Another widespread test of conservative orthodoxy is the acceptance of the counterfactual assertion that Martin Luther King Jr. was an opponent of affirmative action programs and an advocate of quintessentially "conservative" ideas which the civil rights movement later misrepresented. Although some of these positions may be defensible, it is hard to discern anything in them that makes them specifically "conservative." Of course, Republican Party operatives, who seek to crack the black vote and who turn to "conservative foundations" for direction, may pretend otherwise.

It is also possible to see an accommodation of the neoconservative elite that takes the form of equating conservatism with their specific interests: support for the Israeli Right as it engages the Palestinians, the pursuit of a neo-Wilsonian foreign policy, and an affirmation of the "good" civil rights and feminist movements up until the point that these became obnoxious. It is not a question, to emphasize my point again, to evaluate these stands beyond examining whether they can be properly viewed as "conservative."

Do they acquire this quality by being taken less frequently by those on the other side of the centrist spectrum or simply because they are the views of the neoconservatives, who now run the movement? And what eternal "conservative values," supposedly traceable back beyond the recent past, do these stands represent?

We are therefore looking at a situation in which values are a sort of Sunday dress worn to make a good impression. They are articulated mainly by the electoral interests of the Republican Party or by the promoters of neoconservative pet projects. Although the concerns of the Religious Right occasionally appear in conservative movement discussions, they occupy a less exalted place than do other "conservative" interests. There is nothing accidental about how the movement bestows greater attention on waging democratic crusades than on fighting abortion. The Left clearly benefits from this selective attention. Proglobal democratic and Zionistic Joe Lieberman and Christopher Hitchens receive generally favorable treatment from the movement conservative media, even though on every social issue, including late term abortion, they stand decidedly on the Left. In sharp contrast, those Christian opponents of neoconservative-promoted foreign policies who protest gay marriage and abortion have not fared nearly as well.[5]

Undeniably ominous for the residual Rightist character of movement conservatism is the enthusiastic embrace of Bush's war in Iraq by Evangelicals. As James Kurth has argued in *American Interest*, this political stance is fraught with risks. If the engagement turns out well, the mainstream media, which is culturally hostile to Evangelicals, will not likely treat them as heroes. If the war goes south, however, then Bush's Evangelical allies will probably receive more blame than their neoconservative fair-weather friends. Unlike the latter, the Christian Right does not provide the luncheon and TV talking partners of the Democratic liberal establishment.[6]

Any political movement with a recent record of major changes will probably continue to undergo transformations. Why should the trend stop now in the case of the American conservative movement? It will likely come to resemble foreign Right-Center coalitions that have moved unequivocally in the direction of the multicultural Left. In time, the American conservative movement may even attain the rhetorical flexibility of Center-Right parties in Western and Central Europe, where a long-term tropism toward the social Left progresses in a more dramatic fashion. More likely, however, the American conservative movement will continue to stand for the interests of its neoconservative sponsors but waffle on, and thereby effectively support, gay marriage, abortion, and affirmative action. In their general support for Third World immigration, the neoconservative-controlled conservative movement and much of the Republican Party leadership already lean leftward, like the German Union and, until recently, the Chirac government in France.

Such opportunism disguised as adherence to principle has benefited, as the present study attests, from the defective founding of the postwar conservative movement. A weak social base and a shifting identity have both afflicted this movement ever since its beginnings. Neither problem has gone away because American conservatism is now piggybacking on the Republican Party. The establishment by anti-Communists of an anti-Communist movement structured around a single-minded goal and sustained by party-like discipline, set the direction for the new movement. Everything else that it has claimed to be over the decades stands in relation to this founding. The politically useful appeal to mutating values betrays the character of American conservatism's origin, and this practice persisted long after the movement had abandoned inventing overlaps between mid-twentieth-century America prosecuting the cold war and Europe fighting the French Revolution.

Although those who made this implausible comparison between counterrevolutionary Europe and the United States in the mid-twentieth century sometimes believed it, the judgment of European intellectual historian Panajotis Kondylis remains valid here. Only a fool will apply archaic social standards to a contemporary or near-contemporary historical situation, as if the invocation of those standards can bring back what is socially gone. This observation brings me back to the mistakes of Kirk, who should be remembered as by no means the worst of his generation of founding "conservatives" but possibly as the most authentically conservative. Though he made telling points against "value education," he was less cogent in drawing historical parallels and promulgating "conservative principles" intended for individual consumption.

It is necessary to distinguish between cultural traditionalism and the suspect good that the "conservative movement" had to offer as an alternative. Unlike Kirk, his mentor and subject T. S. Eliot shunned any association with *National Review*. Nisbet took a comparably aloof stand with the American conservative movement, even as he continued to write for its publications.[7] Although

by the late eighties Kirk was putting some distance between himself and the movement that he had helped found, he had by then
suffered the fate of becoming a paid fixture within it. Trying to
create for himself a niche as a "cultural conservative" within the
movement was a futile gesture given the particularities of his institutional associations. Kirk was dependent on neoconservative
benefactors, who effectively required him to spend his declining
years manufacturing traditionalist-sounding phrases for their use.

In response to the charge I have been overly selective in my
choice of sources, I would offer this defense: I have not ignored
the major thinkers in the conservative movement in addition to
Kirk but have devoted considerable attention to the popularizers
of "conservative" opinions. These newer publicists resonate better
with the vast majority of today's "conservatives" than do most of
those who received detailed treatment in George Nash's intellectual history. More conservative groupies, one might suspect, read
Jonah Goldberg, David Brooks, and Richard Lowry, and certainly
listen to Hannity and Limbaugh, than know of Kirk, Richard
Weaver, and Frank Meyer. But I have also investigated the more
conceptual thinkers in the movement, and I have bestowed special
regard on Harry Jaffa and his disciples. Such figures were pivotal
for the movement's leftward turn even before the neoconservatives came to lead it.

A look at the list of the ten supposedly most important books
that "have advanced the cause of conservatism and of freedom in
general," to quote the fiftieth-anniversary issue of *National
Review* (December 19, 2005), will confirm my judgments about
the iconic figures whom I have discussed. Allan Bloom and Jaffa
received long commendations, while Kirk and his *The Conservative Mind* were conspicuous by their absence.[8] One rightwing organization, the National Policy Institute, has raised a
question that should at least mildly interest historians of the conservative movement. What major breakthrough in our research
about contemporary history can account for certain noticeable
iconic changes? In 1983, *Human Events* and *National Review*
expressed outrage over proposed congressional legislation for a
Martin Luther King Jr. national holiday, alleging King's Communist
associations, adulterous liaisons, and advocacy of civil disobedi-
ence. But within twenty years, the same sources not only played
down what until a few years earlier had inflamed their editors, but
they were discovering in a once-despised social radical a deeply conservative Christian theologian. The Heritage Foundation has just

uncovered in King's statements about equality nothing less than "the principles of the American founding."[9] This change of face seems to illustrate the irresistible fluidity that has been present in the conservative movement since its inception.

Pointing this out does not mean that everything the movement once believed has disappeared from its publications. Yes, some early beliefs—such as the defense of "orders and degrees," the appalling wickedness of Martin Luther King Jr., opposition to the Civil Rights Act of 1964, and the justification for Southern secession— have been totally expunged, but other positions have endured while becoming less central to the movement's present direction. Thus, the Federalist Society, which usually argues against the inroads of judicial activism, enjoys both widespread movement conservative support and neoconservative philanthropy. But the society rarely, if ever, challenges the landmark civil rights judgments of the fifties or the antidiscrimination legislation of the sixties, as did the conservative movement that existed at that time. Moreover, this group's positions on, for example, judicial activism and original intention as a key for understanding the Constitution, take a backseat in the conservative movement's current order of concerns. The Federalist Society's cares are tangential to the establishment's paramount interests, all of which are recognizably neoconservative ones, particularly a global democratic foreign policy and its domestic ramifications. Among the values and corresponding programs that engage the conservative movement, it is essential to distinguish between primary and secondary interests.

It is also inaccurate to present the neoconservative takeover of the conservative movement in the context of an accelerating campaign against racist and anti-Semitic prejudices. This now prevalent interpretation, which Murray Friedman has recently restated, exaggerates two situations: the impact of the prejudices that Friedman condemned on the preneoconservative Right and the possibility of tracing back to the older neoconservatives the attitudes of younger neoconservatives concerning social questions. The following facts are worthy of note: At least a third of the *National Review* editorial board going back to the fifties was Jewish, a characteristic that also applied to some of those whom William F. Buckley threw "off the bus." The John Birch Society in the fifties and sixties featured both black and Jewish writers. In fact, one of the Birchers' most articulate advocates was the black, former Communist journalist George Schuyler.[10] While the society showcased Schuyler, it summarily expelled the pro-Nazi classicist

Revilo Oliver. A pillar of the isolationist Old Right, Robert Taft, had a Jewish campaign manager, who turned the senator into an ardent Zionist. In 1944, Taft won a close senatorial race in Ohio because of the Democratic Jewish vote that crossed over to him in the Cleveland area. Taft also opposed appropriation bills for Southern states partly on the grounds that they did not provide Negro citizens with equal public facilities.[11]

Although the preneoconservative Right generally took a hard line against the redistributionist and social programs of the central government, it did not practice the exclusionary policy against blacks (and even less against Jews) about which neoconservative publicists like to complain. The postwar Right's opposition to the civil rights movement was never based on racialist theories. This opposition expressed the then reasonable concern that extending federal power to achieve equality for blacks and to mobilize black voters would drive the country politically toward the Left. Whether or not one shares that concern, in retrospect it is unfair to dismiss those who did as racial bigots who needed to be expelled from the Right by the more open-minded neoconservatives.

Even less defensible is the view that the neoconservatives have been preoccupied with the ideal of black equality for as long as they have graced the conservative movement. One would be hard pressed, in looking at issues of *Commentary* or reading the essays of Irving Kristol, Gertrude Himmelfarb, and Norman Podhoretz in the fifties, sixties, and seventies, to find intimations of the future neoconservative celebration of Martin Luther King Jr. and the civil rights movement. What one finds instead are expressions of Podhoretz's distaste for Negroes and grumbling about black anti-Semitism in New York, together with then standard Northern views about the need to prod the Southern states into desegregating. There is no evidence that the older neoconservatives felt differently about Martin Luther King Jr. than the assessment of him that their friend (and distinguished Jewish theologian) Will Herberg provided in *National Review*. Before their ascent to power in the 1980s, most neoconservatives did not promote King as a black role model. Such younger figures as Krauthammer and David Horowitz contributed to this cult of the fallen civil rights leader, but only after they had entered the neoconservative camp from the Left. By the time that the neoconservatives' second generation appeared on the scene in the nineties, this ritual of adoration had acquired an aspect of permanence. But the cult had not been there from the outset. Even the stalwart Jaffa discovered the perennial virtues of King only after he had penned bitter attacks against him in *National Review.*[12]

The neoconservative campaign in the 1980s and afterward against Southern conservatives and, more sporadically, against the vestigial Taft Right was much ado about very little. Buckley's movement had triumphed partly by crushing the older isolationist Right, and by the seventies its founder had begun to distance himself from Southern, neo-Confederate allies, who had never been central to his coalition against Communism. The neoconservatives merely accelerated this process when they went after Southern and Old Right conservatives. Once in charge of foundation monies and generously financed publications, they set about excluding Southern conservatives and others whom they disliked from their movement. If they had acted differently, however, those whom they excluded and sometimes humiliated would not have been in a position to take over the conservative movement. From the Bradford affair in 1981, the neoconservatives went after a declining Southern force, which they aroused for one final battle. But these wars did not have to occur. They took place due to cultural enmity—not because of any danger posed by those who suffered marginalization.

Arguably the most compelling objection to my interpretation is that I wrongly suggest that there were missed opportunities for the Right that were not really available. But there is a difference between finding only modest possibilities for the intact survival of the Right and seeking to push it leftward out of conviction. It is one thing to conclude on the basis of calculation that one has to move in a certain direction if one hopes to keep a movement going, but it is a quite a different matter to believe that this course is morally correct. Let us imagine that the neoconservatives are forced to confront opposition over an issue that matters to them. Let us posit an unyielding public opinion directed against their position on Middle Eastern politics. Would they likely surrender on this particular issue as some of them have done on gay marriage? I repeat an important point one last time: within the neoconservative hierarchy of goods, some issues truly count while others receive little better than lip service because they mean much less to the movement's leaders.

The neoconservatives' current attitude toward the "democratic welfare state" reflects their settled identity as old-fashioned welfare-state Democrats. But this identity does not prevent them from moving closer to a market economy in the matters of marginal tax rates and governmentally negotiated free trade agreements. By association with neoconservative stands, American conservatism has happily embraced not only a lowering of marginal tax rates and free trade agreements but also New Deal programs and the expansion of government that took place in the 1960s, not to mention the liberalization of immigration in 1965. The main reason for support of these liberal achievements is not a calculated belief that their revocation would be difficult to effect without losing votes. The neoconservatives believe in these ideals and programs—and make no attempt to hide their convictions. The others follow their lead because they are accustomed to thinking and acting in that way.[13]

It is therefore misleading to stress exclusively strategic reasons as explanations for why present conservative leaders do not speak and act like Robert Taft in 1950 or Buckley in 1955. Current leaders do not adhere to the notions of limited government put forth by their predecessors in the fifties. And they differ from those reactionaries who bewail the bad hands that History has dealt them, thereby forcing them to compromise with intractable political realities. Neoconservatives affirm the status quo as the best of all possible worlds, as long as they can share power—and as long as they can persuade their fellow Americans to bring American democracy to other societies.

But is contemporary American conservatism, given the configuration of circumstances to which it belongs, the only possible, let alone the best possible, movement on the Right imaginable? Possibly not. Everything might be different without the intervention of certain random conditions that brought about the movement that currently exists. Absent, for example, the nationwide public relations organs long available to neoconservatives or lacking their generally cooperative relations with Center-Left journalists (who remain all too happy to push any other Right out of public respectability), an alternative movement might have developed. Only because of their easy access to the political conversation were neoconservative spokesmen able to offer themselves as mediators between the older conservative movement and the media. And this happened because the older generation of neoconservatives had risen to prominence on the Left before they apparently journeyed rightward. Moreover, the movement in which they would entrench themselves was already predisposed to follow orders from the top. Its struggle against global Communism had so conditioned it. Just how would the political landscape have differed if, contrary to what did occur, the movement that the neoconservatives sought to command had somehow resisted their control?

The establishment Right would not be taking the stands that it currently does. As a consequence, the liberal Left would have a less congenial talking partner, one whose arguments it would have to answer or else ignore. The latter response might entail an attempt to manufacture a tame opposition, which the multicultural Left in Germany is now undertaking by attacking all conservative nationalists as fascists. Given our less disturbing recent history, however, this task might be less feasible for the Left to do here.

The American Left-Center would not have the advantage that it now does have, that of being able to join with the "moderate Right" to demonize those perceived as being to the Right of the neoconservatives. The skeptical judgment that such a Right could not have arisen, because it could not have won over a public that was in the process of becoming more "enlightened," may be an argument after the fact. I am suggesting a different Right, one consistent with positions that the neoconservative-dominated movement abandoned for others. At the very least, such a Right would not establish an expansionist foreign policy litmus test while it drifts toward the center or Left on social questions.

Contingencies and personal decisions, as well as the force of events, have brought about the conservative movement as it now exists. One does not have to favor, much less ardently favor, a hypothetical alternative Right to recognize that such a power might have gained influence in altered circumstances. That this did not happen was hardly because conspiring neoconservatives stole the conservative movement from its well-meaning members. Events did not develop in the way that some paleoconservatives would like to imagine. In the eighties, the neoconservatives swept through the movement as effortlessly as Hitler's armies had marched into Austria in 1938. Resistance to foundational change developed only marginally in the conservative movement, and the neoconservatives could have minimized even that through more tactful conduct.

An alternative Right might have crystallized if one or more of several fairly modest turns had transpired, for example, if the movement that Buckley and his companions had forged had been more open to dissent, if in the seventies and eighties it had been less bureaucratized and less dependent on big government or if it had kept a respectable distance from the Republican Party. Equally imaginable is that the neoconservatives could have come to terms with other Rights—instead of eradicating whatever did not fit the standards that they had brought from the anti-Communist Left and then imposed on a submissive movement. Note we are not speaking here of far-fetched alternatives to what did triumph in the end. But this history developed as it did in a cumulative way so that by now the movement could not be other than it is.

An alternative that seems to have little appeal today is the sort of Right toward which Nisbet leaned in *The Twilight of Authority* and *The Present Age*. Had it survived and flourished, this Right would have defended an older bourgeois civilization and imposed strong restrictions on both the central government and the reach of public administration. Such positions were not alien to the anti–New Deal Right and even, albeit in a contradictory way, to the early phases of the movement that Buckley put together to fight global Communism. This Rightist-style, decentralist, restrained about the use of military force, suspicious of social engineering, and wary of ethnic heterogeneity, seems to be gaining ground now in parts of Europe. The price that it pays there for its relative success is the brandishing of populist rhetoric, often directed against Third World immigration. In the United States , this populist Right exhibits less traction, partly because something else has taken its place in the box marked "conservative." And this "conservative movement" vehemently opposes any alternative to the course it has marked out, in tacit complicity with the Left-Center. Given the balance of forces, it seems unlikely that something resembling the European populist Right will in the foreseeable future replace the American conservative movement.

Another possibility that was never actualized on the postwar American Right was one intensely feared by intellectuals, who wrote about it repeatedly in the sixties, namely, a "radical Right" that Daniel Bell, Richard Hofstadter, and Seymor Lipset all regarded as a growing national danger. McCarthyism and the rise of Goldwater Republicanism were seen as the portents of this emerging Right that was believed to be producing something like fascism, particularly in the South and the West. Anxiety about this putative problem owed much to the trauma of European Nazism, to the identification by intellectuals of anti-Communism with the far Right, and to the popularization of European émigré texts, especially *The Authoritarian Personality*. An anthology published in 1950, this book was the work of avowedly Leftist authors who had fled to the United States from Nazi Germany. It emphasized the psychotic impulses behind both the rejection of the welfare state and opposition to Communism, and it did not shy away from drawing unflattering comparisons between the United States and the "pseudodemocracy" from which its contributors had run away.[14]

The predominantly Jewish New York academics who fulminated against the "radical Right" harked back to nineteenth-century European liberals, who had feared with equal trepidation a rising working-class electorate. Both groups of doom-and-gloom commentators assumed violent scenarios that never came to pass in Western countries. The enfranchised common man generally did not go on a rampage, the exceptions having been starving Parisians during the French Revolution and during the nineteenth-century French repetitions of that upheaval. Workers, once enfranchised, gave power to public administrators, who erected a vast managerial state, for the purpose of providing social programs. Control from the top rather than violent revolution has been the typical outcome of the leap into mass democracy.[15]

In the same way, the "Rise of the Right," which conservative activist William Rusher celebrated in a book by that title, has not been about rustic bigots equipped with pitchforks or Nazi armbands. Those whom Rusher exalted helped to catapult into public view both Beltway operators and the journalistic advocates of Irving Kristol's "democratic capitalist welfare state." Among these political insiders were those who fashioned the latest edition of the conservative movement and who had once expressed fears of the "radical Right." Like their colleagues and coethnics, they had sometimes imagined that the United States was veering perilously rightward. But history has revealed even greater ironies. Waiting at the beck and call of these former spokesmen of the New York elite who have ensconced themselves in neoconservative think tanks are docile enablers, who often started out as professional anti-Communists in Buckley's movement.

Leftwing intellectuals misstated or exaggerated the rightwing threat that they once feared. The evidence that they thought they were uncovering was simply not there. Just as the postwar reaction against Communism at home and abroad failed to turn the country permanently rightward, the "Reagan revolution" in the 1980s did nothing significant to slow the development of a centralized welfare state or the leftward drift of the culture. Similarly, and as recent studies of McCarthyism in the fifties have shown, even this phenomenon did not result in as widespread a blacklisting as the earlier attempts in the forties to punish those who were "soft on fascism." Joe McCarthy's base of support was surprisingly limited and transitory, and he did not meet with a particularly enthusiastic reception from the pre-Buckleyite Right. (Eliot raised an aesthetic objection to his political style when he turned down an invitation by Buckley to write for *National Review*.) Many, and perhaps an absolute majority, of McCarthy's personal supporters were Irish Catholic Democrats, like the Kennedy family, and Southern Democrats, both with strong allegiances to the New Deal.[16] Charges that McCarthy and even his Jewish advisors were anti-Semitic and reminiscent of German Nazis have always verged on the surreal.

One reason why Hofstadter and Bell were not reliable analysts of the American "radical Right" is that the United States was not interwar Central Europe. American anti-Semitism was a dwindling prejudice, which, except in the 1930s, had never amounted to much of a problem; the Right was mostly in the hands of persons whom Europeans would call classical liberals; and the anti-Communism of the fifties gradually turned into what could best be described as a Truman Democratic position. Equally impor-tant, the postwar conservative movement, which was conservative only in a metaphorical sense, did not attract the swarming base of the socially alienated that its critics ascribed to it. Not of inconse-quential significance, the decision of *National Review* to locate business operations in the Northeast put conservatism on the road to becoming an adjunct of the country's most influential regional establishment. By the end of the twentieth century, the conservative network that grew out of the movement would compete with the journalistic Left in its denunciation of McCarthy and his works.

Perhaps the most critical result of the attack on the "fascist" Right was an acceleration of the conservative movement's trans-formation. For many associated with that movement, the denunci-ations linking them to "the paranoid style" and the "prehistory of European fascism" had an unsettling effect. The devastating defeat of Barry Goldwater in 1964 after months of bitter denunciations left his followers stunned and dejected but led to their decision to make a radical break from their previous opposition to the welfare state. From that point on, conservatives marched leftward but hid this move from the public, and perhaps themselves, by pretending that Ronald Reagan and George W. Bush were fulfilling what they

had been waiting for since the 1950s.[17] Although Reagan attained
political eminence as a stellar speaker for Goldwater, his presidency
did not renew the Goldwater assault on the New Deal. Ever since
the Goldwater campaign, no Republican presidential contender
has questioned the welfare state's policies, let alone premises, in
any fundamental way. Goldwater's call to rethink this institution
brought charges of "extremism." Furthermore, his reluctant
opposition to the 1964 Civil Rights Act, as an infringement on the
expressed powers of Congress, led to comparisons between him
and Adolf Hitler—by, among others, Martin Luther King Jr. and
Governor Pat Brown of California.

"Conservative" Republicans would retreat from Goldwater's
opposition to the Civil Rights Act, even though such figures as
Reagan and George H. W. Bush had formerly belonged to this
opposition. Republicans likewise dissociated themselves from
Goldwater's suggestions about reconsidering Social Security, until
some of them recently launched a half-hearted effort to privatize
part of the payments. They would never again raise the indiscreet
topic of denationalizing the Tennessee Valley Authority. The
Right seized on a blander strategy for taking power, generating
government policies that would contain among other elements,
"privatizing initiatives" and reductions in marginal tax rates.
Accompanying such policies would be sustained but often empty
assurances about getting bureaucrats "off our backs." The post-
Goldwater conservative movement, having taken all these precau-
tions against "extremism," went back to value talk and, under
neoconservative guidance, anachronistic appeals to progovernment thinkers of the distant past.

Thus it was that George Will and Gertrude Himmelfarb
praised Aristotle, Edmund Burke, and English Tory prime minister Benjamin Disraeli for their wise emphasis on the state's social
responsibilities. New Deal and Great Society America was realiz-
ing, by whatever term one chose to call it, an essentially conservative vision of governmental solidarity with the working class. Will
commended this view of government as illustrating his dictum
that "statecraft should be soulcraft," a principle that Taft Republicans and Goldwaterites had presumably failed to comprehend.[18]
Himmelfarb warned explicitly against those "who reach for hyper-
bole" in their zeal to "illegitimize legitimate government." The
wife of Irving and the mother of Bill Kristol called on true conservatives in *One Nation, Two Cultures* (1999) to search for the
middle ground between "bureaucratic zealots" and the "armed

fanatics of the Right."[19] Professor Himmelfarb thereby suggested her own application of Aristotle's golden mean. Those on her Left and those on her Right (whoever they may be) have allegedly slighted the teachings of ancient Greek masters, who, in contrast to our rash ideologues, urged prudence and moderation.

Will's comments on "soulcraft" in the eighties and Himmelfarb's warnings against the politics of zealots in the nineties harked back, without acknowledgements, to Kirk and his elegant commentaries on the "politics of prudence."[20] One may easily overlook this pedigree in light of the neoconservatives' explicit distaste for Kirk. It was he, however, in the wake of "Tory Democrat" Peter Viereck, who had proposed a politics that would avoid ideological zeal while pursuing a conservative sense of moderation and respect for existing institutions. Kirk associated prudence with a politics of the possible, but this was a frail remedy for the badly outgunned cultural Right that he and his friends could do little to reinvigorate.

Kirk's once popular definition of "conservatism as belief in a transcendent moral order" bore curious fruit when it surfaced at a conference, "The Conservative Movement," held at Princeton University on December 5, 2005. Attending the conference was the "unabashed ideological liberal" commentator Rick Perlstein, who inquired to whom precisely the designation "conservative" applied. The answers he received in short order were Republicans, "practical conservatives," and "conservatives of principle."[21] Perlstein also had to listen to rote references to "the unchanging ground of our unchanging experience." Movement conservatives were apparently united by the conviction that "there is no such thing as a bad conservative." Someone who disagreed with the speaker was either not a "conservative" or the kind of person "you would not care to be associated with." Perlstein offered this humorous imitation of what he heard from the conference's participants: "Well, maybe he's a Republican. Or a neocon or a paleocon. He's certainly not a conservative." Himself an outsider at the conference, Perlstein grasped the elusiveness of conservatism even for those who championed it. He should not have expected better. Responding to the American establishment Right's wooden language, historian John Lukacs was once driven to observe: "But now we're all social democrats!"[22] To which the appropriate response from the conference's participants would have been: "Yes, but some of us still vote Republican and talk about values."

NOTES

INTRODUCTION

1. Clinton Rossiter, *Conservatism in America: The Thankless Persuasion* (New York: Alfred E. Knopf, 1962).
2. David Brooks, "Don't Worry, Be Happy!" *New York Times*, May 11, 2006.
3. See Robert A. Nisbet, "A Farewell to History" *National Review*, May 22, 1987, pp. 44–46; Richard Nixon's comments on *The Search for Historical Meaning* in "Book Choices of the Year," *American Spectator*, December 1987; and Paul Gottfried, "Richard Nixon: On Power and History: A Conversation with Paul Gottfried," *National Review*, July 14, 1989, pp. 41–42.
4. Manuel Castells, *The Rise of the Network Society* (Oxford: Blackwell, 1996).
5. Nisbet, *Conservatism: Dream and Reality* (Minneapolis: University of Minnesota Press, 1986).

CHAPTER 1

1. Alan Wolfe, "The Revolution That Never Was," *The New Republic*, June 7,1999, pp. 37–38. The exchange between the author and Wolfe is in the same publication, July 12, 1999, pp. 4–5.
2. Correspondence between this author and Kuehnelt-Leddhin, May 14, 1998.
3. Karl Mannheim, *Ideologie und Utopie* (Frankfurt: Vittorio Klostermann, 1995), 4–6, 26–30.
4. Russell Kirk, *The Conservative Mind, from Burke to T. S. Eliot*, 7th rev. ed. (Washington, DC: Regnery Gateway, 1986), 10–11.
5. Ibid., 10, 59–60.
6. Ibid., 9.
7. Ibid., 10–11.
8. Lionel Trilling, *The Liberal Imagination: Essays on Literature and Society* (London: Secker and Warburg, 1951), VII–VIII.
9. Kirk, *The Conservative Mind*, 476.

10. John Dewey, *Liberalism and Social Action* (New York: Capricorn, 1963), 32, 90; and Paul Gottfried, *After Liberalism: Mass Democracy in the Managerial State* (Princeton, NJ: Princeton University Press, 1999), 55–60, 101–7.

11. Arthur Schlesinger Jr., *The Vital Center*, 2nd ed. (Boston: Houghton Mifflin, 1962), XII, 1–10.

12. Ibid., IX.

13. Kirk, *The Conservative Mind*, 7, 40, 115, 194, 217, 222, 263.

14. James T. Patterson, *Mr. Republican: A Biography of Robert A. Taft* (Boston: Houghton Mifflin, 1972); James McClelland and Kirk, *The Political Principles of Robert A. Taft* (New York: Fleet Press, 1967); Ronald Radosh, "A Noninterventionist Faces War," in *Prophets on the Right: Profiles of Conservative Critics of American Globalism* (New York: Simon Schuster, 1975), 119–45.

15. Louis Hartz, *The Liberal Tradition in America: An Interpretation of American Political Thought Since the Revolution* (New York: Harcourt, Brace, and World, 1955), 20.

16. Ibid., 10–11, 253–54.

17. Adam L. Tate, *Conservatism and Southern Intellectuals 1789–1861: Liberty and the Good Society* (Columbia: University of Missouri Press, 2005), esp. 324–31.

18. Barry A. Shain's *The Myth of American Individualism: The Protestant Origins of American Political Thought* (Princeton, NJ: Princeton University Press, 1995) would seem to challenge this picture of a liberal American founding, but the book offers conclusions that are compatible with my argument. While Shain stresses the Calvinist character of late eighteenth- and early nineteenth-century America, he also looks at the modernizing features of early American Protestantism. Individual religious experience and a bourgeois work ethic both belonged to the morally conformist social culture that Shain contrasts to later godless American "individualism."

19. For a polemical but highly informative account of the anti–New Deal Right, see Justin Raimondo, *Reclaiming the American Right: The Lost Legacy of the Conservative Movement* (Burlingame, CA: Center for Libertarian Studies, 1994); see also Gregory L. Schneider, ed., *Conservatism in America Since 1930* (New York: New York University Press, 2003), 5–68; Gottfried and Thomas Fleming, *The Conservative Movement* (Boston: G. K. Hall, 1988); and Gregory P. Pavlik, ed., *Selected Essays of John T. Flynn* (Irvington-on-Hudson, NY: Foundation for Economic Education, 1995).

20. See Sandro Chignola, *Società e costituzione. Teologia e politica nel sistema di Bonald* (Milan: Franco Angeli, 1993), 125; Robert Nisbet, "De Bonald and the Concept of the Social Group," *Journal of the History of Ideas* (1944): 315–31; and Robert Spaemann, *Der Ursprung der Soziologie aus dem Geist der Restauration. Studien über L.G.A. de Bonald* (Munich: Kösel Verlag, 1959), 64.

21. George H. Nash, *The Conservative Intellectual Movement Since 1945*, expanded ed. (Wilmington, DE: Intercollegiate Studies Institute, 1996), 30–73.
22. Ibid., 87–117.
23. John A. Andrew, ed., *The Other Side of the Sixties: Young Americans for Freedom and the Rise of Conservative Politics* (New Brunswick, NJ: Rutgers University Press, 1997), 222.
24. Ibid.; see also Robert J. Bresler's introductory essay to his anthology, *Us vs. Them: American Political and Cultural Conflict from World War II to Watergate* (Wilmington, DE: Scholarly Resources, 2000), 3–93; and Stephen J. Whitfield, *The Culture of the Cold War* (Baltimore: Johns Hopkins University Press, 1991).
25. William F. Buckley, "The Party and the Deep Blue Sea," *Commonweal* 55 (January 24, 1952): 393.
26. Buckley, "Murray Rothbard, RIP," *National Review*, February 6, 1995; Jerome Tucille, "A Split in the Right Wing," *New York Times*, January 28, 1971; and Murray N. Rothbard, "The Transformation of the American Right," *Continuum* (Summer 1964): 220–31.
27. Patrick Allitt, *Catholic Intellectuals and Conservative Politics in America, 1950–1985* (Ithaca, NY: Cornell University Press, 1995).
28. Nash, *The Conservative Intellectual Movement*, 166–67.
29. Buckley, "Footnote to Brown v. Board of Education," *National Review*, March 11, 1961, p. 137; and in the same publication, F. S. Meyer, "Liberalism Runs Riot," March 26, 1968, p. 283; and F. S. Meyer, "The Negro Revolution," June 18, 1963, p. 496.
30. Henry Regnery, *Memoirs of a Dissident Publisher* (New York: Harcourt, Brace, Jovanovich, 1979), 155.
31. Nash, *The Conservative Intellectual Movement*, 67.
32. Kirk, *The Conservative Mind*, 32.
33. Ibid., 63.
34. For an emotionally charged but instructive response to this charge against Kirk, see Taki, "The Fifth Columnist," *The American Conservative*, November 4, 2005, p. 35.
35. See Peter Viereck, *Conservatism: From John Adams to Churchill* (Princeton, NJ: Van Nostrand, 1950); and Viereck, *Conservatism Revisited: The Revolt Against Revolt* (New York: Collier Books, 1962), 145–51.
36. Clinton Rossiter, *Conservatism in America: The Thankless Persuasion* (New York: Vintage Books, 1962), 220–23.
37. Kirk, *Sword of Imagination: Memoirs of a Half Century of Literary Conflict* (Grand Rapids, MI: Eerdmans, 1995).
38. W. Wesley McDonald, *Russell Kirk and the Age of Ideology* (Columbia: University of Missouri Press, 2004), 11–12, 71; see also Gerald J. Russello, "Profile of a Pioneer," *Crisis*, October 21, 2004; and the exchange between McDonald and Russello in letters column, *Crisis*, February 3, 2005. My comments do not exclude the possibility of

reading Catholic elements into Kirk's later work, a hermeneutic possibility that McDonald readily concedes. More problematic, however, is the reading of these elements into Kirk's formative writings, a tendency that, according to McDonald, would not prevail if cultural conservatism had not become allied to the Catholic Right and, more specifically, neo-Thomism.

39. Kirk, *The Conservative Movement: From Burke to Santayana* (Chicago: Henry Regnery, 1953), 8.

40. Ibid., 9; and Kirk, *John Randolph of Roanoke: A Study of American Politics* (Indianapolis, IN: Liberty Press, 1970).

41. This quotation from Rothbard came from an unpublished letter of his from February 9, 1960, which his biographer David Gordon made available to me.

42. Ibid.; see also the essay "Commentator on Our Time: A Quest for the Historical Rothbard" by Sheldon L. Richman that quotes from this letter in *Man, Economy, and Liberty: Essays in Honor of Murray N. Rothbard*, ed. Walter Block and L. H. Rockwell Jr. (Auburn, AL: Mises Institute, 1988), 371.

43. Among works on the relatively recent origin of the state are Ettore Rotelli and Pierangelo Schiera, ed., *Lo stato moderno*, 3 vols. (Bologna: Mulino, 1971–1974); Charles Tilly, ed., *The Formation of Nation States in Western Europe* (Princeton, NJ: Princeton University Press, 1975); and Wolfgang Reinhard, *Geschichte der Staatsgewalt. Eine vergleichende Verfassungsgeschichte Europas von den Anfängen bis zur Gegenwart* (Munich: C. H. Beck Verlag, 1999), see especially the bibliography for further relevant readings.

44. Frank S. Meyers, *In Defense of Freedom: A Conservative Credo* (Chicago: Henry Regnery, 1962), 40.

45. Ibid., 41; and Meyers, ed., *What Is Conservatism?* (New York: Holt Rinehart and Winston, 1964).

46. See the comments on Meyer in Gottfried's *The Search for Historical Meaning: Hegel and the Postwar American Right* (DeKalb: University of Northern Illinois Press, 1986), XII–XV, 83–87, 88–91.

47. Karl Marx, *Die Frühschriften*, ed. Siegfried Landshut (Stuttgart: Kröner Verlag, 1953), 117, 143–45.

48. Harry V. Jaffa, "Lincoln and the Cause of Freedom," *National Review*, September 21, 1965, pp. 827–28; and also by Jaffa, *Crisis of a House Divided* (Chicago: University of Chicago Press, 1982).

49. Jaffa, *A New Birth of Freedom* (Lanham, MD: Rowman and Littlefield, 2000), 6.

50. Jaffa, *American Conservatism and the American Founding* (Durham, NC: Carolina Academic Press, 1984), 255.

51. Walter Berns, "Congress Is Saying, Give Peace a Grant," *Wall Street Journal*, August 2, 1982, p. 14.

52. Ibid., 148–56.

53. Jaffa, *How to Think About the American Revolution* (Durham, NC: Carolina Academic Press, 1978), 142.

54. Ibid. and 13–48. See also Jaffa's "Equality, Justice and the American Revolution," *Modern Age* 21, no. 2 (Spring 1977): 114–26, written in response to the Southern Agrarian critic of Lincoln, M. E. Bradford. Rendering the arguments of Jaffa's now deceased adversary (see, e.g., "The Heresy of Equality," *Modern Age* 20, no. 1 [Winter 1976]: 62–77), especially noteworthy was Bradford's affinity for the mindset of European counterrevolutionaries. His statements are reminiscent of a classical conservative, appealing to unwritten custom, social deference, and the moral qualities of landed aristocracy. Attacks on his "bigotry" reflected either bewildered shock on the part of his critics or attempts to neutralize his appeal to "the reactionary imperative." See M. E. Bradford, *The Reactionary Imperative* (Peru, IL: Sherwood Sugden, 1980).

55. Jaffa, *How to Think About the American Revolution*, 13.

56. Buckley and Charles R. Kesler, ed., *Keeping the Tablets: Modern American Conservative Thought* (New York: Harper Collins, 1988).

57. See Jaffa, *American Conservatism*, XIV and passim XI–XIV; and Kesler's essay that follows, 1–17, which had been originally published as "The Special Meaning of the Declaration of Independence," *National Review*, July 6, 1979.

58. Jaffa, "On the Nature of Religion and Civil Liberty," in *Did You Ever See a Dream Walking? American Conservative Thought in the Twentieth Century*, ed. Buckley, 221–38 (Indianapolis, IN: Bobbs-Merrill, 1968).

59. Kirk, "The Conservative Movement Then and Now," in *Reclaiming a Patrimony: A Collection of Lectures*, Lecture 1 (Washington, DC: Heritage Foundation, 1982).

60. Peter J. Stanlis, *Edmund Burke and the Natural Law* (Ann Arbor: University of Michigan Press, 1958); Stanlis, *The Relevance of Edmund Burke* (New York: P. J. Kennedy and Sons, 1964); and Stanlis, *Edmund Burke: The Enlightenment and Revolution*, introduction by Kirk (New Brunswick, NJ: Transaction Publishers, 1991).

61. Nash, *The Conservative Intellectual Movement*, 60–61.

62. Patrick Allitt, *Catholic Intellectuals and Conservative Politics in America 1950–1985* (Ithaca, NY: Cornell University Press, 1993).

63. For works that contextualize this German "Basic Law conservatism," see Martin Kriele, *Einführung in die Staatslehre. Die geschichtlichen Legitimitätsgrundlagen des demokratischen Verfassungsstaates*, 5th ed. (Stuttgart: Kohlhammer, 2003); Joachim Ritter, *Metaphysik und Politik. Studien zu Aristoteles und Hegel*, exp. ed. with an afterward by Odo Marquard (Frankfurt: Suhrkamp, 2003); and Frank Bösch, *Die Adenauer-CDU. Gründung, Aufstieg und Krises einer Erfolgspartei, 1945–1969* (Munich: Deutsche Verlagsanstalt, 2001).

64. Robert Spaemann, *Zur Kritik der politischen Utopie. Zehn Kapitel politischer Philosophie* (Stuttgart: Kohlhammer, 1977).

65. See Gottfried, "How European Nations End," *Orbis* 49, no. 3 (Summer 2005): 259–69.

66. Bosbach's comments on *Leitkultur*, December 2, 2004, are available at CDU/CSU Fraktion, http://www.cducsu.de/section.

67. For the nitpicking that attended this debate on *Leitkultur*, December 2, 2004, see FDP-site, http://www.michael.goldmann.de/rede. A resourceful social researcher for the Konrad-Adenauer-Stiftung, Stefan Eisel devotes one issue of the institute's monthly *Die Politische Meinung* (December) to documenting the erosion of electoral support for the CDU-CSU Union since 2002. According to Eisel, this dwindling vote was related to the decision to play down traditional social positions "at a time of rapid change, when men are looking for stability and orientation." Both waffling on social issues lest it give offense and "reducing family politics to mere economics" actually cost the union many votes. What disguised this downward trend in 2005, however, was that the Socialists did even worse in the federal elections.

68. On the centrality of Middle Eastern policy as a determinant of political identity, see Philip Weiss's "George Soros's Right-Wing Twin," *New York* (August 1–8, 2005): 26–31, 88.

69. See National Review Online, posted January 21, 2002, available at http://www.nationalreview.com/goldberg/goldberg; and on the same Web site, the earlier comments on Maistre, posted July 26, 2000.

70. Jaffa, *New Birth of Freedom*, 117–21.

71. See Jaffa, "The False Prophets of American Conservatism," delivered at the Claremont Institute's Lincoln Day Conference on February 12, 1998, available at Claremont Institute Writings, http://www.claremont.org/writings; and Vincent J. Cannato's "Culture vs. Creed," *Claremont Review of Books* 4, no. 4 (Fall 2004); Patrick Garrity's "Wilson's World," *Claremont Review of Books* 3, no. 2 (Spring 2003); and Dennis J. Mahoney's "Un-American Activities," *Claremont Review of Books* 4, no. 4 (Fall 2004).

72. Allan Bloom, *The Closing of the American Mind* (New York: Simon and Schuster, 1987), 153.

73. Ibid., 27.

74. Claes G. Ryn, *America the Virtuous: The Crisis of Democracy and the Quest for Empire* (New Brunswick, NJ: Transaction Publishers, 2003).

75. See Ernst van den Haag's "The War Between Paleos and Neos," *National Review*, February 24, 1989, pp. 21–23; and the subsequent exchange between van den Haag and S. T. Francis in letters column, *National Review*, April 7, 1989, pp. 43–45.

76. Schwartz on Trotsky, June 11, 2003, available at http://www.national review.com/comment/comment; and Gottfried, "Mussolini and the Mideast," *American Conservative*, July 4, 2005, pp. 3–25.

77. Michael Massing, "Trotsky's Orphans," *New Republic*, January 22, 1987, pp. 18–20.

78. Claes Ryn, conversation with the author, July 1987. The connection between cultural conservatives and the Republican Party, and particularly Ronald Reagan and his entourage, should be clear from Lee Edwards's authorized history of America's most visible promoter of cultural conservatism, Intercollegiate Studies Institute. See Lee Edwards, *Educating for Liberty: The First Half Century of the Intercollegiate Studies Institute* (Washington, DC: Regnery, 2003). For full disclosure, the reader is referred to a symposium in Intercollegiate Studies Institute's publication "The State of Conservatism," *Intercollegiate Review* (Spring 1986), in which I participated with Russell Kirk and others mentioned in this chapter concerning changes on the American Right. My commentary on pages 19–21, which Edwards discusses (see *Educating for Liberty*, 181–84), suggests that the "Old Right" will take back the conservative movement because it stands for the conservative rank and file. At that time I was still leaning toward the conservatism that was present in the original *National Review*, before its transitory character had become fully apparent.

CHAPTER 2

1. Thomas Hobbes, *Leviathan*, ed. Michael Oakeshott (New York: Macmillan, 1962), 39–40; and André Robinet, "Pensée et langage chez Hobbes," *Revue Internationale de Philosophie* 33, no. 129 (1979): 443–51.

2. Karl Mannheim, *Konservatismus: Ein Beitrag zur Soziologie des Wissens* (Frankfurt: Suhrkamp Verlag, 1984), 137–84.

3. Ibid., 146–54, 120–27, 218–20.

4. Ibid., 133–53, 220–23; and Mannheim, *Ideologie und Utopie*, 8th ed. (Frankfurt: Vittorio Klostermann, 1995), 134–43.

5. See Christoph Groffy's introductory essay to Mannheim, *Konservatismus*, 11–37.

6. Mannheim, *Konservatismus*, 169.

7. See Paul Gottfried, *The Search for Historical Meaning: Hegel and the Postwar American Right* (DeKalb: University of Northern Illinois Press, 1986), 104–34; and the review essay for this work by Robert Nisbet, *National Review*, May 22, 1987, pp. 39–44.

8. See Henry Regnery, "Russell Kirk and the Making of the Conservative Mind," *Modern Age* 21 (Fall 1977): 338–53; W. Wesley

McDonald, "Russell Kirk of Piety Hill," *The Alternative*, February 1971, pp. 9–11; and Russell Kirk, *The Surly Sunken Bell* (New York: Fleet Publishing, 1962).

9. See two illustrations of latter-day American historical conservatism: Donald Livingston, *Philosophical Melancholy and Delirium: Hume's Pathology of Philosophy* (Chicago: University of Chicago Press, 1998); and Clyde N. Wilson, ed., *A Defense of Southern Conservatism: M. E. Bradford and His Achievement* (Columbia: University of Missouri Press, 1999).

10. Mannheim, *Konservatismus*, 158–59 and 195–97; and Klaus Epstein, *The Genesis of German Conservatism* (Princeton, NJ: Princeton University Press, 1966), 1–70.

11. Eugene Genovese, *The Southern Tradition: The Achievement and Limitation of an American Conservatism* (Cambridge, MA: Harvard University Press, 1994). Genovese combines sympathy for his subject with a residual social determinism, traceable to his Gramscian-Marxist background.

12. See Richard M. Weaver, *Ideas Have Consequences* (Chicago: University of Chicago Press, 1947); Joseph Scotchie's biography *Barbarians in the Saddle: An Intellectual Biography of Richard Weaver* (Columbia: University of Missouri, 1995) and the anthology of Weaver essays, Scotchie, *The Vision of Richard Weaver* (New Brunswick, NJ: Transaction Publishers, 1996); and Ted J. Smith, ed., *Collected Shorter Writings of Richard M. Weaver* (Indianapolis, IN: Liberty Press, 2001). The construction of a comprehensive biography for Weaver remains a project waiting to be done. Two scholars who undertook this work with the assistance of University of Missouri Press, Ted Smith and John Attarian, both friends of this author, died suddenly at relatively young ages. Scotchie, who produced a monograph on Weaver, celebrates him for his Southern conservative thinking and as someone whose hometown, Weaverville, is adjacent to Scotchie's native city, Asheville.

13. Frank S. Meyer, "Richard M. Weaver: An Appreciation," *Modern Age* 14 (Summer 1970): 243.

14. See Carlo Galli, *I Controrivoluzionari. Antologia di scritti politici* (Bologna: Il Molino, 1981), esp. intro.; Panajotis Kondylis, *Konervativismus. Geschichtler Gehalt und Untergang* (Stuttgart: Klett, 1986); and Nisbet, *Conservatism: Dream and Reality* (Minneapolis: University of Minnesota Press, 1986).

15. Mannheim, *Ideologie und Utopie*, 208–9; Mannheim, *Konservatismus*, 142–46, 184–85; and Mannheim, "Historismus," *Archiv für Sozialwissenschaft und Sozialpolitik* 52 (1924): 1–60.

16. Kondylis, *Konservativismus. Geschichtlicher Gehalt und Untergang*, (Stuttgart: Klett, 1988), 51, 387–441. See also Gottfried, "Panajotis Kondylis and the Obsoleteness of Conservatism," *Modern Age* 39, no. 4 (Fall 1987): 403–10.

17. Carl Schmitt, *Politische Romantik*, 3rd ed. (Berlin: Duncker and Humblot, 1968). For more nuanced formulations of Schmitt's attack on Müller and the political romantics in general, see Friedrich Meinecke, *Weltbürgertum und Nationalstaat*, 8th edition, ed. Hans Herzfeld (Munich: Oldenbourg Verlag, 1962), esp. 113–42; and Gottfried, "Kunst und Politik bei Burke und Novalis," *Zeitschrift für Ästhetik und Allgemeine Kunstwissenschaft* 19, no. 2 (1974): 240–51.

18. Mannheim, *Konservatismus*, 25–36, 187–97, 200–205, 213–23; Mannheim, *Ideologie und Utopie*, 202–4; the short sketch of Savigny in Carpar Schrenck-Notzing, ed., *Lexikon des Konservatismus* (Graz: Stocker Verlag, 1996), 476–77; and Gottfried, "German Romanticism and Natural Law," *Studies in Romanticism* 4 (Summer 1968): 231–42.

19. Adam Müller, *Über König Friedrich II und die Natur, Würde und Bestimmung der preussischen Monarchie* (Berlin: n.p., 1810), 49.

20. Mannheim, *Konservatismus*, 216–20.

21. A shorter version of Mark C. Henrie's "Understanding Traditionalist Conservatism" is available in Peter Berkowitz. ed., *Varieties of Conservatism in America* (Palo Alto, CA: Hoover Press, 2004); the citations are from the longer Web site text, August 5, 2005, available at "The New Pantagruel," http://www.newpantagruel.com/issues/2.2/understanding_traditionalist_c.php.

22. Ibid.,13.

23. Marist Poll, released on August, 12, 2005, showing growing Republican support for Hillary Clinton; see "Presidential Election of 2008," *New York Times*, February 22, 2005, p. F22.

24. Kevin P. Phillips, *The Emerging Republican Majority* (New Rochelle, NY: Arlington House, 1969); and Gottfried, *The Conservative Movement*, rev. ed. (New York: Macmillan-Twayne, 1993), 30–50.

25. Murray Friedman, *The Neoconservative Revolution: Jewish Intellectuals and the Shaping of Public Policy* (Cambridge: Cambridge University Press, 2005), 200.

26. Ibid., 225.

27. Ibid.; and William F. Buckley, "Toast to Tomorrow," *National Review*, December 22, 1997, pp. 46–49.

28. For references to this now largely forgotten incident, see Gottfried, "Looking Back," *The World and I* 8 (August 1986): 460–64.

29. John B. Judis, "The Conservative Crackup," *American Prospect* 3 (Fall 1990): 30–39; I. L. Horowitz, conversation with the author, May 7, 1989; and John B. Judis, "The Conservative Wars," *New Republic*, August 11, 1987, pp. 15–16.

30. Friedman, *The Neoconservative Revolution*, 7, 196–204. Like other proponents of neoconservatism, particularly Mark Gerson (*The Neoconservative Vision: From the Cold War to the Culture Wars* [Lanham: Madison Books, 1996]), who speaks vaguely about "Catholic

neoconservatives," Friedman treats as "neoconservatives" writers who may have received neoconservative patronage and those who are in some way affiliated with neoconservative-funded organizations. By this inclusive definition, I too could fall into Friedman's category by virtue of having taken funding, unbeknownst to myself, from one of his confreres. Friedman repeatedly credits his movement with intellectual enterprises that they have funded. Still, it is hard in the end to connect projects like Charles Murray's work on the genetic basis of intelligence or anti-abortion Catholic magazines to recognizable neoconservative interests.

31. See *American Conservative*, November 8, 2004, for the comment by editor Scott McConnell endorsing John Kerry in the presidential race; P. C. Roberts's vitriolic invectives directed against Bush and his "brownshirt" administration is available at http://www.lewrockwell.com/roberts/roberts-arch.html; http://www.counterpunch.org/roberts; and http://www.antiwar.com/roberts; and still growing followings, which are as fierce as any group on the American Left in their attacks on Bush and the Republican Party.

32. Gary Dorrien, *The Neoconservative Mind: Politics, Culture, and the War of Ideology* (Philadelphia: Temple University Press, 1993), 369.

33. Richard J. Neuhaus, "Will Herberg Pluralist," *National Review*, January 22, 1988, p. 54.

34. Victor S. Navasky, *A Matter of Opinion* (New York: Farrar, Strauss, Giroux, 2005), 419.

35. See Eliso Vivas's *The Moral Life and the Ethical Life* (Chicago: University of Chicago Press, 1950); George H. Nash, *The Conservative Intellectual Movement in America Since 1945* (Wilmington, DE: Intercollegiate Studies Institute, 1996), 49–74; and just about every issue of *Modern Age* from 1956 on.

36. An exploration by Murray Rothbard of ethical values within the framework of a liberty-maximizing society can be found in *Man, Economy, and the State: a Treatise on Economic Principle*, 2 vols. (Princeton, NJ: Van Nostrand, 1962); and Rothbard, *The Ethics of Liberty* (Atlantic Highlands, NJ: Humanities Press, 1982). See also the essays on liberty and morality in Rothbard, *Man, Economy, and Liberty*, 195–268.

37. See Dorrien, *The Neoconservative Mind*, 180–82; and Norman Podhoretz, "The Culture of Appeasement, " *Harper's* 255, no. 1529 (October 1977): 32.

38. Friedman (*The Neoconservative Revolution*, 196–97) highlights the NAS's commitment to neoconservative activists and neoconservative goals. See also David Horowitz's related Web site publication http://www.frontpagemag.com, particularly its revealing "War Room" series. The neoconservative daily the *New York Sun* produced an editorial (February 27, 2006, pp. 1, 7) expressing enthusiastic approval that the controversial historian David Irving, who in Austria was

accused and found guilty of "Holocaust denial," was sentenced to three years imprisonment. Whether the 67-year-old historian was actually guilty as charged was not clear from the contemptuous coverage, nor could one discern from reading the report any questioning of a judicial process whereby a British visitor to Austria was seized upon arrival and imprisoned for having taken an interpretive position, however ill conceived, that the Austrian government had decided to criminalize. The *New York Sun* defended Austria's action as "a kind of atonement by a country starting to recognize that its great error of the twentieth century was not only the authoritarianism [of its past] but the anti-Semitism itself." This came from a neoconservative publication that steadily upholds intellectual freedom when defending those who hold its views on the war in Iraq or Israeli-Palestinian relations.

39. Peter Steinfels, *The Neoconservatives: The Men Who Are Changing America* (New York: Simon and Schuster, 1979), 55.

40. Podhoretz's books are mostly autobiographical and, despite their distribution as inspirational reading to members of the onetime Old Right Young Americans for Freedom, focus on nothing more important than their subject's spats with other New York Jewish intellectuals. See Podhoretz's *Making It* (1969), *Breaking Ranks: A Political Memoir* (1979), *Bloody Crossroads: Where Literature and Politics Meet* (1996), and *Ex-Friends* (1999). The interpretation of such name-calling as high literature raises doubts about the claim that American conservatism has elevated its intellectual horizons since the 1980s.

41. A now largely forgotten study of neoconservatives dealing with the narrowly restricted social world of their beginnings is Alexander Bloom's *Prodigal Sons* (New York: Oxford University Press, 1986).

42. Dr. Samuel T. Francis, conversation with the author, July 5, 1986; and Christopher Hitchens, "A Modern Medieval Family," *Mother Jones* (July 1986): 52–56 (first installment); (August 1986): 74–76 (second installment).

43. Steinfels, *The Neoconservatives*, 39–46; Daniel Bell, *The End of Ideology* (New York: Free Press, 1962); and Chaim Waxman, *The End of Ideology Debate* (New York: Funk and Wagnalls, 1968), an anthology.

44. Buckley, ed., *Did You Ever See A Dream Walking? American Conservative Thought in the Twentieth Century* (Indianapolis, IN: Bobbs-Merrill, 1968), 228.

45. For a devastating critique of Jaffa's hortatory rhetoric masked as moral reasoning, see David Gordon's review of *New Birth of Freedom* in *Mises Review* 7, no. 2 (Winter 1995): 16–22; and for the still unpublished source of this critique, see David Gordon, "Jaffa on Equality, Democracy, Morality," lewrockwell.com, available at http://www.lewrockwell.com/gordon/gordon5.html. Gordon provides a devastating response in the *Mises Review* (Winter 1995) to Dinesh

D'Souza's *The End of Racism* (New York: Free Press, 1995), the work of a self-identified neoconservative reprising Jaffa's attacks on "cultural relativism." Gordon explains that D'Souza misunderstands the nature and implications of the relativism that he condemns. According to Gordon, neoconservatives, including D'Souza, equate Max Weber's "fact-value distinction" with a relativist ethic. They thereby misrepresent what Weber understood as facts and values and betray how little of his work they have read.

46. See Irving Kristol, "'Family Values'—Not a Political Issue," *Wall Street Journal*, December 7, 1992, p. 14; and Gerson, *The Neoconservative Vision*, 328–33.

47. See the yearly report *Jewish Political Studies* published by Jerusalem Center for Public Affairs, ed. Daniel J. Elazar 11, no. 11 (Spring 1999); and for an informative but partisan study of the same issue, *International Religious Report* (2000).

48. Kristol, " The Coming Conservative Century," *Wall Street Journal*, February 1, 1993, p. 18.

49. See Kristol, *Neoconservatism: The Autobiography of an Idea* (New York: Free Press, 1995), 386.

50. Willmoore Kendall, "Do We Want An 'Open Society'?" *National Review*, January 31, 1959, p. 493; and *The Conservative Affirmation* (Chicago: Regnery, 1963), 108–16.

51. Linda C. Raeder, *John Stuart Mill and the Religion of Humanity* (Columbia: University of Missouri Press, 2002), 234–67; Joseph Hamburger, *John Stuart Mill on Liberty and Control* (Princeton, NJ: Princeton University Press, 1999); and Maurice Cowling, *Mill and Liberalism* (Cambridge: Cambridge University Press, 1963).

52. William A. Donahue, *Twilight of Liberty: The Legacy of the ACLU* (New Brunswick, NJ: Transaction Publishers, 1994).

53. Mannheim, *Ideologie und Utopie*, 70–76.

54. Allan Bloom, *The Closing of the American Mind* (New York: Simon and Schuster, 1987), 202.

55. Barry Shain, conversation with the author, July 15, 2005; and Shain's review of M. J. Zuckert in *Modern Age* 45, no. 2 (Fall 2003): 366–68.

56. Bloom, *The Closing of the American Mind*, 142.

57. Kristol, *Neoconservatism*, 163–64.

58. Ibid., 165–78.

59. See Benjamin Hart, *The Third Generation: Young Conservative Leaders Look Toward the Future* (Washington, DC: Regnery, 1987), introductory note by President Reagan and 11–28.

60. Ibid., 255–70.

61. George Will, "Silliness on Stem Cell Research," *Washington Post*, August 7, 2005.

62. William Bennett, *The Broken Hearth: Reversing the Collapse of the Family* (New York: Doubleday, 1996), 47–66.

63. In "Der lange Marsch der CDU nach links," German political historian Karlheinz Weissmann presents an argument about "value conservatism" similar to mine in explaining the "leftward lurch" of the Christian Democrats on social and national questions under Helmut Kohl and even more under Merkel. According to Weissmann, in the 1970s the center-right CDU decided to exchange the defense of "structural conservatism," identified with the family, church, army, and nation, for a less confrontational "Wertekonservatismus," a position that signified a "dwindling of its conservative content." Instead of rising to the defense of German refugees from Eastern Europe, upholding the honor of its nation and the traditional concept of marriage, Christian Democratic leaders could leave behind divisive issues, which were likely to draw charges of flirting with fascism from the left, and to focus on inoffensive electoral slogans. In Germany, Weissmann insists that this substitution was deliberate and took place for opportunistic reasons. See the *Junge Freiheit* Web site for August 18, 2000, at http://www.jf.de/archiv00/340yy46.htm.

CHAPTER 3

1. Philip Weiss, "The George Soros of the Right," *New York* (August 1–8, 2005): 88.
2. Ibid., 89.
3. Paul Gottfried, *The Conservative Movement*, rev. ed. (New York: Macmillan, 1993), 118–41; Roger Williams, "Capital Clout," *Foundation News* 30, no. 4 (July/August 1989): 40;George Archibald's report on Heritage funding in *Washington Times*, December 2, 1991, p. A7.
4. Gottfried, *The Conservative Movement*, 124–36.
5. Weiss, conversation with the author, April 6, 2005.
6. For a particularly spirited attack on his neoconservative opponents, see Murray Rothbard's presidential speech to the John Randolph Club, "A Strategy for the Right," January 18, 1992, cited from the original manuscript; and William McGurn, "Pat Buchanan and the Intellectuals," *National Review*, February 17, 1992, pp. 41–42.
7. See Suzanne Garment's comments in "There's Nothing Like a Liberal Trial for an Education," *Wall Street Journal*, October 11, 1985, p. 28; and James Nuechterlein's review of John Judis's biography of William F. Buckley in *Commentary* 85, no. 6 (June 1988): 31.
8. See Stephen Schwartz, "What Is Islamo-Fascism?" *Weekly Standard*, August 17, 2006, available at http://www.weeklystandard.com/Contest/Public/Articles.
9. Irving Kristol, "The Neoconservative Persuasion: What It Was and What It Is," *The Weekly Standard*, August 25, 2003, p. 2.

10. Ibid., 2, 3.

11. See "Conservative Lament Movement's Founders Win a Few but Not the Big One," *Washington Times*, August 24, 2003, available at http://www.washingtontimes.com/commentary/archive/long.

12. An Evangelical opponent of the war in Iraq, Lawrence M. Vance has documented the Religious Right's attitude of submissiveness toward the Bush administration in his article "Christianity and the War," available at http://www.levrockwell.com/vance/vance81.html. Vance also wrote a book on the same topic, *Christianity and War* (Pensacola, FL: Vance Publications, 2005); Grace Halsell, *Prophecy and Politics: The Secret Alliance Between Israel and the U.S. Christian Right* (New York: Lawrence Hill, 1989); the same tendency can be found in Jerry Falwell's weekly "Newsletter to the Moral Majority Coalition and the Liberty Alliance," particularly the August 25, 2005, issue, which equates opposition to the Iraqi war with "hate-Bush, hate-America, hate-capitalism."

13. Samuel T. Francis, *Beautiful Losers: Essays on the Failure of American Conservatism* (Columbia: University of Missouri Press, 1993); and an essay on the same themes, Samuel T. Francis, monthly column, *Chronicles* 15 (May 1990): 14–17. Because of his deadly wit and no-holds-barred style, Francis became one of the more penetrating but hated critics of the postwar Right. His literary brilliance and analytic power have never been equaled among commentators on the postwar conservative movement; nonetheless, Francis suffered for his merits by being driven out of the later conservative movement as an "extremist."

14. This now ritualistic emphasis on the profundity of neoconservative scholarship is evident in, among other works, William A. Rusher's *The Rise of the Right*, rev. ed. (New York: National Review, 1993), 165–68.

15. See Charles Krauthammer, "Neoconservatism and Foreign Policy," originally delivered at a banquet to honor I. Kristol, in *The National Interest*, October 2004, available at http://www.inthenationalinterest.com/Articles/october2004/october2004/Krauthammer.

16. Joel Mowbray, "General Zinni, What a Ninny!" Townhall.com, December 31, 2003, available at http://townhall.com/columnists/JoelMowbray/2003/12/31/general_zinni,_what_a_ninny; and Michael Lind, "A Tragedy of Errors," *The Nation*, February 23, 2004, pp. 2–7.

17. Lee Edwards, *The Conservative Revolution* (New York: Free Press, 1999); and Jerome L. Himmelstein, *To the Right: The Transformation of American Conservatism* (Berkeley: University of California Press, 1990). Himmelstein's work may not really deserve its title, since it ignores significant "transformations" of the movement that it sets out to treat.

18. Mark Gerson, *The Neoconservative Vision: From the Cold War to the Culture Wars* (Lanham: Madison Books, 1996), 309–20; and Gottfried,

"The Conservative Crackup," *Society* (January/February 1994): 23–24.

19. Peter Brimelow, conversation with the author, July 24, 2002; and Brimelow's *Alien Nation: Common Sense About America's Immigration Disaster* (New York: Random House, 1995).

20. M. E. Bradford, interview with the author, July 10, 1987; and Bradford, *The Neoconservative Vision*, 313.

21. George H. Nash, *The Conservative Intellectual Movement in America Since 1945* (Wilmington, DE: Intercollegiate Studies Institute, 1996), 329–41.

22. See Gottfried, "Toward a New Fusionism," *Policy Review* 42 (Fall 1987): 64–71; Paul Piccone, "The Crisis of Conservatism," *Telos* 74 (Winter 1987–1988): 3–29; and S. Churcher, "Radical Transformation," *New York Times Magazine*, July 6, 1989, 30–31.

23. Nash, *The Conservative Intellectual Movement*, 159–66.

24. See Jonathan M. Schoenwald, *A Time for Choosing: The Rise of Modern American Conservatism* (Oxford: Oxford University Press, 2001), esp. 190–265. The omission from this generally reliable survey of all references to conservative wars or splits on the Right since the 1980s may be the result of the outcome of these struggles. Since neoconservative power over the movement is no longer in doubt, Schoenwald assumes that it represented a natural progression from whatever came before.

25. Friedrich Julius von Stahl, *Die gegenwärtigen Parteien im Staat und Kirche* (Berlin: W. Hertz, 1863), 2.

26. See F. Carolyn Graglia's *Domestic Tranquility: A Brief Against Feminism* (Dallas: Spence, 1998), esp. 40–41, 140–43, for a critique of moderate or "classical liberal feminists." Graglia poses the question whether or not the neoconservative model of restrained feminism, represented by Christine Hoff Sommers, which seeks to return selectively to the ideas of Betty Friedan, has departed significantly from the current feminism. The feminism that precedes its present radicalized form, according to Graglia, is its precondition and not its bourgeois alternative.

27. For Secretary of State Condoleezza Rice's remarks on March 8, 2006 on the occasion of International Women's Day, available at http://www.state.gov/secretary/rm/2006/62735.htm.

28. See, for this neoconservative reconstruction of Martin Luther King Jr., David Horowitz's columns on *FrontPage Magazine.com*, August 19, 2002, and January 20, 2003, available at http://www.frontpagemag.com/Articles/index.asp. The latter begins by explaining (without really proving) that "Martin Luther King was a great man and a conservative one, which is why the Left turned its back on him." A work that inter alia refutes such assertions while focusing on King's unacknowledged use of borrowed texts for his dissertation is Theodore Pappas's *Plagiarism and the Cultural War: The Writings*

of Martin Luther King Jr. and Other Prominent Americans, expanded edition with introduction by Eugene Genovese (Tampa, FL: Hallberg, 1998).

29. Ralph Peters, *New Glory: Expanding America's Global Supremacy* (Denville, NJ: Dimension Books, 2005).

30. Rich Lowry "Rice on Tour," *National Review Online*, February 11, 2005, available at http://www.nationalreview.com/lowry/lowry 200502110734.asp.

31. Peter Steinfels, *The Rise of the Neoconservatives: Intellectuals and Foreign Affairs, 1945–1994* (New Haven, CT: Yale University Press, 1996), 55–58, 65–67, 172–73, 260–63.

32. Jurgen Habermas, *The New Conservatives*, trans. and ed. Shierry Weber Nicholsen (Cambridge: Massachusetts Institute of Technology Press, 1991); and Thomas Fleming's incisive review of this book in *Society* 28, no. 3 (March/April 1991): 92–94.

33. David Brooks, "The Power of Marriage," *New York Times*, November 22, 2003, p. A15; and Brooks, "America Is Being More Virtuous," *New York Times*, August 7, 2005, p. A15.

34. I. Kristol, "The Neoconservative Persuasion," 2, 3.

35. See the dossier on Adler and other French journalists who identify criticism of the United States or of Israel and opposition to free trade with "*judéophobie*" in: Alain de Benoit, "Revue de la nouvelle judéopholie," *Elements* 117 (Summer 2005): 40–49; Pierre-André Taguieff, *La nouvelle judéophobie* (Paris: Mille et une nuit Presse, Paris, 2002); J.-F. Revel, *Antiamericanism*, trans. Diarmid Cammel (San Francisco: Encounter Books, 2003); and Gottfried, "Les tentations du pouvoir," *Catholica* (Fall 2003): 32–38.

36. I. Kristol, "The Neoconservative Persuasion."

37. Wanniski (until his death in 2005) and Roberts both distrusted the neoconservatives because of their perceived Jewish nationalism, which they alleged had taken over the conservative movement and the Republican Party. See the columns of Roberts and Wanniski, condemning the Iraqi war as an unwise neoconservative adventure, on http://www.antiwar.com.

38. Gottfried, *Multiculturalism and the Politics of Guilt*: Toward a Secular Theocracy (Columbia: University of Missouri Press, 2002), 81–84.

39. See Robert Kagan and William Kristol, "Toward a Neo-Reaganite Foreign Policy," *Foreign Affairs* (July/August 1996): 25–34.

40. Two books addressing the transitions in the development of the welfare state with special reference to Germany are Meinhard Miegel's *Die deformierte Gesellschaft: Wie die Deutschen ihre Wirklichkeit verdrängen* (Berlin: Ullstein, 2005); and Miegel, *Epochenwende: Gewinnt der Westen die Zukunft* (Berlin: Propyläen, 2005); also Gottfried, *After Liberalism: Mass Democracy in the Administrative State* (Princeton NJ: Princeton University Press, 1999); and Gottfried, *The*

Strange Death of Marxism: The European Left in the New Millennium (Columbia: University of Missouri Press, 2005).

41. See Norman Podhoretz, "My Negro Problem and Ours," *Commentary* 35, no. 2 (February 1963): 93; and Podhoretz, *Breaking Ranks* (New York: Harper and Row, 1979), 53. A far more interesting turnaround on race relations, though the volte-face was never made explicit, related to Ernst van den Haag (1914–2005), who spent the fifties and sixties as a "scientific" expert testifying in court cases, most notably *Stell v. Savannah-Chatham Board of Education* (1963), on black cognitive inferiority and the merits of segregation. By the eighties, however, van den Haag, originally a Dutch Jew who later became a Catholic, threw in his lot with the neoconservatives, vigorously taking their side at *National Review*. See John P. Jackson, *Science for Segregation: Race, Law, and the Case against Brown v. Board of Education* (New York: New York University Press, 2005), 131–37.

42. Ronald Radosh, "Why Conservatives Are So Upset with Thomas Woods's Politically Incorrect History," History News Network, available at http://hnn.us/articles/10493.html. See also the Joseph Bishop, "The End of Senator McCarty," *American Spectator* 16 (December 1983): 16–20, which includes invectives against McCarthy, together with a drawing on the cover that shows him plunged into a garbage can and covered with litter. One might wonder whether *Commentary* would have featured the same denunciations ten years earlier that its associates later put into the neoconservative *American Spectator*.

43. I. Kristol, "The New York Intellectuals," *Commentary* 47, no. 6 (July 1969): 14.

44. I. Kristol, "Civil Liberties 1952: A Study in Confusion," *Commentary* (March 1952): 233–34.

45. For comments on the neoconservatives' uses of the Religious Right by someone who obviously supports this practice, see Murray Friedman, *The Neoconservative Revolution: Jewish Intellectuals and the Shaping of Public Policy* (Cambridge: Cambridge University Press, 2005), 214–22. Illustrating how Christianity was treated in *Commentary* prior to its strategic turn in the late eighties are Norman Ravitch, "The Problem of Christian Anti-Semitism," *Commentary*, April 1982; Ruth Wisse, "The Delegitimation of Israel," *Commentary*, July 1982; Henryk Grynberg, "Appropriating the Holocaust," *Commentary*, November 1982; and Hyam Maccoby, "Christianity's Break with Judaism," *Commentary*, August 1984. Almost all of these articles trace the roots of the Holocaust to Christian anti-Semitism going back to the Gospels. According to the most uncompromising of these critics of the Christian tradition, Wisse, Israel has suffered delegitimation because of Christian anti-Semitism, which has now spread to the pro-Palestinian Left. Although the Religious Right's pro-Zionist politics had been apparent for years, the neoconservatives

may not have immediately noticed it. It is also possible that anti-Christian members of the neoconservatives' older generation needed time to adjust psychologically to a changed political situation. Thus it took several years after the Christian Right's Zionist enthusiasms had become clear before *Commentary* ceased to attack the New Testament as a source of anti-Semitism. For a well documented treatment of *Commentary's* attacks on Christianity, see Thomas Piatak's "Ecrasez l'infame" in *Chronicles* (April 2007), 14–16.

CHAPTER 4

1. See John Lukacs, *The Last European War, September 1939/December 1941* (Garden City, NY: Anchor Press, 1976); and Lee Congdon, "Reactionary Loyalties," *Modern Age* 45, no. 3 (Summer 2003): 232–34. A discussion of Italian fascism's appeal to the American democratic Left well into the 1930s is available in John P. Diggins, *Mussolini and Fascism: The View from America* (Princeton, NJ: Princeton University Press, 1972); and Wolfgang Schivelbusch, *Entfernte Verwandtschaft: Faschismus, Nationalsozialismus, New Deal 1933–1939* (Munich: Carl Hanser Verlag, 2005), esp. 23–52. Schivelbusch's study might have been better if it were less discursive (much of it centers on city planning under the vigorous governments of the Depression years) and if it were less full of disclaimers about not wishing to compare such progressive Democrats as FDR to European dictators. Either the author should point out the programmatic and characterological similarities between the governments, as James Burnham does in *The Managerial Revolution*, repr. ed. (Wesport, CT: Greenwood, 1972) or he should pick another theme that he can treat with fewer inhibitions. In the early thirties FDR and his Braintrusters (ibid., 31–36) admired Mussolini as a reformer, contrasting him to Hitler, whom they considered a Teutonic brute. Less clear is whether the New Dealers, who had been mostly Wilsonians, disliked the Nazi regime because it was German or because they foresaw the ugly German version of fascism.

2. Renzo De Felice, *Mussolini il fascista: l'organizzazione dello stato fascista 1925–1929* (Turin: Einaudi, 1968), 243–96.

3. Ernst Nolte, *Der europäische Bürgerkrieg 1917–1945: Nationalismus und Bolschewismus* (Berlin: Propyläen, 1987), 46–106; and Johannes Rogalla von Bieberstein, *Jüdischer Bolschewismus: Mythos und realität*, intro. by Ernst Nolte (Dresden: Edition Antaios, 2002).

4. De Felice, *Mussolini il fascista*, 223–43; and Franklin H. Adler, *Italian Industrialists from Liberalism to Fascism: The Political Development of the Italian Bourgeoisie, 1906–34* (New York: Cambridge University Press, 2002). Two worthwhile studies of the Italian Fascist

attempt to look back to the rural past as well as forward to the urban, industrial future are by Danilo Breschi; "Il regime fascista: Tra rural-ismo e industrialismo," *Mondo Operaio* 1 (January-Feburary, 2006), 109–18; and "Nuova ricognizione sul fascismo," in *Annali della Fondazione Ugo Spirito* 14 and 15 (2002-2003), 123–76; see also the thematic issue on Fascism, edited by Frank H. Adler, of the jour-nal *Telos*, 133 (Winter 2006).

5. See Alistair Hamilton, *The Appeal of Fascism: A Study of Intellectuals and Fascism, 1919–1944* (New York: Macmillan, 1971); and Pareto's letter to Mussolini from July 1923 in the appendix to *Le trasfor-mazioni della democrazia*, ed. Mario Missiroli (Milan: Cappelli Edi-tore, 1964), 169–70.

6. W. Etschmann, *Die Kämpfe in österreich im Juli 1934* (Vienna: öster-reich Lexikon, 1984); and L. Reichhold, *Die Vaterländische Front und ihr Widerstand gegen den Anschluss, 1933–38: Eine Dokumenta-tion* (Vienna: österreich Lexikon 1984). A uniquely interesting study of the transition from traditional conservatism to various Rightest movements in Austro-German society is Arnim Mohler and Karl-heinz Weissmann, *Die Konservative Revolution in Deutchland 1918–1932: Ein Handbuch* (Graz: Leopold Stocker Verlag, 2005). The authors show how thoroughly "conservative revolutionary" groupings of the interwar years disappeared or were suppressed after the Nazis came to power.

7. Francois Furet and Ernst Nolte, *Fascisme et communisme* (Paris: Hachette, 1998).

8. Ibid., 33–41, 129–41; Nolte, *Der Faschismus in seiner Epoche*, 10th ed. (Munich: Piper, 2000); and Nolte, *Marxismus und industrielle Revolution* (Stuttgart: Klett-Cotta, 1983).

9. De Felice, *Storia degli Ebrei sotto il fascismo* (Turin: Einaudi, 2005).

10. Furet and Nolte, *Fascisme et communisme*, 83–84; see also the inter-view with Furet on De Felice's accomplishment in *Ideazione* 3, no. 4 (Summer 1996): 19–28.

11. Carl Schmitt, *Positionen und Begriffe im Kampf mit Weimar-Genf-Versailles: Die Dreigliederung der politischen Einheit*, 3rd ed. (Ham-burg: Hanseatische Verlagsanstalt, 1935), esp. 58–62; and Paul Gottfried, *Carl Schmitt: Politics and Theory* (Westport, CT: Green-wood, 1990), 101–22.

12. Furet and Nolte, *Fascisme et communisme*, 61–67.

13. Jean Ranger, "L'évolution du vote communiste en France depuis 1945," *Le communisme en France* (Paris: Armand Colin, 1969), 211–54; and Stéphane Courtois and Marc Lazare, *Histoire du parti communiste*, 2nd ed. (Paris: Presses Universitaires de France, 2000).

14. For a defense of this Leftist politics of nostalgia and "anti-fascist" militancy by a longtime German Communist spokesman, see Gregor Gysi, *Ein Blick zurück: Ein Schritt vorn* (Hamburg: Hoffmann and Campe Verlag, 2001); and Gottfried, *The Strange Death of European*

Marxism: The European Left in the New Millennium (Columbia: University of Missouri Press, 2005), 1–26.

15. German public health expert Jost Bauch has written about multicultural indoctrination as a form of managed health care in "Freiheit und Solidarität," in *Festschrift für Horst Baier* (Konstanz: Harung-Gorre Verlag, 1998), 241–73; Bauch, "Erlaubt ist nur noch, was erlaubt ist," *Junge Freiheit*, August 12, 2005, p. 18; and Bauch, "Gesundheit im Wandel," in *Gesundes Österreich* 7, no. 2 (June 2005): 16, 17; and Bauch, "Wer bringt die Verhältnisse zum Tanzen," *Sezession Heft* 12 (2006): 14–20. The last text, which had been previously given as a lecture at the Institut für Staatspolitik, incorporates the arguments of the German edition of my book *Multiculturalism and the Politics of Guilt* (*Multiculturalismus und die Politik der Schuld*) (Graz: Leopold Stocker Verlag, 2005). Although leading racial nationalists Jared Taylor and Michael Levin stress the importance of cognitive differences between blacks and other races and endorse restrictions on immigration, their political views are for the most part libertarian bordering on anarchist. Taylor's *Paved with Good Intentions: The Failure of Race Relations in Contemporary America* (New York: Carroll and Graf, 1992) and Levin's *Feminism and Freedom* (New Brunswick, NJ: Transaction Publishers, 1987) are polemics against social engineering combined, in Levin's case, with data about biologically rooted gender differences. Levin's other sociobiological opus, *Why Race Matters* (New York: Praeger, 1997), which is a painfully researched study on IQ differences among the races, includes nothing that contradicts his declared libertarian-atheist beliefs.

16. Leon P. Baradat, *Political Ideologies: Their Origin and Their Impact*, 9th ed. (Upper Saddle River, NJ: Prentice Hall, 2005), 234–35.

17. Donald T. Critchlow, *Phyllis Schlafly and Grassroots Conservatism* (Princeton, NJ: Princeton University Press, 2005), 271–304.

18. Ibid., 12–17.

19. George H. Nash, *The Conservative Intellectual Movement in America Since 1945* (Wilmington, DE: Intercollegiate Studies Institute, 1996), 214–35; and Willmoore Kendall, *Contra Mundum*, ed. Nellie D. Kendall (New Rochelle, NY: Arlington House, 1971), 360.

20. David Brooks, "The Power of Marriage," *New York Times*, November 22, 2003, p. A25; and Brooks, "Americans Have Become More Virtuous," *New York Times*, August 7, 2005, Section 4, p. 12.

21. Margot Hentoff, "Unbuckled," *New York Review of Books*, December 10, 1970, p. 19.

22. John B. Judis, *William F. Buckley, Jr.: Patron Saint of the Conservatives*, 2nd ed. (New York: Simon and Schuster, 2001), 324–27.

23. "Merkel: Weichenstelling wie 1949," *Frankfurter Allgemeine Zeitung*, August 28, 2005, p. 1; *Junge Freiheit*, September 3, 2005, p. 4.

24. Editorial, *Junge Freiheit*, September 3, 2005, p. 5; "Merkel mess 45 Prozentholen," *Süddeutsche Zeitung*, August 28, 2005, pp. 1, 2; Bauch, "Die sozialdemakratisierte CDU," in *Zahnärzteblatt Schleswig-Holstein* 11 (2005): 35.

25. For an exhaustive critique of this banning of rightwing rivals instigated by union politicians, see Josef Schüsslburner's *Demokratie-Sonderweg Bundesrepublik: Analyse der Herrschaftsordnung in Deutschland* (Fulda: Lindenblatt Media Verlag, 2004), esp. 127–218; and Gottfried, "How European Nations End," *Orbis* (Spring 2005): 559–69.

26. See Samuel T. Francis, *Beautiful Losers: Essays on the Failure of American Conservatism* (Columbia: University of Missouri Press, 1993); two issues of a decidedly rightwing periodical, *Occidental Quarterly* (Spring/Summer 2005), were devoted to Francis's work of redefining the American Right as a social movement for dispossessed "Middle Americans" and marginalized, self-conscious "Euro-Americans."

CHAPTER 5

1. See Robert A. Nisbet, "Moral Values and Community," *International Review of Community Development* 5 (1960).

2. Noam Scheiber, "Spent Force," *The New Republic*, October 10, 2005, p. 6.

3. Rick Santorum, *It Takes A Family: Conservatism and the Common Ground* (Wilmington, DE: Intercollegiate Studies Institute, 2005), esp. 189–94.

4. Ibid., 7, 193, 213–14, 300–301.

5. See Jack Fowler, "The Specter of Defeat," March 23, 2004, available at http://www.nationalreview.com/comment/fowler200403231002.asp; and Joe Feuerherd, "Conservatives Haunted by Specter of Santorum's Leftwing Drift," *National Catholic Reporter*, May 14, 2004, p. 5.

6. Paul Gottfried, "What Santorum Really Said," *Insight*, May 27, 2003.

7. Ibid., 213–14. Curiously, one of the recent fervent advocates of King's values, Harry Jaffa, bitterly inveighed against him during his lifetime in *National Review*, September 10, 1968, pp. 911–12.

8. John Hallowell, "Modern Liberalism: An Invitation to Suicide," *South Atlantic Quarterly* 46 (October 1947): 460.

9. George H. Nash, *The Conservative Intellectual Movement in America since 1945* (Wilmington, DE: Intercollegiate Studies Institute, 1996), 35–45.

10. See Hallowell, "Politics and Ethics," *American Political Science Review* 38 (August 1944): 651–52.

11. See, for example, John Courtney Murray, *We Hold These Truths: Catholic Reflections on the American Proposition* (New York: Sheed and Ward, 1960).

12. Heinrich Rommen, *Der Staat in der katholischen Gedankenwelt: DieLehre vom Naturrecht* (Paderborn: n.p., 1935), 69.

13. Eliso Vivas, *The Moral Life and the Ethical Life* (Chicago: University of Chicago Press, 1950), IX, 126–29; and A. Campbell Garnett, "A Search Remembered," *Christian Century* 68 (February 7, 1951): 175.

14. Rommen, *Der Staat in der katholischen Gedankenwelt*, 101–02; and my essay on Savigny and historicism in the forthcoming jurisprudence volume edited by Bruce Frohnen for University of Missouri Press, 2008.

15. Max Scheler, *Schriften zur Anthropologie* (Stuttgart: Reklam, 1994), 263–86; Claes G. Ryn, *Will, Imagination and Reason* (Chicago: Regnery, 1986); and J. N. Findlay, *Language, Mind and Value* (London: George Allen and Unwin, 1963).

16. See Herbert J. Muller, "The Revival of the Absolute," *Antioch Review* 9 (March 1949): 99–110.

17. Pascal Bruckner, *Le sanglot de l'homme blanc: Tiers-monde, culpabilité, haine de soi* (Paris: Seuil, 1983), 1–16, 178–180; and Claude Lévi-Strauss, *Anthropologie structurale, II* (Paris: Plon, 1973), 410.

18. Harry V. Jaffa, "The False Prophets of American Conservatism," Claremont Institute, February 12, 1998, available at http://www.claremont.org/publications/pubid.670/pub_detail.asp.

19. Ibid., 5–7.

20. See the Web site for Larry P. Arnn, who is the president of Hillsdale College and vice chairman of the Claremont Institute, and his institute projects at http://www.claremont.org/projects.

21. One of the few studies I have encountered that investigates this overlap between Jaffa's and the once mainstream Left-liberal interpretations of the American past is Clyde N. Wilson's "American Historians and Their History," *Continuity* 6 (Spring 1983): 1–16.

22. Pope Benedict XVI's passionate concern about the spread of "relativism" can be seen in his pastoral work *Ohne Wurzeln. Der Relativismus und die Krise der europäischen Kulturen* (Augsburg: Sankt Ulrich Verlag, 2005).

23. See Michael Novak's syndicated column "Human Rights at Christmas," *Washington Times*, December 24, 1988; and Gottfried, "At Sea with the Global Democrats," *Wall Street Journal*, January 19, 1989.

24. Nisbet, *The Twilight of Authority* (New York: Oxford University Press, 1975); and Nisbet, *The Present Age: Progress and Anarchy in Modern America* (New York: Harper and Row, 1988); and Brad Lowell Stone, *Robert Nisbet: Communitarian Traditionalist* (Wilmington, DE: Intercollegiate Studies Institute, 2000). For a thematically

related study written from a similar perspective, see Bertrand de Jou-
venel, *On Power: The Natural History of Its Growth*, trans. J. F.
Huntington and introduction by D. W. Brogan (Indianapolis, IN:
Liberty Fund, 1993).

25. Max Weber, *Gesammelte Aufsätze zur Wissenschaftslehre*, 7th ed., ed.
Johannes Winckelmann (Tübinger: Mohr-Siebeck, 1988), 508.

26. Ibid., 531–34, 536–37.

27. Ibid., 574.

28. Ibid., 582–613; and "Science on Calling" and "Politics on Calling,"
Gesammelte Politische Schriften, in the same series, 505–60; Max
Weber, *Gerammelte Politische Sehriften*, ed. Wolfgang J. Mommsen
and Birgitt Morgenbrod (Tübinger: Mohr-Siebeck).

29. Carl Schmitt, "Die Tyrannei der Werte" in *Die Tyrannei der Werte*,
ed. Carl Schmitt, Eberhard Jüngel, and Sepp Schelz (Hamburg:
Lutherisches Verlagshaus, 1979), 40; and Nicolai Hartmann, *Ethik*,
3rd ed. (Berlin: W. de Gruyter, 1949), 546–50.

30. Schmitt, "Die Tyrannei der Werte," 31–32.

31. Charles R. Kesler, "Democracy and the Bush Doctrine," Claremont
Institute, January 26, 2005, available at http://www.claremont.org/
writings/crb/winter2004/kesler.html.

32. Ibid., 7.

33. Qtd. in ibid., 3.

34. Ibid., 7.

35. Ibid., 7–8; also Gottfried, "Armies of the Right?" *The American
Conservative*, February 27, 2006, pp. 26–27.

36. The author was present at this address by David Brooks on August
25, 2005 at the Omni Shoreham Hotel in Washington, DC.

37. See Jonah Goldberg's commentary "Golden Days," National Review
Online, October 27, 2005, available at http://www.nationalreview
.com/goldberg/goldberg200510270832.asp; and Larry Auster's
observation "McCain: A Danger More Reflecting the Triumph of
Clintonism," Newsmax, March 6, 2000, available at http://
www.newsmax.com/articles/?a=2000/3/5/121256. Typical of the
journalistic establishment's attempt to create a light version of neoconservatism, if the present neoconservative leadership falls into dis-
repute over the war in Iraq, is the space that the *Sunday New York
Times* ("After Neoconservatism," excerpted from Fukuyama, *America at the Crossroads* [New Haven, CT: Yale University Press, 2006])
February 19, 2006, Section 6, p. 62, gave to the mildly dissident
neoconservative, and self-declared Straussian, Francis Fukuyama.
Except for the question of whether the current American military
presence in Iraq fits the "neo-Wilsonian" and democratic missionary
aims that Fukuyama shares with other neoconservatives, it is hard to
tell their views apart. The publication of this tepid dissent may be the
closest to a rightwing debate that the *New York Times* editors are
willing to bestow on their readers. But more likely, the space

accorded to Fukuyama's apparent break is intended to bring to the fore a tolerable opposition to the liberal media that may please the Left-Center even more than the neoconservatives identified with the *Weekly Standard*. See Paul Gottfried, "The Invincible Wilsonian Matrix," *Orbis* 51.2 (Spring 2007), 239–250; and "Lunging Leftward," *National Observer* 71 (Summer 2006), 57–66.

CHAPTER 6

1. E. J. Dionne, "The Right's Practical Intellectual," *Washington Post*, October 11, 2005, p. Al7.
2. Jonah Goldberg, "Golden Days," National Review Online, October 27, 2005, available at http://www.nationalreview.com/goldberg/goldberg200510270832.asp.
3. Ibid., 3.
4. Paul Gottfried, *The Search for Historical Meaning: Hegel and the Postwar American Right* (DeKalb: University of Northern Illinois Press, 1986), esp. 105–34.
5. Goldberg, "Golden Days," 4.
6. A highly polemical work that sets out to refute this view of the Old Right is Justin Raimondo's *Reclaiming the American Right: The Lost Legacy of the Conservative Movement* (Burlingame, CA: Center for Libertarian Studies, 1994).
7. For investigations of the lost feminist legacy, see Allan C. Carlson, *Family Questions: Reflections* (New Brunswick, NJ: Transaction Publishers, 1988); and Ken Myers's interview with Carlson in "The American Way: Family and Community in the Shaping of American Identity," *Mars Hill Audio Journal* (June 2004): 67.
8. For a characteristically neoconservative statement of "moderate feminism," see Daphne Patai, *Heterophobia: Sexual Harassment and the Future of Feminism* (Lanham, MD: Rowman and Littlefield, 1998); and for two critical reviews of this book, see mine in book review section of *Society* 37, no. 2 (January/February 2000): 78–80; and Carol Iannone's incisive commentary in *Academic Questions* 14, no. 1 (Winter 2000/2001): 27.
9. See William F. Buckley, James Burnham, and Frank S. Meyer, "The John Birch Society and the Conservative Movement," *National Review*, October 19, 1965, pp. 914–20, 925–29.
10. For informative but partisan comments on this phase of the postwar conservative revival, see Murray Rothbard, "Requiem for the Old Right," *Inquiry*, October 17, 1980; and Marcus Epstein, "Buckley Fiction," LewRockwell.com, March 25, 2003, available at http://www.lewrockwell.com/orig/epstein11.html.
11. See Buckley, "Thoughts on Eichmann," *National Review*, April 22, 1961, pp. 238–39; and even more compromising, Buckley, "Let's All

Hate Germany, Comrade," *National Review*, March 25, 1961, p. 172. Peter Novick, in *The Holocaust in American Life* (New York: Houghton Mifflin, 1999), 130–31, is correct to point out that Buckley's comments "represented the sort of backlash Jewish organizations feared." Although Buckley's statements are certainly defensible, they are stated with shocking tactlessness. Moreover, they came from a magazine—and possibly the pen—of someone who was later hailed as an embattled enemy of the anti-Semitic Right.

12. Walter Karp, review of *The Jeweler's Eye* in "Book World," II, *Washington Post*, June 30, 1968, p. 14.

13. John Patrick Diggins, *Up From Communism: Conservative Odysseys in American Intellectual History* (New York: Harper and Row, 1975), esp. 405–13.

14. Meyer, *The Moulding of Communists: The Training of the Communist Cadre* (New York: Harcourt, Brace, 1961); and Kevin J. Smant, *Principles and Heresies: Frank S. Meyer and the Shaping of the American Conservative Movement*, foreword by M. Stanton Evans (Wilmington, DE: Intercollegiate Studies Institute, 2002).

15. Andrea Ragusa, *I comunisti e la società italiana* (Rome: Editore Lacaita, 2003); Annie Kriegel, *The French Communists: Profile of a People*, trans. Elaine P. Halperin (Chicago: University of Chicago Press, 1994), esp. 60–64; and Aileen S. Kraditor, *"Jimmy Higgins": The Mental World of the American Rank-and-File Communist, 1930–1958* (Westport, CT: Greenwood, 1988).

16. Kraditor, *"Jimmy Higgins,"* 80–87.

17. Maie-Claire Lavabre and Francois Platone, *Que reste-t-il du Parti Communiste* (Paris: Autrement CEVIPOF, 2003), 53–54, 81–82.

18. Kraditor, *"Jimmy Higgins,"* 222–32.

19. Ragusa, *I comunisti e la società italiana*, 45, 95–98; Kraditor, *"Jimmy Higgins,"* 80. The PCI never went as far as their Soviet patrons in trying to isolate the non-Communist Left. Despite their break with the Italian Socialists over taking sides in the cold war, Italian Communists cultivated the PSI in order to form parliamentary coalitions.

20. See Murray Rothbard, "Pat Buchanan: Accused of Anti-Semitism," *Conservative Review* 1, no. 7 (November 1990): 10–14; and Allan Brownfeld, "False Anti-Semitism Charge Inhibits Free Discussion," *Washington Inquirer*, October 20, 1990, p. 5; and for an unsympathetic presentation of the targets of this recrimination, see Martin Durham, *The Christian Right, the Far Right, and the Boundaries of American Conservatism* (Manchester: University of Manchester Press, 2001), 147–68.

21. See George H. Nash, *The Conservative Intellectual Movement in America since 1945* (Wilmington, DE: Intercollegiate Studies Institute, 1996), 329–41; and James Lobe, Inter Press Service correspondent in Washington, "Pentagon Office Home to Neocon Network,"

August 7, 2003, available at http://www.antiwar.com/ipr/lobe 080703.html.

22. See, for example, Max Boot, "Incorrect History," *Weekly Standard*, February 15, 2005, a scathing review of Thomas E. Woods's *Politically Incorrect Guide to American History* (Washington, DC: Regnery, 2004); and Woods's response in "A Factually Correct Guide to Max Boot," *The American Conservative*, March 28, 2005.

23. See Jeffrey Hart, "Buckley at the Beginning," *New Criterion*, November 24, 2005; and Hart's celebratory book *The Making of the American Conservative Mind: National Review and Its Times* (Wilmington, DE: Intercollegiate Studies Institute, 2005).

24. On the deliberately misleading term "Islamo-fascism," see my essay "Mussolini in the Middle East," *The American Conservative*, July 5, 2005, pp. 23–25.

25. See Ragusa, *I comunisti e la società italiana*, 215–20; and Gottfried, *The Strange Death of Marxism: The European Left in the New Millennium* (Columbia: University of Missouri Press, 2005), 60–66.

26. A proper discussion of neoconservative self-enrichment since the early nineties has yet to be written. My own detailed analysis, which can be found in Gottfried, *The Conservative Movement*, rev. ed. (New York: Macmillan, 1993), esp. 118–41, is probably outdated, mostly because it understates the now likely higher figures for the accumulation of neoconservative philanthropic wealth. In *A Gift of Freedom: How the John M. Olin Foundation Changed America* (San Francisco: Encounter, 2006), John J. Miller mentions that huge sums of money have passed from "conservative foundations" to neoconservative beneficiaries. A current *National Review* editor, Miller seeks to justify this distribution of grants, but despite his statements to the contrary, he fails to refute my characterization of the grant recipients as "neoconservative."

27. See *National Review*, July 14, 1989, pp. 4–8; Richard J. Neuhaus, "Neuhaus on Rockford"; and Nash, *The Conservative Intellectual Movement in America*, 328–41.

28. Pat Buchanan, "Crackup of the Conservatives," *Washington Times*, May 1, 1991, commentary page; and the angry responses by David Frum, "Conservative Bully Boy," *American Spectator* 24, no. 7 (July 1991): 2, 3, 12; and Norman Podhoretz, "Buchanan and the Conservative Crackup," *Commentary* 93 (May 1992): 30–34.

29. See Joshua Muravchik, "Patrick J. Buchanan and the Jews," *Commentary* 91 (January 1989): 12–14.

30. Cited from the original manuscript, which Rothbard showed me, of his speech "Strategy for the Right"; see also the response in William McGurn, "Pat Buchanan and the Intellectuals," *National Review*, February 17, 1992, pp. 41–42.

31. See the editorial note in "Four More Years," *National Review*, February 17, 1992, p. 12; and Buckley's comments in "Score One for Buchanan," *National Review*, March 16, 1992, p. 55.

32. Daniel Lazare, "Thunder on the Right," *Present Tense* (December 1989): 30; Sara Diamond, "Rumble on the Right," *Z Magazine* (December 1990): 24–25; and S. Churcher, "Radical Transformations," *New York Magazine* (July 6, 1989): 30–31; Daniel McCarthy, "The Failure of Fusionism," *American Conservative*, January 29, 2007, revisits this long lost hour when it seemed that the anti-neoconservative forces on the American Right might rally to gain national prominence. According to McCarthy, it was the role of Murray Rothbard, as a bridge between the libertarians and the Old Right, even more than the presidential run of Buchanan, that made this resurgence possible.

33. See Ralph Z. Hallow, "Conservatives Split into Warring Camps," *Washington Times*, June 2, 1987, pp. A1, A2.

34. The revised edition of *The Conservative Movement*, esp. 132–38, provides a discussion of the degree to which the Unification Church, which owns the *Washington Times*, has supported neoconservative projects. The Unification Church-owned newspaper began to purge columnists from its commentary section in the nineties. Among those who suffered in this purge were Samuel T. Francis, Joseph Sobran, Pat Buchanan, and more recently, Paul Craig Roberts, all of whom offended the overwhelmingly neoconservative editorial and advisory boards. The likelihood of such a purge was already evident when I worked for the Washington Times Corporation between 1986 and 1989. The newspaper's editor-in-chief, Arnaud de Borchgrave, was so deferential to the son of Norman Podhoretz and Midge Decter, who then served as an editor, that the younger Podhoretz was given the sobriquet "Normanson." Despite the efforts of well-placed neoconservative editors to limit my influence and, if possible, have me sacked, I then enjoyed the protection of Unification Church officials. I was also insulated by virtue of my post as an editor of another one of the corporation's publications, *The World and I*.

35. A recent Italian anthology, James J. Lobe and A. Olivieri, ed., *I nuovi rivoluzionari: il pensiero dei neoconservatori americani* (Milan: Feltrinelli, 2003), provides further evidence of the aggressive Wilsonian tendencies now dominating the movement. See also Victor Davis Hanson, "What the President Might Say," National Review Online, April 30, 2004, available at http://www.nationalreview.com/hanson/hanson200404300833.asp; Larry Auster's response, "Liberal Universalist With a Gun," View from the Right, available at http://www.amnation.com/vfr/archives/002266.html; and Gary Dorrien, *Imperial Designs: Neoconservatism and the New Pax Americana* (New York: Routledge, 2004).

36. Ramesh Ponnuru, "A Conservative No More," National Review Online, October 11, 1999, available at http://www.nationalreview.com/11oct99/ponnuru101199.html.

CONCLUSION

1. Russell Kirk, *Decadence and Renewal in Higher Learning: An Episodic history of American University and College since 1953* (South Bend, IN: Gateway Edition, 1978), 253.

2. Kirk, *The Politics of Prudence*, intro. by Mark C. Henrie (Wilmington, DE: Intercollegiate Studies Institute, 2004), 191–203.

3. See, for example, Charles Krauthammer's invective, "Trent Lott Must Resign," directed against the Mississippi Senator for being overly indulgent toward the ex-segregationist centenarian senator Strom Thurmond in Townhall.com, December 12, 2002, available at http://www.townhall.com/columnists/CharlesKrauthammer/2002/12/12/trent_lott_must_resign.

4. See Irving Kristol, *On the Democratic Idea in America* (New York: Simon and Schuster, 1972) and I. Kristol, "A Conservative Welfare State," *Wall Street Journal*, June 14, 1993, p. 14; and William Kristol, "The Future of Conservatism in the U.S.," *The American Enterprise* (July/August 1994): 32–37.

5. See the two thick volumes of D. L. O'Huallachain and J. Forrest Sharpe, eds., *Neoconned: Just War Principle: A Condemnation of War in Iraq* (Vienna, VA: HIS Press, 2005), edited and mostly written by conservative Catholic opponents of the American invasion of Iraq.

6. James Kurth, "The Protestant Deformation," feature article in *The American Interest* 1, no. 2 (December 2005).

7. See Robert Nisbet's "A Farewell to History," *National Review*, May 22, 1987, pp. 137–38; and Nisbet, *The Present Age: Progress and Anarchy in America* (Indianapolis, IN: Liberty Fund, 2003). The fact that Nisbet's blurb for Kristol's book *On the Democratic Idea in America* speaks of a "modern classic" did not prevent him from eventually turning away from neoconservatism, a change of stance that is evident in his review of my book.

8. See "Books, Arts, and Manners," *National Review*, December 19, 2005, pp. 102–11.

9. See "The 'Conservative' Legacy of Martin Luther King," National Policy Institute, January 17, 2006, available at http://www.nationalpolicyinstitute.org/article.php?PortID=59; and "Why a King Holiday?" *Human Events*, October 15, 1983, p. 1; Jesse Helms, "The Radical Record of Martin Luther King," *Human Events* supplement, October 15, 1983.

10. George H. Nash, *The Conservative Intellectual Movement in America since 1945* (Wilmington, DE: Intercollegiate Studies Institute, 1996), 100. It is not necessarily the case that blacks who consider themselves to be "conservatives," are uniformly on the side of the well-heeled, supposedly problack neoconservatives. A highly literate, black social commentator and *American Conservative* contributor, Elizabeth Wright, who edits the Web site monthly *Issues and Views*, leans strongly toward the paleos. The same is true of other black contributors to her publication. Wright herself is openly opposed to the war in Iraq as an exercise in neo-Wilsonian politics. In 2000 Pat Buchanan's running mate in the presidential race on the Reform Party ticket was a black California public school teacher Ezola Foster (1938–), who, like George Schuyler, had been associated with the John Birch Society.

11. James Patterson, *Mr. Republican: A Biography of Robert A. Taft* (Boston: Houghton Mifflin, 1972), 174–75, 280–82.

12. See Harry Jaffa, "The Limits of Dissent," *National Review*, September 10, 1968, pp. 911–12; and Will Herberg, "A Religious 'Right' to Violate the Law," *National Review*, July 14, 1964, pp. 579–80. Professor Herberg's remarks about the favorable responses he had elicited from later neoconservatives to his criticism of King came in conversation with and letters to me. A chapter of my memoirs, which I have contracted to write, will discuss Herberg's posthumous reconstruction as a neoconservative precursor.

13. Works that show this militant pro-democracy tropism are Norman Podhoretz, *Breaking Ranks: A Political Memoir* (New York: Harper and Row, 1979); Michael Novak, *The Spirit of Democratic Capitalism* (New York: Simon and Schuster, 1982); Ronald Radosh, *Divided They Fall: The Demise of the Democratic Party 1964–1996* (New York: Free Press, 1998); and Joshua Muravchik, *Exporting Democracy: Fulfilling America's Destiny* (Washington, DC: American Enterprise Institute, 1992).

14. Theodor W. Adorno (with Else Frenkel-Brunswick, Daniel J. Levinson, and R. N. Sanford), *The Authoritarian Personality* (New York: Harper and Brothers, 1950), esp. 36–57, 442–84. Indicating the connection between social engineering and mainstream cold war liberalism, according to Christopher Lasch's *The True and Only Heaven: Progress and its Critics* (New York: Norton, 1991), 449–54, was the support for the study on anti-Semitism from the American Jewish Committee, which also became the sponsor of *Commentary*. Two later neoconservative spokesmen, S. M. Lipset and Daniel Bell, both expressed high regard for this 1950 study of rightwing prejudice in America.

15. See Paul Gottfried, *After Liberalism: Mass Democracy in the Managerial State* (Princeton, NJ: Princeton University Press, 1999), esp.

30–49, for a survey of nineteenth-century bourgeois liberal fears about the coming of mass democracy.

16. For a recent, dispassionate assessment of McCarthy and his effects, see Arthur Herman, *McCarthy: Reexamining the Life and Legacy of America's Most Hated Senator* (New York: Free Press, 2000); and the comments by Robert Weissberg in *Political Tolerance: Balancing Community and Diversity* (Thousand Oaks, CA.: Sage, 1998), 96–109, which also deal with the overall effects of the Smith Act, which was passed in 1940 and which addressed the threat of violence and subversion against the American government. Weissberg goes into the often-inflated claims about academic persecution in the early fifties. He points to two aspects of the war against subversion that are routinely overlooked, its almost entirely rightwing and Trotskyist targets until well after the Second World War; and the fact that the Communist Party and its supporters did not complain about governmental restrictions on political speech until they were directly affected during the cold war. See also Daniel Bell, *The Radical Right: The New American Right*, exp. ed. (Garden City, NY: Doubleday, 1963); Richard Hofstadter, *The Paranoid Style in American Politics and Other Essays* (New York: Knopf, 1965); and for a more sympathetic treatment of Hofstadter's concern, see David S. Brown's exhaustive biography of the Columbia University historian, *Richard Hofstadter: An Intellectual Biography* (Chicago: University of Chicago Press, 2006).

17. See Jonathan M. Schoenwald, *A Time for Choosing: The Rise of Modern American Conservatism* (Oxford: Oxford University Press, 2001), 147–61. Schoenwald understates the sharp transformation of the movement after 1964 when he explains: "Conservatives did not drop their ideological tenets; they merely subverted them to more pragmatic politics, which would draw people into their vision for America" (161).

18. George Will, *Statecraft as Soulcraft: What Government Does* (New York: Simon and Schuster, 1983), 86–87.

19. Gertrude Himmelfarb, *One Nation: Two Cultures: The De-moralization of Society* (New York: Knopf, 1999), 78.

20. See the incisive review essay of W. Wesley McDonald's *Russell Kirk and the Age of Ideology* by James E. Pierson Jr. in *Modern Age* 47, no. 4 (Fall 2005): 344–48.

21. Rick Perlstein, "I Don't like Nixon Until Watergate: The Conservative Movement Until Now," *The Huffington*, December 19, 2005, 4.

22. See John Lukacs, "The Stirrings of History," *Harper's Magazine* 281, no. 1683 (August 1990): 41. Lukacs's comment that "we're all social democrats now" was meant to expose both the futility and dishonesty of the pretended revival of free market capitalism as the result of certain governmental economic policies.

INDEX

Breinigsville, PA USA
26 July 2010
242472BV00002B/152/P